Improving
Reading

Improving Reading

Nancy V. Wood
Director
Study Skills and Tutorial Services
The University of Texas at El Paso

Holt, Rinehart and Winston

New York   Chicago   San Francisco   Pliladelphia
Montreal   Toronto   London   Sydney
Tokyo   Mexico City   Rio De Janeiro   Madrid

Library of Congress Cataloging in Publication Data

Wood, Nancy V.
Improving reading

Includes bibliographies and index.
1. Reading (Higher education)   2. Reading reading
comprehension.   3. Developmental reading.   I. Title.
LB2395.W633   1984   428.4′ 3′ 0711   83-18584

ISBN 0-03-059318-2

CBS COLLEGE PUBLISHING
Holt, Rinehart and Winston
The Dryden Press
Saunders College Publishing

For my parents
Gus and Marianne Hagglund

Preface

This developmental reading textbook is written for students who may have difficulty at times doing their college reading assignments. The primary purpose is to teach students to become active readers who take notes on, summarize, study, remember, and make critical judgments about all types of college reading assignments. Another purpose is to expand students' reading rates and to improve their flexibility so that they can do college reading and research more efficiently and improve their leisure and vocational reading skills. Text and exercises are designed to clarify not only the reading process but the writing process as well. Because of its scope, this text can be appropriately used in reading classes, reading and study skill classes, and reading and writing classes.

Rationale for the Organization

The organization of this book follows, as closely as possible, the process that experienced readers naturally follow when they read. First, they make some quick judgments about the source of the material, its author, its relative difficulty for them, and their own reasons for reading it. Once they have placed the material to be read in a context for reading, they then set out to read it as rapidly as possible. When the material is too difficult or their purpose is too demanding to yield adequate comprehension quickly, they then go back to read the material closely and critically. This tendency to try to read rapidly before making the commitment to read closely and critically provides the logic for the organization of this book. Thus, rapid-reading skills—including surveying, skimming, scanning, selective reading, and speed-reading—are taught before close and critical reading skills. Students are taught to heighten their awareness and sharpen their ability to make preliminary judgments in Part I, to read rapidly in Part II, and to read closely and critically in Parts III and IV.

In our classroom testing of this book, we discovered that teaching rapid-reading skills before close and critical reading skills has an added advantage. Most students who take reading improvement want to see some obvious and immediate gains as soon as possible. They will experience such gains as well as improved reading confidence as they work through the rapid-reading exercises in Part II. This confidence will then provide them with the motivation to do the more difficult types of reading demanded in Parts III and IV.

Chapters and Exercises

The chapters are written for easy comprehension. The exercises are designed to introduce students to all types of college reading material including textbooks from many disciplines, library resource materials, current periodicals, and samples of prose from past centuries. Each chapter begins with chapter goals and proceeds with explanations, examples, and brief in-chapter exercises designed to help students make immediate applications. Additional exercises at the end of each chapter invite students to write summaries, to practice what they have just learned on additional reading exercises, to participate in discussions and class activities, and to improve their vocabularies. Other exercises urge students to go a step further to apply their new skills to the "real" reading they do outside of this textbook. It is assumed that students studying this textbook will be taking other classes in which they are also required to read.

Reading Level

All of the students who test-read this book while it was in manuscript form demonstrated that they were able to comprehend the text and complete the exercises without difficulty. These readers possessed a variety of reading comprehension scores before they began to read. They were given the Nelson-Denny Reading Test, Form C, as a pre-test, and eight weeks later when they finished the manuscript, Form D as a post-test. On the pre-test, student comprehension scores ranged from grade 6.6 to 15. The strongest readers (grade 15) maintained their scores and reported that *Improving Reading* taught them to do their college reading more effectively and with greater insight. All of the other readers demonstrated gains that ranged from one year to four years in reading levels. The two weakest readers in the group, who both began with comprehension scores of grade 6.6, ended with scores of 7.5 and 10.6, or net gains of one and four years respectively during the eight-week reading period. Neither of these students reported difficulty in comprehending the text or exercises. Their classwork, in fact, demonstrated a steady increase in their general reading competency. The student who registered the four-year gain reported improved comprehension and better grades in all of his other college courses. This comparative testing suggests that this book can be effective in improving the college reading skills of students who pre-test at the sixth-grade reading level and up.

Other Special Features

Other features of this book are as follows: (1) An *evaluation* in Chapter 2 actively involves students in an assessment of their present reading habits, attitudes, and current reading responsibilities and preferences. (2) There is an emphasis throughout on *active, involved reading* rather than on reading about reading. (3) *Natural vocabulary development that emphasizes context* is featured in every chapter. Instruction is reinforced with a *vocabulary review* at the end of every chapter and a *glossary* at the end of the book. (4) *A Vocabulary Builder* in the Appendix teaches dictionary skills as well as systematic ways to improve vocabulary. (5) *Text-marking symbols* lead student eyes to focus on those elements and relationships most important to effective comprehension. A key to the text-marking symbols used in this book is on page xvii. (6) *Instruction and practice in summary writing* is provided at the end of every chapter. (7) A *holistic approach to reading* teaches students first to perceive the structure or organizational plan of the entire written message and then to attend to paragraph organization and words and sentences. (8) A consistent effort is made throughout to *broaden students' expectations of what is likely to appear on the printed page.* (9) A *"read" page in the first chapter* shows the interactive relationship between reader and author. (10) There is *ample opportunity for group work and teacher intervention.* In fact, there is a governing assumption in this book that reading is an act of communication, that the reader must stretch to understand the author, and that if the student cannot stretch far enough, the teacher will be present to give the extra boost. (11) *The questions are mainly open-ended rather than multiple choice,* and focus student attention on applying reading theory rather than on answering questions correctly. (12) An *Instructor's Manual* is also available, which contains readability information about all chapters and exercises as well as test questions on each chapter.

Acknowledgments

I have had valuable help from a number of people in preparing this manuscript. Particular thanks go to Ruth Pepin, who first tested it in a reading classroom. Her encouragement and perceptive criticism helped me make it ready for other classrooms. I am also grateful to the students in her class who read the text and worked the exercises. These students were generous in pointing out what they liked and disliked, what was difficult for them to understand, and what changes should be made. These students are Claudia Guillaume, Imelda Zapata, Carol Jean Hall, Ki Huyn Kim, Benjamin A. Freeman, Dan V. Heuer, and Gary J. Mann. Their recommendations had considerable influence in shaping the final published version of this book. I am grateful to James A. Wood, who has helped me generate and think about many of the ideas in this book, particularly those on organization and critical reading. I also appreciate the help that Sam, David, and Joe Wood have given me. They were often the first to read and test particular exercises. I am especially grateful to Jo Willems, who not only prepared an accurate and attractive manuscript, but also told me where it needed rewriting. I want to thank a number of other individuals around the country who have read and commented on the manuscript. They are: Madelyn Bowlin, Livingston University; Jane Bracy, St. Louis Community College at Florissant Valley; Suzette Cohen, Cleveland State University; Leila Gonzalez-Sullivan, Rockland County Community College; Judith Kean, Community College of Philadelphia; Thomas W. Lackman, Temple University; and Janith Stephenson, College of the Mainland, Texas City. Their positive criticisms encouraged me, and their recommendations for changes helped me improve the final text. Finally, at Holt, Rinehart and Winston special thanks go to editors Anne Boynton-Trigg and Charlotte Smith, and to Ruth Stark, who saw the project through from manuscript to book.

N. V. W.

El Paso, Texas
February 1984

To The Student

The purpose of this book is to help you develop the habits, skills, and insights that you will need to read your college assignments successfully. Instruction in rapid reading precedes that of close and critical reading because most of us want to know how to get through the great quantities of reading material we face each day as quickly and effectively as possible. There is ample instruction, however, to help you read the assignments that must be read slowly, closely, and critically.

An important aim of this book is to encourage you to read actively and with concentration. You will learn what to expect in a text and how to mark important matter as you read. Consequently, you will need to have a pencil in your hand at all times while you are reading this book.

Another aim of this book is to help you improve your present vocabulary. So, in addition to the pencil, you will also need to have a dictionary handy while you read. In each chapter ten or fifteen words that are important to the meaning of the text have been circled or underlined for you. You will be instructed to write brief definitions of these words in the margins and to define them again at the end of each chapter. You will also be encouraged to use context clues to help you discover definitions.

As you read this textbook some other special features will catch your eye. For instance, special text-marking symbols are recommended for your use in reading both this and your other textbooks as well. A key to these symbols is on page xvii. Space is provided at the end of each chapter for your own summary writing. This activity will help you concentrate and understand as you read. Summaries are also useful for exam review. If this book works as it should, you will soon be writing summaries in all of your textbooks. Finally, reading exercises throughout the book will encourage you to practice your new reading skills and also to use them when you do your other college reading.

The students who test-read this book before it was published found that it helped them improve both their confidence and skill in completing their college reading assignments. You will find that it can help you in the same way.

Contents

Text-Marking Symbols   Introduced in

boldface	specialized vocabulary	Chapter 1
circled	general vocabulary	Chapter 1
wavy line	allusions	Chapter 1
[square brackets]	reader's original ideas	Chapter 1
underlining	main ideas	Chapter 3
MI	main idea	Chapter 3
SI	subidea	Chapter 3
SM	supporting material	Chapter 3
boxed	transitions	Chapter 3
TS	topic sentence	Chapter 8

Improving Reading

PART I
Preliminaries to Active Reading

Part I of this book will help you develop the active reading skills that you will need to do all types of college reading. The following ideas will be given special emphasis in the next three chapters:

1. Active readers use a number of special activities when they read to help them concentrate and comprehend.
2. Some of these activities are defining important words, marking the text, summarizing, and asking questions while reading.
3. Active readers know what they can expect to find on most printed pages, and they look for it as they read in order to keep a high level of comprehension.

Prepare for your reading of these first three chapters by trying to answer the following questions. This activity will encourage you to predict what might be in the chapters, and thereby improve your concentration and comprehension.

1. What is active reading?
2. What are your favorite methods for improving your vocabulary?
3. What do you do now to improve your concentration?
4. Do you ever ask questions about material you read? What are they?
5. What are your present strengths and weaknesses as a reader?
6. How do you read difficult material?
7. How do you discover the most important ideas in the material you read?
8. Do you know how to summarize material you have read?

CHAPTER 1

How To Become an Active Reader

In this chapter you will learn:

How to improve your vocabulary.
How to use an active reading process to improve comprehension.
How to use active reading strategies.
How to mark a text.
How to summarize a text.

Pick up a pencil, pull out your dictionary, and begin reading.

Imagine for a moment that you see two students studying together in your student union. One of these students is reading aloud from a physics textbook. The other, a blind student, listens but stops the first student occasionally so that she may dictate into a tape-recorder. Which of these students would you say from your observation is reading? Mark your answers.

The student reading aloud.   —— yes   —— no

The blind student.   —— yes   —— no

Both.   —— yes   —— no

Why? _____

This is, frankly, a trick question. You may not be able to answer it adequately without more information. The student who is reading aloud is an English major who has never taken physics nor does she ever intend to. She reads fluently and with good intonation. Yet, as she reads, her mind wanders, and, if she were asked to stop and summarize what she had just read, she would be unable to do so. The blind student, on the other hand, is an engineering major who is working for an A in her physics course. She has employed the English major to read to her. She listens intently to the reader, organizes the ideas in her mind, relates them to what she already knows, asks that certain material be reread, and then stops the reader so that she may summarize what she has heard into a tape-recorder. She also asks the English major to repeat certain key vocabulary words and to define them for her. She then adds these words and definitions to her tape. Later she will listen to the tape until she knows it well enough to take an exam on it.

You may now want to revise your answer to the question about who is actually reading in the situation. *The blind person is the only person who is reading.* The English major sees the words and says them aloud, but no meaning registers in her brain. She is not reading.

Unlike the English major, the blind student is comprehending the text. She is an *active* reader because she is concentrating, she knows why she is reading, and she knows what she wants to learn. She is also understanding as much as her background permits, and she is asking questions about what she does not understand. The English major, on the other hand, is *passive*. As a reader she is more blind than the person to whom she is reading. She sees and hears the words, but she understands nothing.

Are you usually an active or a passive reader? Stop now, reflect, and check below the percent of time that you have been actively concentrating and understanding the material that you have read so far in this chapter: 100% _____ 75% _____ 50% _____ 25% _____ 0% _____ of the time. If you are often passive, you can start right now, as you continue to read this book, to use some of the blind student's methods to help you become more active. To begin, notice that the blind student questioned the meanings of the words she did not know.

Isolate and Learn Vocabulary

There are three types of words that you will need to define in order to understand what you read. They are (1) **specialized terms,** which from now on in this book will be set in **bold-face type;** (2) general vocabulary words, which from now on will be circled; and (3) allusions, which will be identified with a wavy line. All three types of words will also be reproduced in the margins of this book with space where you can write brief definitions for them.

Define:
**active
reader**

_____

_____

Define:
strategy

_____

_____

Instructors of every subject use some specialized terms to talk about their subject matter, and this is true also of the subject of reading. Notice the specialized term **active reader** that appears in the title of this chapter. Other examples are **frustration** in psychology, **recombinant DNA** in biology, **momentum** in physics, **credits** in accounting, and **symbolism** in English. In most textbooks, specialized terms are introduced in boldface or in italics, or are written and defined in the margins or glossary at the back of the book. It is important to take time to learn exactly what is meant by such terms so that you can understand the instructor, the textbook, and even the examination questions. An effective strategy for learning a specialized vocabulary word is to underline it, read the author's definition in the text that surrounds it, finish reading the chapter, and then go back and try to define it. If you need more information, look it up in the dictionary or glossary and, finally, jot a short definition in the margin.

The word "strategy" was just circled to identify it as a general vocabulary word. Sometimes strategy describes military maneuvers. Here it describes a special activity or skill that you can use to improve your vocabulary. It is not a specialized term that you would associate with a particular field of study. You might, in fact, find it in a number of different contexts. Besides the general vocabulary words already circled in the text, you may want to select and circle other words that interest you and define them also in the margin. Do not interrupt your reading to

Define:
context

_____

Define:
jot

_____

Define:
allusion

_____

define words, however. Instead, mark the words, read to the end of the chapter, and then go back to write definitions. If possible, use **context** to discover meanings. Consult the dictionary only if the information in the text is insufficient to help you. When you consult the dictionary, find a meaning for the word as it is used in the text and then jot that meaning in the margin.

An allusion is a brief mention or reference to a person, a place, or an event that the author obviously recognizes but that you may not. In order to understand authors well, you need to have the same information about such allusions as they do.

At first, as you read this text, you may find it somewhat distracting to encounter words written in boldface type, circled, or underlined with wavy lines. These marking symbols are used here to lead your eyes to the words you may not know. This will help you develop the habit of identifying such words in your other books, which, in turn, will help you improve your present vocabulary and become an active reader.

Use an Active Reading Process

Recall that the blind student related new ideas to those she already knew and then organized them in her mind. These activities were only part of an active reading

Figure 1.1

THE FAMILY CIRCUS   By Bil Keane

Copyright 1982
The Register and Tribune
Syndicate Inc

"Just this morning I was reading on the cereal box that . . . ."

The Family Circus by Bil Keane, reprinted courtesy The Register and Tribune, Syndicate, Inc.

Define:
process
_____
_____

process that she used to understand her physics assignment. All active readers follow a process to understand a text whether it be a magazine, letter, textbook, or the back of a cereal box. This **process** takes varying amounts of time and effort depending on the material being read. Figure 1.2 describes such a process. Even though this is a step-by-step process, if one part does not yield sufficient information for the later steps, the reader may always backtrack and repeat a step. As you work to improve your reading, you will learn to adapt this process to different kinds of reading assignments. The object of this process is to gain adequate reading comprehension.

Define:
**active
reading
strategies**
_____
_____

Included in this process is a variety of **active reading strategies,** which involve reading, writing, and thinking. All of them are directed toward getting the author's meaning. You may use some of these strategies already; others you may never have tried. By the time you finish reading the chapters and working the exercises in this

Figure 1.2   This process focuses mainly on reading for information. It could easily be modified to include fiction or poetry.

The Reading Process

Define:
anticipate
_____

Before reading

The reader is motivated (or is assigned) to read about a particular topic.
    The reader selects material to read that will give information about the topic.
    The reader looks through the material forming questions and trying to predict the organizational plan and the pattern of ideas that the author will follow. The reader begins to (anticipate) what might be in the text.

While reading

The reader uses various strategies to read and understand the author. The reader is rarely satisfied that the author has been understood perfectly. Eventually, however, the reader decides that enough has been gained and stops reading.

Define:
**private
product**
_____

After reading

The reader puts the information and ideas learned from the text into a final form. They may be thought about briefly and forgotten, organized and committed to memory, laughed over, written out in notes and summaries, and/or reflected upon, evaluated, or used to generate other ideas. The material from the text, however, becomes a **private product,** the property of the reader and no one else.

Define:
Interactive
_____
_____

textbook, you will be skilled at using them. The following questionnaire will help you focus your attention on some active and **interactive** reading strategies that you can begin to use now to improve your comprehension. They require you both to take meaning from the text and also to contribute meaning from your own background. Final comprehension becomes a fusion of what the author says and what you already know.

In-Chapter Exercise 1

Check the active reading strategies that you presently use. Circle the numbers of the interactive strategies that encourage you to contribute meaning from your own background.

	Often	Sometimes	Never
1. I look for ideas rather than stare at words.	___	___	___
2. I jot the important ideas in the margin.	___	___	___
3. I stop and summarize ideas from time to time either in writing or mentally.	___	___	___
4. I think of my own examples of a difficult concept.	___	___	___
5. I study all pictures, graphs, and other visual materials.	___	___	___
6. I visualize descriptive passages in my mind.	___	___	___
7. I study new words in context to understand them better.	___	___	___
8. I relate what I am reading to what I already know.	___	___	___
9. I ask mental questions of myself as I read and try to answer them.	___	___	___
10. I read an especially interesting passage aloud to someone else and then discuss it.	___	___	___
11. I mentally argue and disagree with the author at times.	___	___	___
12. I think ahead and try to predict what the author will say.	___	___	___
13. I take a guess at the meaning once in awhile when it is not clear.	___	___	___

14. I number the parts of a text as I read so
that I can see the chunks that make up
the whole. Then I go back and reread the
difficult parts until they are clear.   ____   ____   ____

15. I stop and write out an original idea of
my own that is inspired by the text.   ____   ____   ____

Did you omit questions number 2 and 3, which asked about writing in the text
itself? It is difficult for many students to learn to write in their books because they
have been told not to for so many years in public school. You may, however, write
in the books that you own. Careful markings will make them more valuable to you.

Mark the Text as You Read

The blind student used the active reading strategy of taking notes while she read.
She could have taken reading notes in braille. She preferred, however, to record
her notes on the tape-recorder and listen to them later. Both ways are effective
because both encourage active reader participation.

Your books will look like you have read them and be easy to review if you
mark them skillfully. Some specific types of markings and notes you can make are
(1) circling words and jotting their meanings in the margin; (2) underlining important ideas; (3) jotting main ideas in the margin; (4) writing brief summaries at the
end of sections, chapters, and the book itself; and (5) writing your own ideas and
reactions in [square brackets]. Use the top or bottom of the pages or the inside of
the front or back covers. The square brackets are a special marking symbol to show
that these ideas are yours.

Figure 1.3 shows a "read page" from a book owned by Mark Twain. The
jottings in the margins are Twain's own. They come as close to anything we have
of a public record of what went through Twain's mind when he read this page.
These jottings are interesting to students of Twain because they give an insight into
what Twain thought about another author's description of two people slipping and
clinging to a mountainside. They were useful to Twain himself because they helped
him clarify his own thinking and because they provided him with a record of his
thoughts. We can see from this page that Twain was an active reader.

Note that Twain's jottings are really directed to himself rather than to an
outside audience. When he wrote them, he did not expect you to be looking at
them some day. Many libraries own books from the collections of well-known
people that contain such marginal notes. We preserve and study these notes because
they give us insights into the private thoughts of well-known people.

Your marginal notes in your books may never be preserved and studied, but
they can be as useful to you as Twain's were to him. They are a record of your
thoughts and what you perceived as important the first time you read the text. Such

Define:
generate

a record is useful for review and also for (generating) your own creative thinking
about the ideas in the text.

Figure 1.3   A "read" page from a book owned by Mark Twain.

THE TWINS OF TABLE MOUNTAIN.   93

But the giddy girl had darted past him, and, face to the wall of the cliff, was creeping along the dangerous path.   Rand followed mechanically.   Once or twice the trail crumbled beneath her feet, but she clung to a projecting root of *chapparal*, and laughed.   She had almost reached her elected goal when, slipping, the treacherous *chapparal* she clung to yielded in her grasp, and Rand, with a cry, sprung forward. But the next instant she quickly transferred her hold to a cleft in the cliff and was safe.   Not so her companion.   The soil beneath him, loosened by the impulse of his spring, slipped away; he was falling with it, when she caught him sharply with her disengaged hand, and together they scrambled to a more secure footing.

"I could have reached it alone," said the Pet, "if you'd left me alone."

"Thank Heaven, we're saved," said Rand, gravely.

"*And without a rope,*" said Miss Euphemia, significantly.   *Just so!*

This is more than marvelous. It is impossible.

To diabet.

From Francis Bret Harte, *The Twins of Table Mountain, and Other Sketches.* (Boston: Houghton, Mifflin, and Company, 1881), p. 93. S. L. Clemens' annotated copy located at the Mark Twain Papers, The Bancroft Library, Berkeley, California. All previously unpublished words by Mark Twain quoted here are copyright 1984 by the Mark Twain Foundation. Published with the permission of the University of California Press and Robert H. Hirst, the General Editor of the Mark Twain Papers. Photographic reproduction courtesy of Mark Twain Papers, The Bancroft Library.

Figure 1.4 shows a page from an economics textbook that has been read by a student. This page is actually overmarked. It would be too time-consuming to mark all pages in such a book this extensively. The page serves to make public, however, a student's private reading and studying. It is also intended to demonstrate to you the kinds of mental activities that might take place in your own mind as you read similar material. It also demonstrates some ways to mark a text. Note particularly how the student reader has used the following text markings. They are numbered for cross-reference to Figure 1.4.

1. *Underlined* key ideas and details.
2. *Circled* and defined key words.
3. *Outlined* the key ideas in the margin in order to see the pattern of ideas and how they relate to each other.
4. *Graphed* the statistical data so that it could be visualized and thus understood and remembered more easily.
5. *Reflected* on the main problem, which is noted in square brackets.
6. *Related* material to a past experience, in this case a movie, which is also noted in square brackets.

Figure 1.4. A page read by a student.

⑥→ [remember contrast between dignity of country life and corruption of city life in Bolivian film *Blood of the Condor*.

② **Need for ⨀Rural⨀ Development**

① Throughout the world, less developed countries are (urbanizing) rapidly—far more rapidly than today's developed countries did at comparable stages of their own growth. The reasons for this urbanization are complex. Partly the modernity and the promise of a better life in the city attract people. Partly the problem is education systems that do not emphasize agricultural topics. Whatever the causes, cities are not able to meet the aspirations of all those who arrive in them. Urban unemployment rates are very high. Many people who are employed work in tertiary services—from shining shoes to hustling—that contribute little to economic development or to the development of the individuals. Huge shantytowns surrounding third world cities are the rule rather than the exception. ©

Current rates of urbanization far exceed the potential for industrial development in most poor countries. One study calculated that, just to keep urban unemployment from rising in a typical less developed country, industrial output would have to grow at 18 percent per year.* Even in Brazil, which has had outstanding success with industrialization and urban development, industrial growth has run at only 15 percent per year. To get rid of the 20 to 25 percent unemployment common in cities of less developed countries, industry would have to grow at something like 30 to 35 percent per year for a decade.

When urban unemployment and the food problem are considered together, it is not surprising that many development economists believe that the real hope for the less developed countries lies in the countryside. The hope is to hold people on the land and to make them productive there within a meaningful community structure. If the third world nations can do that, they may be able to feed themselves, distribute what little they have more equitably, meet the nonmaterial aspirations of their populations, and retain their independence. That, at least, is what the advocates of rural development say. They all recognize that there are problems, though.

⑤→ [problem: how to motivate people to stay on the farm]

(rural) - country
(urban) - city

③ A. People moving to cities
B. Problems in cities
C. Not enough industrial output
   Ex. Brazil

④ need 35% industrial growth
   25% unemployment now
   15% indus. gr. now

D. Unemployment = hunger
   Hope lies in farms

---

* David Turnham, *The Employment Problem in Less Developed Countries* (Paris: Organization for Economic Cooperation and Development, 1971), as cited by Power and Holenstein, *World of Hunger*, pp. 74–75.

In-Chapter Exercise 2

The following is a passage from a psychology textbook for you to read and mark as in the example above. Try to use as many of the ways for marking just described as you can.

Personal Space

The physical responses you make toward other people also influence the initial attitudes you arouse in others. California psychologist Robert Sommer has for many years studied what he called **personal space.** Sommer believes that you carry an ''invisible bubble'' around your body that encloses what you consider to be your own, personal psychological space. He notes that in a number of studies, subjects have shown a dramatic increase in nervousness when an experimenter moved to within a foot or so of them. Most of the subjects ''defended their territories'' by either moving away from the intruder, or by becoming increasingly hostile.

Sommer states that the size of your own personal space bubble is influenced by such factors as your personality, your status, and your culture. For middle-class Americans, this private area extends outward about two feet from any part of the body. For Arabs, the space is usually much smaller. For Scandinavians, the bubble is typically larger. People with great status (that is, people whom almost everyone respects) often command a larger personal space than do individuals with little or no status. We approach a prince, a pope, or a president with care and caution, lest we come too close. But we approach babies, young children, and animals as closely as we wish, because we typically perceive them as having little if any real status.[1]

Summarize as You Read

Define:
summarize
_____

Recall that the blind student stopped her reader from time to time so that she could summarize sections of material in her own words onto the tape. Summarizing is an extremely effective means for improving reading comprehension. You will need the instruction that some of the later chapters will provide as well as considerable practice to learn to write summaries easily and skillfully. Still, it is not too soon to start to learn this skill.

Two questions you can ask to help you learn to summarize are: (1) What is the subject? and (2) What did the author say about it? You can ask these questions about short sections of material as well as about chapters and even books. Section summaries may be written in the white space at the end of sections, chapter summaries in the blank space at the end of chapters, and book summaries on the back and inside covers of a book. A summary retells, in language you can easily understand, the ideas that you think the author wants you to understand and remember.

Textbook authors usually write chapter summaries in complete sentences at the end of each chapter. You will find such summaries at the end of the chapters

---

[1] From _Understanding Human Behavior_, 3rd edition, by James V. McConnell (New York; Holt, Rinehart and Winston, 1980), p. 692. Copyright © 1974, 1977, 1980 by Holt, Rinehart and Winston, CBS College Publishing.

in this book. Use them to help you check your understanding of the material. Your own summaries, however, need not be this complete. They will be more useful to you, in fact, if you jot them in outline form so that you later can reread and study them.

At the end of each chapter in this book, a space is provided for you to write a summary. To help you organize your ideas, use the topic headings that appear in bold-face type throughout the chapter as the main headings in your outline.

In-Chapter Exercise 3

The following are summary notes that you might make on the introduction and first section of this chapter. Continue this summary by adding some brief notes about the active reading process.

Summary of Chapter 1

What is the subject?

1. *Ways to become an active reader*

What did the author say about it?

1. *Blind student active — concentrating, comprehending*
2. *reader passive — no meaning*

Learn Vocabulary

3 types:

1. *specialized — assoc. with subject — boldface*
2. *general — used for any subject — circled*
3. *allusions — place, people, events — wavy line*
select interesting words
define briefly in margin
use context and dictionary

The Active Reading Process

Develop the Active Reading Habit

Develop the habit of active reading by practicing the active reading strategies presented in this chapter as you read the rest of this book. Write brief definitions of words and mark the text, just as you did on page 00, as you go along. Finally, write your own chapter summaries at the end of each chapter. In the first three chapters of the book, headings will be provided to help you organize your summaries. Later you will be expected to provide your own.

Next, use the skills you are practicing here when you read your other college assignments. Be careful, however, not to identify too many unfamiliar words or to take too many marginal notes so that you become discouraged. In your other books, select only the words that interest you or that you must know in order to understand the subject. Underline selectively, write an occasional marginal note, and write summaries at the end of sections and of chapters. Finally, turn to your instructors to help you read difficult material. They can explain, provide background, even read passages aloud in class and comment on them. Instructors' comprehension will probably be imperfect, just like yours, but because of their familiarity with the subject, they can help you stretch to their level of comprehension. Working together

Define: collaborate

for the comprehension of a difficult passage can be a rewarding collaborative effort between instructor and student. Such effort usually results in both parties improving their comprehension of the text.

Your goal by the time you finish this book is to make this and all of your other books look like "read" books that you can go back and quickly review and understand again. Now continue with your active reading practice by reading the chapter summary and then writing your own summary of this chapter in outline form.

Chapter Summary

Active readers use various methods to understand reading material that include defining unfamiliar vocabulary; looking for main points; jotting down ideas; summarizing; thinking of examples; drawing pictures; relating unfamiliar material to familiar; asking questions; mentally arguing with the author; predicting what the author may say; guessing at times about meaning; and writing out original ideas inspired by the text. The results of reading are private. We may understand another person's reading only by listening to or reading about those experiences. The "read" pages in this chapter demonstrate ways in which a reader may take notes on a text. The sample summary above demonstrates how to write a brief summary in outline form that answers the questions, "What is the subject?" and "What did the author say about it?" Practice using both active and interactive reading strategies to become an active reader of this and other texts. The symbols for identifying the three types of vocabulary introduced in this chapter are boldface for specialized terms, circles for general vocabulary, and wavy lines for allusions. Square brackets identify your own ideas.

Your Summary

(Use outline form as in In-Chapter Exercise 3 on page 12.)

What is the subject of this chapter?

What did the author say about it?

Learn Vocabulary

The Active Reading Process

Mark the Text

Summarize

Become Active

END-CHAPTER EXERCISES

I. Practice

A. Go back now and write the definitions of the specialized terms and general vocabulary introduced in this chapter in the spaces provided in the margins. Remember to use the dictionary only when the context does not tell you enough. Repeat this activity when you finish reading each chapter in this book.

B. List three reading activities from this chapter that you will use while reading your other textbooks.

a. _____

b. _____

c. _____

C. In this chapter you studied a "read" page from a book owned by Mark Twain and another from an economics textbook. Then you read and marked a page yourself from a psychology textbook. Now actively read and mark the following passage from a physics textbook. Think a moment first about what you already know about nuclear power plants and then get started. Use the same marking techniques that you learned to use in this chapter. Review the example on page 10 if necessary.

Safety Problems with Nuclear Power Plants

As more reactors are being built around the country, there is justifiable concern about their safety and about their effect on the environment. This is particularly true in light of the 1979 near disaster at Three Mile Island in Pennsylvania. These subjects are so vast that we can only touch upon them here.

One of the primary concerns of the public seems to be the fear of a nuclear explosion. Fortunately, the use of water as a moderator limits this possibility—and in an interesting way. As the temperature in a boiling water reactor increases, the water is boiled faster. But this results in steam, rather than water, being present between the fuel elements. Steam, however, contains far fewer molecules in a given volume than does water, and since water molecules are necessary as a moderator, the number of neutrons which are moderated is reduced. The final result is less fission and a slowing down of the reaction.

The same limiting feature occurs for the pressurized water reactor, although the pressure vessel may have to be ruptured before the water would change to steam and shut down the reaction.

A more real danger is the possibility of the water flow being interrupted so that the cooling of the reactor stops. As explained earlier, the production of steam would decrease the rate of fission, but heat would continue to be produced from the great amount of radioactive fission fragments within the core. The temperature could conceivably build to the point where the fuel elements melt, the bottom of the reactor melts, and the ground below the reactor melts. This possibility is referred to, appropriately enough, as the **China syndrome.**

In addition to the China syndrome, a regular non-nuclear explosion may occur because of the tremendous heat produced, causing radioactive materials to be spread through the area surrounding the power plant. To prohibit such an event, all reactors are built with a back-up cooling system which is supposed to go into operation if the regular system fails.

Another concern about nuclear power plants is the everyday release of radioactive materials to the environment. It is apparently almost impossible to prevent small leaks of fission fragments from the fuel elements into the water of the cooling loop. Notice, though, that this water is recycled rather than being continuously released into the environment. In fact, in the pressurized water reactor, cooling water is two cycles away from the water that contains radioactive materials. Nevertheless, slight leaks do develop, and some radioactivity is released into the stream.

There are also some radioactive materials released in a gaseous form from ''smokestacks'' at the reactor site. The total amount of radioactivity that any nuclear facility may release into the water or atmosphere is regulated by the Nuclear Regulatory Commission. Still, the question of what are safe limits is constantly debated.

The disposal of radioactive materials when the reactor core is replaced is another problem. This material contains such highly radioactive isotopes that it is literally *hot* and must be cooled for some time after removal from the reactor. It must then be stored in such a way that there is no chance that it will be released to the environment. At present, sealing it in deep salt mines seems to be the most promising solution.

A major concern about the proliferation of nuclear power plants is the danger of sabotage at reactor sites and the danger of nuclear fuel (or waste) being stolen during transport. One reason for fear is, of course, the fact that the materials could be used to make an atomic bomb. And aside from dangers due to its radioactivity, plutonium is one of the most poisonous materials known to man. It is frightening to imagine plutonium in the hands of terrorists, but the very fact that highly radioactive material is so difficult to handle and transport makes such terrorism much less likely.

A consequence not associated with radioactivity per se is the thermal effect on the cooling stream. So much stream water is required to cool the reactor's water after it has passed through the turbine that the river is measurably warmer downstream from a reactor. The heat affects living organisms within and adjacent to the river. In some cases the effect may be considered beneficial and in others detrimental, but in any case this factor must be taken into consideration in the location of nuclear power plants.[2]

Your Summary

What is the subject?

What does the author say about it?

Be critical of your own understanding. Complete the following statements:

a. I already knew _____
about this subject before I began to read.
b. The easiest parts for me to understand were _____

_____

c. I'd have been able to read this better if I had understood what

the author meant by _____

_____

d. The most interesting and important information for me in this

passage was _____

_____

[2] From *Physics in Your World*, 2nd edition, by Karl F. Kuhn and Jerry S. Faughn (Philadelphia: Saunders College,1980), pp. 517–519. Copyright © 1980 by Saunders College/Holt, Rinehart and Winston. Reprinted by permission of Holt, Rinehart and Winston, CBS College Publishing.

II. Application to Your Other Reading.

Marking the text and summarizing it are difficult for most readers, and you have just practiced these activities on college textbook material. You may have felt some frustration as you tried these tasks. All readers experience dissatisfaction with their comprehension from time to time. The important fact is that you have now tried some active reading strategies on one important type of material you will have to read, your college textbooks. You will become more successful and confident in reading such material as you practice using these strategies in your other books.

A. Read and mark a page in one of your other textbooks as you have practiced doing here. Bring it to class to be checked by the instructor or compare your reading and marking with a classmate's.

III. Discussion and Class Activities

A. Do you now have different ideas about what is required of a reader than you did before you read this chapter? How have your ideas changed?

B. Read a passage aloud. Now read one silently. When was your concentration and comprehension best? Some people are visual learners. They learn best by seeing written words. Others are aural learners who learn best by hearing the words. Still others learn by using both methods. Which are you? Try to use techniques that give you the highest degree of comprehension for a particular text.

C. Discuss your reading of the passage on nuclear reactors. What active strategies did you use? How did you answer the final questions? Are you satisfied with the degree of comprehension you achieved in reading this passage?

IV. Vocabulary Review

Try now to define the words introduced in this chapter from memory. Write a *brief* definition next to each word. If you cannot remember the meanings, look back at what you wrote in the margin, and then rewrite it here. Writing the meanings a second time will help you learn them.

A. Specialized Terms

1. active reader _____

2. context _____

3. process _____

4. active reading strategy _____

5. private product _____

6. interactive _____

B. (General Vocabulary)

1. strategy _____

2. jot _____

3. allusion _____

4. anticipate _____

5. generate _____

6. collaborate _____

CHAPTER 2
Active Readers Ask Questions

In this chapter you will learn:

> How to think about reading as communication.
> How to ask questions to help you read actively.
> How to determine the level of difficulty of selected reading material.
> How to evaluate your present reading skills, habits, and responsibilities.

Define:
**reading
communi-
cation
process**
————
————

This chapter, like Chapter 1, is devoted to breaking passive reading habits. One of the active reading strategies you learned in Chapter 1 was to practice asking questions as you read. Mentally posing and asking questions before, during, and after reading will help you keep your mind on the text and improve comprehension. The questions presented in this chapter have been selected to help you analyze the elements in the **reading communication process**. Asking them will help you think of reading as a real act of communication that takes place between two people via a text.

Reading as Communication

Reading involves an author, a text about a subject, and a reader. When meaning is transmitted from the author's mind to the reader's mind about the subject through the text, then communication takes place. A diagram (see Figure 2.1) of the requirements for author–reader communication will clarify what is actually involved as well as some of the problems that can occur for the reader. As you look at the diagram, one thing may become obvious to you. Authors have an advantage over readers. They select from the world what will appear in their text, and readers may or may not have sufficient knowledge and experience to understand it. When your experience, knowledge, and vocabulary equals or is greater than that of the author's, the text will seem easy to you. You will be able to read it fast and with little difficulty. On the other hand, if the author knows much more about the subject than you do and describes it in words you have never seen, the text will seem difficult. You may feel too discouraged to try to read it.

Define:
empathy
————
————

The reader's comprehension of the text is most close to being perfect when the author and reader share a common language, a similar educational background, a comparable vocabulary, similar interests and experiences, a common empathy, compatible opinions, similar cultures, and when they occupy the same time and

Figure 2.1

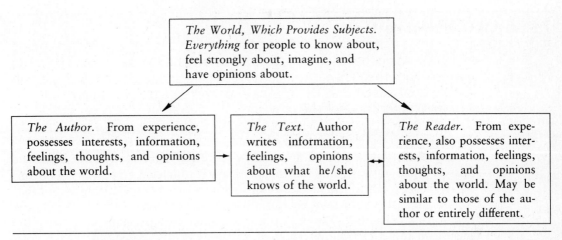

How Authors Communicate with Readers

The World, Which Provides Subjects. Everything for people to know about, feel strongly about, imagine, and have opinions about.

The Author. From experience, possesses interests, information, feelings, thoughts, and opinions about the world.

The Text. Author writes information, feelings, opinions about what he/she knows of the world.

The Reader. From experience, also possesses interests, information, feelings, thoughts, and opinions about the world. May be similar to those of the author or entirely different.

Define: funnel

place in history. Even under those ideal circumstances, comprehension is probably never so perfect that thought is funneled into the reader's mind exactly as it was originally formed in the author's mind.

This does not mean, however, that it is permanently impossible for you to read difficult texts. If you cannot at first bring enough meaning of your own to a text to read it successfully, then you need to read other material, study with a good teacher, and ask the questions you will learn to ask in this chapter. All this will help you stretch to meet the demands of a difficult text.

Who is Emerson?

Perhaps you have already had the experience at the beginning of a semester of trying to read a textbook that made no sense at all. At the end of the semester, however, after reading other material and listening to the instructor lecture, you have returned to the book for final review and have found that it is much easier to read. Ralph Waldo Emerson said that a good reader makes a good book. He meant that a good reader brings sufficient knowledge and skill to the text to be able to read it effectively. The questions that follow will help you think about each part that contributes to the communication process: the author, the subject, the text, and the reader.

Questions To Ask about the Author

Who Wrote the Text?

Begin by asking questions about the author as a person. You form opinions of people when you converse with them. Think of reading as a form of conversation, and as you read–converse, form an opinion of the man or woman who produced the text you are reading. Discover information about the author in the introduction or preface to the book or in headnotes or footnotes to a particular piece or chapter. If there is no such information, try to answer at least some of the questions as you read the text itself.

In-Chapter Exercise 1

Practice reading the following excerpt from an essay written by an Australian businessman. Then answer the author-as-a-person questions as they pertain to this text. Notice that the footnote to this passage will supply you with information for some of the answers.

The Special Joys of Super-Slow Reading

I discovered [the] worth [of super-slow reading] years ago, in the infamous Changi prison-of-war camp in Singapore. I was nineteen, an artillery sergeant, when the city fell to the Japanese on February 15, 1942. Waiting with other Australian POWs to be marched off, I tried to decide what I should take in the single pack permitted. The only limit was what a weary man could carry the seventeen miles to Changi. Our officer thoughtfully suggested, "Each man should find room for a book."

Define: macabre

So I stuffed into my pack a copy of Lin Yutang's *The Importance of Living*—a title of almost (macabre) appropriateness—and began a reading habit that was to keep me sane for the next three and a half years. Previously, if I had been really interested in a book, I would race from page to page, eager to know what came next. Now, I decided, I had to become a miser with words and stretch every sentence like a poor man spending his last dollar. . . .

It took me something like two months to read Lin Yutang's book. By then, his philosophy on tea-making had become my philosophy on reading: You can do it fast, but it's a whole lot better done slowly. I held to the method, even after we had persuaded the Japanese to give us several hundred books from the famous Raffles library in Singapore. . . .

Beyond giving me the will to survive in Changi, slow reading helps me today. . . . I can skim an inter-office memo as fast as the next person. But when faced with a real problem, to clear my mind of everyday clutter I will sit down quietly at home and slowly read myself into another world.[1]

Questions about the Author as a Person	Your Answers

1. What is the author's name?

2. Education?

3. Nationality?

4. Background and interests?

[1] Sydney Piddington, "The Special Joys of Super-Slow Reading," *Reader's Digest*, June 1973, pp. 157–160. Reprinted with permission of the author and *Reader's Digest*.

Questions about the Author as a Person	Your Answers

Define:
deceased

_____

5. Living or dead?

6. If (deceased,) when?

7. What sort of person?

8. Strong opinions or values?

9. Sense of humor?

10. Seem to like people?

11. Why qualified to write on this subject?

When you have formed an estimate of the author as a person, you may then put yourself in the author's place and consider some of the decisions that this author had to make. While writing, authors plan ideas, make decisions, and follow strategies in order to communicate. You can assume, for instance, that the author made decisions about a purpose for writing, the probable background and interests of the audience (readers), and the occasion for writing. It will narrow the distance among the author, the text, and you the reader, if you ask questions that will help you think about the author's decision making during the writing process.

Why Did the Author Write the Text?

Define:
persuade

_____

Define:
dominant

_____

Authors have purposes for writing. The main purposes are: (1) *to give information;* (2) *to change your mind and behavior* or *to* (persuade) *you;* (3) *to express personal feelings or values;* or (4) *to entertain and delight you.* Authors usually have more than one purpose for writing, and these purposes will overlap in much of what you read. Try to identify the author's primary or (dominant) purpose. In all communication it is useful to know what the other person wants and expects of you even though you may not always respond exactly as expected.

In-Chapter Exercise 2

Answer the following purpose questions about the passage on super-slow reading that you just finished reading.

Questions about the Author's Purpose	Your Answers

1. What is the author's *main* purpose (to inform, persuade, express, or entertain)?

2. What are the other purposes?

Who Did the Author Write the Text for?

Besides having a purpose, all authors imagine readers as they write. The authors of your textbooks imagine you as college students who want to read their texts. The authors of junk-mail letters that ask for contributions imagine you as concerned readers who are willing to contribute. As readers we sometimes fit the author's imagined audience and sometimes we do not. Communication is the most effective when we do fit.

Define:
conform

The following are questions you can ask to help you determine how the author thought about the audience and how well you conform to the author's ideas.

_____

In-Chapter Exercise 3

Read the following passage and then practice answering the audience questions.

Building Better Body Language
You know you're intelligent, confident, and capable, but your body may be telling the world you're insecure. Women speakers have special trouble with negative body language because traditionally feminine behavior often conveys insecurity to an audience, according to the Atlanta speech-consulting firm Speakeasy Inc. Among the firm's suggestions:

Stand balanced on both feet, keeping them about six or eight inches apart. The fashion-model stance—knees close together with one ankle wrapped behind the other—makes you appear weak even if the audience can't see your legs. It says, "I can't stand on my own two feet."[2]

**Questions about the Author's Attitude
toward the Audience**   **Your Answers**

1. What type of audience did the author have
   in mind?

2. How well do you fit?

3. What do you need to do to become more
   like the intended audience?

What Caused the Author to Write the Text?

What was
the
Gettysburg
Address?

Authors are not only influenced by their purpose for writing and their imagined audience. The occasion for writing also affects the way they present their ideas. You know, for instance, the occasion of the Gettysburg Address, and knowing that improves your comprehension of the speech. Develop the habit of asking what outside event motivated or caused an author to write a particular text.

_____

[2] Reprinted by permission from the 1981 issue of *Insider*. © 1981, by 13-30 Corporation.

In-Chapter Exercise 4

Look at the passage you just read about building better body language and answer the question as it pertains to it.

Question about the Author's Occasion for Writing: **Your Answer**

1. What event caused the author to write this?

Questions To Ask About the Subject and Its Development

What Is the Text About?

When you wrote your summary at the end of Chapter 1, you answered the questions, "What is the subject?" and "What did the author say about it?" These are useful questions to ask every time you read because they focus your attention on the subject, where it belongs.

In-Chapter Exercise 5

Read the following passage and then try to answer the subject questions below. If you have difficulty, look forward to additional information in the next chapter to help you answer such questions more easily.

Next Lecture, Take Note of the System

If you're having trouble taking notes in some of your classes, it could be because you're hearing the lecture but not really listening to it. The secret to taking good notes, according to Dr. Lyman Steil, a professor in the rhetoric department at the University of Minnesota, is not only hearing the lecture content but also listening for the method the professor uses to present the lecture. Some of the most common techniques:

Point system. "The professor walks into class, announces that three topics will be covered in the lecture, and then proceeds to take those points one by one," says Steil. "It's a very predictable and easily organized lecture."

Problem cause and effect. "The professor declares that a problem exists and then explains why. The lecture is built around examining the reasons."

Chronology. "A subject like a medieval war is selected and then discussed in the order that it occurred. This usually makes for very easy note-taking."

Pictorial. "A visual example is given for every point of the lecture. Sometimes this can really help when trying to remember major points later."[3]

---

[3] Reprinted by permission from the 1981 issue of *Insider.* © 1981, by 13-30 Corporation.

Subject and Development Questions	Your Answers

1. What is the subject?

2. What is the main source of information—research or author experience?

3. What are the main ideas?

4. Are the main ideas in a pattern? What
   is it?

5. How does the author develop these
   ideas with subideas and supporting material? What types and why?

6. Does the author use transitional material? Where and why? How does it help
   you understand the text?

7. Is the style formal or informal?

Questions To Ask about the Text

What Type of Text Is It?

Define:
classify

_____

Define:
fiction text

_____

Define:
**nonfiction
text**

_____

You will find it easier to think about how to read a particular text if you first classify it accordingly to its general type. Ask first whether it is a fiction or nonfiction text. Then ask, what type of fiction or nonfiction text? Some common classifications of **fiction texts** are short stories, poems, plays, or novels. Some common classifications of **nonfiction texts** are magazine articles for the general public, specialized scholarly articles, newspaper articles or editorials, textbooks, expository and persuasive books for the general public, and specialized scholarly books. You will be able to think of other classifications yourself. From your past reading experience you can reasonably expect certain distinct characteristics to be associated with each different type of text. You will learn, if you have not already, to actually change your reading strategies to adapt to the type of text you read.

How Difficult Is the Text?

It was pointed out earlier that some texts will be easy for you to read, some will be relatively difficult, and some will be just plain difficult. The intent of the following questions is to encourage you to make a judgment about the level of difficulty of each text you read. They are also meant to persuade you to try to read difficult texts if they can be of any use or value to you.

As you ask questions about the text, develop the attitude that it will be permissible for you to take some chances with a difficult text by guessing at some of the author's meaning. It will even be acceptable to miss part of the meaning. Your aim in reading is to comprehend as much as your present background and experience permit. Note, when you have finished reading, how much communication has taken place and how useful it is to you.

When faced with the task of reading a difficult text, bring all you can to the experience. Remember and think about what you know about the subject already. Then, look for anything familiar—a word, an allusion, an idea—in the next few paragraphs. Finally, *read to the end* even though you do not understand it all. Go back and reread some of the difficult passages. Stop and summarize in your mind or on paper what you have understood from your reading.

In-Chapter Exercise 6

Passage 1 comes from a theoretical book about readers and reading and Passage 2 from a periodical about communication. The questions will help you classify and determine the level of difficulty of the two passages.

Passage 1

The Four Kinds of Meaning
It is plain that most human utterances and nearly all articulate speech can be profitably regarded from four points of view. Four aspects can be easily distinguished. Let us call them *Sense, Feeling, Tone,* and *Intention.*
1. *Sense.*
We speak *to say something,* and when we listen we expect something to be said. We use words to direct our hearers' attention upon some state of affairs, to present to them some items for consideration and to excite in them some thoughts about these items.
2. *Feeling*
But we also, as a rule, have some feelings *about these items,* about the state of affairs we are referring to. We have an attitude towards it, some special direction, bias, or accentuation of interest towards it, some personal flavour or colouring of feeling; and we use language to *express* these feelings, this nuance of interest. . . .
3. *Tone*
Furthermore, the speaker has ordinarily *an attitude to his listener.* He chooses or arranges his words differently as his audience varies, in automatic or deliberate *recognition of his relation to them.* The tone of his utterance reflects his awareness of this relation, his sense of how he stands towards those he is addressing. . . .
4. *Intention*
Finally, apart from what he says (Sense), his attitude to what he is talking about (Feeling), and his attitude to his listener (Tone), there is the speaker's intention, his aim, *conscious or unconscious,* the effect he is endeavouring to promote. Ordinarily he speaks for a purpose, and his purpose modifies his speech. The understanding of it is part of the whole business of apprehending

his meaning. Unless we know what he is trying to do, we can hardly estimate the measure of his success. Yet the number of readers who omit such considerations might make a faint-hearted writer despair.[4]

Passage 2

They Learn from Pupils

Some cultures search one another's eye pupils for nonverbal signals, according to anthropologist Edward T. Hall, who has helped train American diplomats for overseas service. In the Middle Eastern countries, for example, people tend to stand about two feet apart instead of the five feet customary to Americans. This way they see the size of each other's pupils, according to Hall, and can use this as an indicator of how the other person is responding to a situation. For example, a person's pupils tend to dilate when he's interested and contract upon hearing something he dislikes.[5]

Questions about the Type of Text and Level of Difficulty	Your Answers	
	Passage 1	Passage 2
1. How would you classify this text? (fiction/nonfiction and type)		
2. Is the subject familiar? What do you know about it already?		
3. Is the vocabulary familiar or unfamiliar?		
4. Are there unfamiliar allusions?		
5. Are the sentences easy to comprehend or long and difficult?		
6. Are the concepts familiar or brand new to you?		
7. Can you find the major topic divisions or changes of subject?		
8. Is the text easy, relatively difficult, or just plain difficult for you?		

Questions To Ask about Yourself as the Reader

How Will the Text Benefit Me?

You have practiced answering questions about the author, the author's purpose, the audience, the occasion, the subject, the type of text, and the difficulty of the

---

[4] I. A. Richards, *Practical Criticism* (New York: Harcourt Brace, 1929), pp. 175–176.
[5] Reprinted by permission from the 1981 issue of *Insider*. © 1981, by 13-30 Corporation.

text for you. The next questions will help you think about the fourth and most important element in the reading communication process: you the reader. Without you and other readers, the book has no reason to exist. Without your active involvement, communication may fail, and the act of reading will have had no benefit or use for you.

In-Chapter Exercise 7

Think about your reading of the first two chapters of this book, and practice answering these questions as they apply to those chapters.

Questions To Ask about Yourself as Reader	Your Answers
1. Why did you select this text to read? Or, why was it selected for you?	
2. How do you feel about reading this text?	
3. What is your purpose for reading the text?	
4. What are your strengths or limitations as a reader that will help or hinder your reading of this text?	
5. How have you been affected by this text? Were you moved, entertained, persuaded, informed?	
6. What is the value of this text to you? What final use will you make of it?	

Question 6 is the most important of these questions. You should try to answer it for everything you read. To be entertained or to escape, by the way, is an acceptable use of a text. You do not have to read everything for educational profit.

At this point, you are not to suppose that you should answer all of the questions listed so far for everything you read each time you read it. Rather, you are being encouraged to develop the habit of becoming aware of the elements in the communication process and to think about them before, during, and after reading a text in order to improve your active involvement with the text.

Chapter Summary

The reading communication process involves an author, a subject, a text, and a reader. It is difficult for readers to achieve perfect understanding of the author's ideas because the experience and background of the two people are never equal.

One way to improve understanding is to ask questions about the author as a person; about how the author regarded the audience; about the author's purpose and occasion for writing; about the subject and its development; about the type and level of difficulty of the text; and about the final value of the text to you the reader. Questions should be asked before, during, and after reading to improve the reader's active involvement with the text.

Your Summary

What is the subject of this chapter?

What does the author say about it?

Reading as Communication

Questions To Improve Comprehension

END-CHAPTER EXERCISES

I. Practice
A. Read the following selection and practice answering the questions presented in this chapter about the Author, the Subject, the Text, and the Reader. Although you would not always answer all of these questions for every text, practicing them here will demonstrate again some of the many things that active readers can be aware of as they read.

I Was a 49-Pound Weakling

by DON AKCHIN*

As a kid I would have given my buck teeth for O. J. Simpson's speed, Chris Evert's cool grace or Arnold Schwarzenegger's biceps. Instead, I was slow, awkward and had lots of sand kicked in my face.

I wanted badly to be a football player. Instead I became what is known in gym class as a capital–J Joke. The hierarchy of a gym class, you recall, is crowned by an aristocracy of natural athletes who can do anything in any sport with perfect grace, superb power and no apparent effort. Next on the pecking order are those who are only average but cover their shortcomings under a barrage of yap. What's left are the Jokes. When the sides are chosen up for a game, the Jokes are left standing around until somebody says, "Okay, we'll take him and you get him. (Snicker, snicker) Boy, what a Joke."

Jokes like me got this reputation by scoring somewhere between below average and abysmal on every skill test of the year, year after year. The chin-up, sit-up, somersault test, the run-pass-kick test, the 30-second layup test, the one-mile run test—you name it, I flunked it.

Now as I say, I didn't start out to be a Joke. I started out as a football player, back in the first grade, but got off to a shaky start. Everybody on the team was supposed to buy his own red jersey. My mom couldn't find a single red jersey in town, so she bought what she thought was the next best thing: maroon. When I showed up for the first practice, there were 20 guys in red, two in maroon. "Okay," says the coach, "let's divide up into two teams here and run a few plays. Everybody in red is one team, and you two purple guys are the other team. You two see if you can stop the red fellas."

We didn't do all that well against the other 20, but from that moment on, the coach had me pegged as a defensive lineman, no doubt in recognition of my size and brains. I was all of 3-foot-6, weighed almost 50 pounds including shoulder pads, and was the only guy on the team who could spell encyclopedia. Like the rest of the big dumb linemen, I crouched down at the line, listened for the work "hike," and tried to push those giant 4-foot brutes on their cans before they pushed me. They always won. After awhile I took to sidestepping them altogether. Later in the season, someone accused me of biting him—through a helmet, chin strap and mouthpiece, no less. I left the game in tears and my mom assured me I would never have to play again. I was relieved. So was she. She thought football was too dangerous. That may have been in the back of her mind when she bought me a maroon jersey.

It was a short hop, step and jump from touch football washout to full-fledged Joke. All it took was a steady diet of negative reinforcement and continuous doses of the Old Fitness.

*Staff writer Don Akchin is a 149–pound New Fitness enthusiast.

Old Fitness versus New Fitness

The Old Fitness refers to physical education as I learned it (or learned of it) in public secondary schools. It was:

Exclusively physical. Mind and body were treated as separate. It was assumed that most people had either brain or brawn; only rare specimens had both. One was irrelevant to the other.

Comparative. Every student's performance was ranked against a national standard for that age group—not unlike the standarized tests in the classroom. Your ranking told you whether you were normal, better than normal or a Joke.

Competitive. The idea was always to beat everybody else in the class—just like in academics. This was especially true for team sports. V–I–C–T–O–R–Y! Victory! Victory! Is Our Cry!

Punitive. Physical exercise was a punishment for misbehavior. "What did you say, son? Okay, son, take 45 quick laps around that backstop out yonder while the rest of us stay inside where it's cool and play some basketball. Now take off."

The Old Fitness and I were not suited for each other. I was obviously a loser by its rules. Meanwhile I was making "A's" in everything but gym class. I believed in the mind–body split. It was clear that my mind was doing well; my body was not. So I rationalized that my body was just not important. If I were never going to be O. J. Simpson or Arnold Schwarzenegger or Rod Laver or Hank Aaron, then who needed it? Big deal. Could Einstein do layups?

The Old Fitness is still irrelevant to me. For years I thought that was the only fitness there was.

Fortunately for me, and many others who have been turned off over the years by the Old Fitness, it is no longer the only system. If you read the latest literature on sports and exercise, you'll notice a distinct change. The experts are taking a turn to the East—borrowing concepts and attitudes from Oriental philosophies—and also a turn to the new branches of psychology which emphasize human potential. From my viewpoint, those are turns for the better.

This New Fitness is:

A body-mind integration. The physical, mental and spiritual are all interrelated. The body is not a machine that needs maintenance to run efficiently and works independently of the mind; it is a part of the whole person. Physical well–being improves mental alertness, relieves anxiety and tension, even helps you sleep better.

Noncomparative. You don't rate yourself against a "norm"; you set your own standards, based on your own needs and objectives. You also are free to set your own pace.

Noncompetitive. You compete with no one, not even with yourself. There are no losers, only a winner—you. Some people are just noncompetitive by nature and by body type. One exercise physiologist says 70 percent of all body types are not represented at the Olympics because competitive sports are only appropriate for certain bodies. There are sports and activities, though, for every body.

Fun. Exercise and activity are to be enjoyed, not taken like medicine. If your only motivation for doing something is that you *should* because it's good for you, you probably won't continue it for long. You're also missing the point. Sport and recreation aren't supposed to be work or punishment. The play's the thing.

After reading some literature by members of the New Fitness school, I have embarked upon a fitness program of my own. Nobody is more surprised than me. I don't expect to ever look like O. J. or Arnold (or Chris), but that isn't important.

The New Fitness recognizes that you don't have to be an athlete to be fit; and better yet, that you need not train like an athlete to be a fit nonathlete. The idea is to meet your own needs for your own body and your own life. You don't have to work at it; it's far better for you to play. And you don't *have* to do anything. . . .

Putting Together Your Personal Fitness Program

What exactly is fitness? How do you know whether you are fit?

Under the Old Fitness this question is answered by taking a few tests and comparing your performance to the "norm". The New Fitness leaves every individual to arrive at his or her own answer, based upon individual needs, personal goals and different life styles.

The New Fitness definition is less precise but more flexible: you are fit if you can work effectively all day at your normal tasks; if you have enough energy left at the day's end to invest in leisure activities; and if you have the stamina and strength to withstand an unexpected physical emergency—running a block to catch a bus, for instance, or rearranging all your furniture.

By this definition, a healthy, physically fit accountant would not be in the same shape as a healthy, physically fit lumberjack. But there's no need to be.

Fitness can be divided into three basic factors: endurance, strength and flexibility.

Of the three, endurance is the factor that is most often cited as the key indicator of fitness. And the exercises which build endurance have the greatest effect on your overall health. If you perform a rhythmic or "aerobic" exercise long enough, often enough and hard enough, some definite physical changes take place inside your body. The arteries leading into you heart enlarge; new capillaries develop around the heart; the heart pumps more efficiently, forcing more blood through the body with each stroke and resting longer between strokes. The lungs also work more efficiently, processing more oxygen with each breath. These changes are called "training effect."

The exercises which can provide you with training effect include jogging, swimming, bicycling, brisk walking, rowing, rope–skipping, some forms of dancing, skating, hiking, cross–country skiing, and vigorous games of basketball, handball, squash, hockey, tennis (singles) and soccer. But the physical changes happen only if you do three things:

1. Exercise at enough intensity to increase your heart rate to between 70 and 85 percent of its maximum rate. (The maximum is roughly 220 minus your age for males, 226 minus your age for females; for a 20–year–old male, the

maximum rate is 200 beats per minute, and exercise must be intense enough
to achieve a rate of 140 to 170 beats per minute.)
2. Keep your heart rate at 70 to 85 percent of maximum for at least 10 minutes,
and eventually for 20 minutes or more.
3. Perform this intensive exercise regularly, at least three times a week (pref-
erably every other day).

It's an all–or–nothing proposition. All three of these requirements must
be met, or no training effect takes place. It takes several months of regular
exercise to accomplish the physical changes.[6]

Questions about the Author as a Person   **Your Answers**

1. What is the author's name?

2. Education?

3. Nationality?

4. Background and interests?

5. Living or dead?

6. If deceased, when?

7. What sort of person?

8. Strong opinions or values?

9. Sense of humor?

10. Seem to like people?

11. Why qualified to write on this subject?

Questions about the Author's Purpose

1. What is the author's *main* purpose (to
inform, persuade, express, or entertain)?

2. What are the other purposes?

Questions about the Author's Attitude toward the Audience

1. What type of audience did the author
have in mind?

2. How well do you fit?

3. What do you need to do to become
more like the intended audience?

[6] Reprinted by permission from the 1977 issue of *Insider*. © 1977 by 13-30 Corporation.

Questions about the Author's Occasion for Writing	**Your Answers**

1. What caused the author to write this?

Subject and Development Questions

1. What is the subject?

2. What is the main source of information—research or author experience?

3. What are the main ideas?

4. Are the main ideas in a pattern? What is it?

5. How does the author develop these ideas with subideas and supporting material? What types and why?

6. Does the author use transitional material? Where and why? How does it help you understand the text?

7. Is the style formal or informal?

Questions about the Text

1. How would you classify this text?

2. Is the subject familiar? What do you know about it already?

3. Is the vocabulary familiar or unfamiliar?

4. Are there unfamiliar allusions?

5. Are the sentences easy to comprehend or long and difficult?

6. Are the concepts familiar or brand new to you?

7. Can you find the major topic divisions or changes of subject?

8. Is the text easy, relatively difficult, or just plain difficult for you?

Questions To Ask about Yourself As Reader

1. Why did you select this text to read? Or, why was it selected for you?

Questions To Ask about Yourself As Reader	Your Answers

2. How do you feel about reading this text?

3. What is your purpose for reading the text?

4. What are your strengths or limitations as a reader that will help or hinder your reading of this text?

5. How have you been affected by this text? Were you moved, entertained, persuaded, informed?

6. What is the value of this text to you? What final use will you make of it?

II. Application to Your Other Reading

A. Select a passage from one of your textbooks or from a magazine, newspaper, or book. Describe it briefly, and answer the following questions about it. Submit your answers to your instructor.

1. What type of text is it? Classify it (fiction, nonfiction, textbook, magazine, etc.).
2. Who wrote it?
3. What was the author's purpose for writing it?
4. What type of audience did the author write it for?
5. What outside circumstances caused the author to write it?
6. What is it about?
7. How difficult is it for you to read?
8. How will it benefit you?

III. Evaluate Your Present Reading Skills, Habits, Attitudes, Responsibilities, and Preferences

Answer the following questions to help you and your instructor form some opinions about *you as a reader* at the present time.

1. How would you classify your own present reading skills?
   poor _____   average _____   excellent _____
2. How would you describe your usual comprehension of most of the material that you read?
   poor understanding _____   mediocre understanding _____
   (less than 25% of the text)   (25%–50% of the text)
   very good understanding _____   excellent understanding _____
   (50%–75% of the text)   (more than 75% of the text)
3. How would you rank the speed at which you do most of your reading?   extremely slow _____   somewhat slow _____   about average, compared to my friends _____   faster than average ___

extremely fast _____. (Your actual, present reading speed and comprehension will be tested in Part II.)

4. How would you classify your present degree of interaction with the text? I am a passive reader most of the time. _____
I am an active reader when the material is interesting. _____
I am almost always an active reader. _____

Describe your present reading habits.

1. What do you voluntarily select to read on a regular, routine basis (mention

   everything, including billboards and food labels)? _____

   _____

2. Name some types of material that are *easiest* for you to read (because you are interested and bring some background and experience to such

   material). _____

   _____

3. If possible, name some hobbies or special interests that you have learned

   about by reading. _____

   _____

What are your present attitudes toward reading?

1. Do you *enjoy* reading any particular type of material? _____

   What? _____

2. Do you *hate* reading any particular type of material? _____

   What? _____

3. Are you *afraid* to try to read any particular type of material? _____

   What? _____

4. Check all of the following that are true of you.

   ___ I dread reading and successfully avoid it most of the time.

   ___ I think of reading as an unpleasant necessity and do it as little as possible.

   ___ I don't mind reading material I select, but I hate to read assignments.

___ I don't read very much because I lack confidence in my ability to comprehend.

___ I think of reading mainly as a tool to help me gain information.

___ I think of reading as a reward for completing a difficult task.

___ I would rather curl up with a book or magazine in my free time than do anything else.

___ I read to relax and get my mind off other problems.

___ I think it is important to read to develop values and ideas about life.

___ I believe that reading helps me generate and think through ideas of my own.

5. Are you satisfied with your present attitudes toward reading?

yes _____ no _____   Why? _____

What are your current reading responsibilities?

Make a list of all of the reading that you believe you will do in the next three or four months. Include specific textbooks, secondary sources, library research materials, and other such materials.

_____

_____

_____

_____

Describe your reading preferences.

1. How do you get ideas about what you would like to read? Check all that apply.
   _____ recommendations from family and friends
   _____ recommendations from professors
   _____ book reviews in newspapers and journals
   _____ browsing in the bookstore
   _____ browsing in the library
   _____ getting ideas for subjects from newspaper and magazine articles
   _____ seeing TV programs and movies that make you want to read the book or read more on the subject

   _____ other _____

2. List one thing that you would like to read right now:

_____

Describe your present reading ability.

Look back over your responses to the above questions and also to those in Chapter 1 (pp. 7—8). Write a few sentences in which you describe either why you are now satisfied with yourself as a reader or how you would like to improve as a reader.

_____

_____

_____

_____

_____

_____

_____

_____

_____

_____

This evaluation should give both you and your instructor some insights to help you plan your future reading instruction so that it will help you meet your reading goals.

IV. **Discussion and Class Activities**
   A. Discuss how asking author questions changes the way you think about a text as you read it.
   B. Give examples of material you have read whose main purpose was (1) to give information; (2) to persuade; (3) to express personal feelings or values; and (4) to entertain or delight. Can you give similar examples of television programs?
   C. Give examples of texts you intend to read this year that are difficult, relatively difficult, and easy for you. Would everyone in your class regard their level of difficulty as you would? Why or why not?
   D. List at least three strategies presented so far for reading difficult texts.
   E. What is the value of this chapter to you?
   F. If your past experience has made you a good reader, what effect will additional experience have?

V. Vocabulary Review

Follow the same instructions for vocabulary review given at the end of Chapter 1. Write brief definitions from memory. Check the margins to review the meanings of words you cannot remember.

A. Specialized Terms

1. reading communication process _____

2. fiction text _____

3. nonfiction text _____

B. General Vocabulary

1. empathy _____

2. funnel _____

3. macabre _____

4. deceased _____

5. persuade _____

6. dominant _____

7. conform _____

8. classify _____

C. Allusions

1. Ralph Waldo Emerson _____

2. Gettysburg Address _____

CHAPTER 3
Active Readers Know What To Expect

In this chapter you will learn:

>How to broaden your present expectations of a text.
>How to find the subject and focus.
>How to identify main ideas, subideas, supporting material, and transitions.
>How to follow the author's train of thought.
>How to read when the author breaks the usual rules.

Define:
assume

A major purpose of this book is to help you broaden your expectations of what is likely to appear on the printed page. Active readers assume, for instance, that everything they read will have a main subject, and that one of their responsibilities in reading will be to discover it. Besides a main subject, there are other common characteristics that you can expect to find in most of the texts you read, and this chapter will identify them for you. When you finish reading, you will know much better what to expect when you attempt the rapid, close, and critical reading in the other chapters in this book.

What You Can Expect of a Text

Define:
conven-
tional

We are all taught rules about using language from the time we start to use it. We learn to think and express our ideas in established patterns, we learn conventional word order, and we learn the rules of grammar. Writers assume that you know these rules about language. They also assume that you will either consciously or unconsciously notice how the rules have been followed or broken in the material they write. This chapter will remind you of some of the most important terms and rules about language. You have been introduced to them before in your English and speech classes. You may never have thought until now, however, of looking for them in the work of other authors.

Specifically, you can expect everything you read to have a subject and a focus; main ideas, subideas, and supporting material that tell more about the subject; transitions that separate the main ideas; and a logical train of thought that you can follow. This chapter will help you recognize and use these special features of a text to improve your reading comprehension.

How To Find the Subject and Focus

Define:
subject

_____

Define:
focus

_____

Define:
purpose
or
thesis
sentence

_____

_____

Everything you read will have a main **subject** and a **focus.** The subject is the overall main idea or topic, such as *my high school days, my neighborhood, inflation,* or *the draft.* The focus is the main point the author makes *about* the subject, such as *my high school days were happy, my neighborhood was a great place to grow up, inflation creates problems for retired people,* or *the draft should be voluntary.* The rest of the material in a selected passage, chapter, or book tells more about the subject and the focus.

Authors often state the subject and focus in a **purpose,** or **thesis sentence,** which usually can be found in the first paragraph. This is not always the case, however. Sometimes an author does not state the purpose until midway or even at the end of the text. At times no purpose is directly stated, and you will have to ask when you have finished reading, "What was the subject?" and "What was the main point the author made about it?" The title can also often help you answer these questions.

In-Chapter Exercise 1

Read the next two passages that come from the beginning of a chapter. Write in the blanks provided what you think the subject and the focus of the rest of the material in the chapters will be.

Passage 1

Chapter 4. Listening

Listening, then, is one of the most frequent activities in which we engage. Despite this fact our experience shows that much of the listening we and others do is not at all effective. We misunderstand others and are misunderstood in return. We become bored and feign attention while our minds wander. We engage in a battle of interruptions where each person fights to speak without hearing the other's ideas.

As you'll soon read, some of this poor listening is inevitable. But in other cases we can be better receivers by learning a few basic listening skills. The purpose of this chapter is to help you become a better listener by giving you some important information about the subject. We'll talk about some common misconceptions concerning listening and show you what really happens when listening takes place. We'll discuss some poor listening habits and explain why they occur.[1]

What is the subject of this chapter? _____

What is the focus? _____

[1] From *Understanding Human Communication* by Ronald Adler and George Rodman (New York: Holt, Rinehart and Winston, 1982), p. 90. Copyright © 1982 by CBS College Publishing. Reprinted by permission of CBS College Publishing.

Passage 2

Chapter 5. The Importance of Rome

The contribution of Rome to the development of Western civilization is tremendous. In fields like language, laws, politics, religion, and art Roman culture continues to affect our lives. The road network of modern Europe is based upon one planned and built by the Romans some two thousand years ago; the alphabet we use is the Roman alphabet; and the division of the year into twelve months of unequal length is a modified form of the calendar introduced by Julius Caesar in 46 B.C. Even after the fall of the Roman Empire the city of Rome stood for centuries as the symbol of civilization itself; later empires deliberately shaped themselves upon the Roman model.[2]

What is the subject of this chapter? _____

What is the focus? _____

How To Discover the Important Ideas

Everything you read can be separated into bits and chunks of material and labeled as **main ideas, subideas, supporting material,** or **transitions.** You do not have to try to recognize any other types of material in the texts you read. These are, furthermore, used by authors in various combinations. Being able to recognize a main idea, spot a transition, and understand how subideas and supporting material are used to develop main ideas will enable you not only to discover the important ideas, but also to follow along and see how these ideas are developed and related to each other.

A Review of Outline Form and Content

Define:
outline

_____

Before you read further, recall for a moment what you know about **outline** form. Recall specifically that:

1. Outlines provide a visual picture of ideas and their relationships to each other.
2. A title at the beginning of an outline usually states the main subject.
3. Main ideas are written next to the margin and labeled with roman numerals.
4. Other materials on an outline tell more about the main ideas. They are indented and labeled with numbers or letters.
5. Outlines are used by authors to help them think about their ideas and put them in an order. Then it is easier for the author to write.

[2] From *Culture and Values: A Survey of the Western Humanities* by Lawrence Cunningham and John Reich (New York: Holt, Rinehart and Winston, 1982), p. 196. Copyright © 1982 by CBS College Publishing. Reprinted by permission of CBS College Publishing.

6. Readers try to discover the author's outline. This helps them understand and remember the author's ideas more easily.

7. There are many forms an outline might take. One outline might look like this:

Title
I. Main Idea
    A. Subidea
        1. Supporting material
    B. Subidea
        1. Supporting material
        2. Supporting material
        (transition to Main Idea 2)
II. Main Idea
    A. Subidea, and so on.

Define:
component

Now read on about the characteristics of these different parts of the outline that are also the (component) parts of every text you read.

The Characteristics and Functions of Main Ideas

Define:
main idea

Main ideas set forth the author's major line of thought in the text. In final summaries, where you find them stated by themselves, they are often almost meaningless because they do not tell enough. On an outline the main ideas appear at the Roman numeral level. Examples are:

> Main idea: Surveying textbooks is a useful study aid.
> Main idea: Good readers follow conscious reading strategies.

It is important to locate main ideas so that you will have the topics you will be reading about clearly in mind. You need to read on, however, to gain the additional and supporting information you need to understand these ideas.

The Characteristics and Functions of Subideas

Define:
subidea

Define:
restrict

The major function of **subideas** is to give you more information about main ideas. Subideas may (restrict) a main idea by telling what will not be discussed, or they may expand or give additional information about it. They appear at the A and B level on an outline. Examples are:

Main Idea   I. Surveying textbooks is a useful study aid.
Subideas   A. Survey to understand the pattern of ideas before you read.
             B. Survey as a final review.
             C. The following steps describe how to survey.

OR

Main Idea   I. Good readers follow conscious reading strategies.
Subideas   A. They isolate and learn unfamiliar vocabulary.
             B. They ask questions as they read.
             C. They look for main ideas.

Sometimes the only additional information you are given about a main idea is at the subidea level. When this is the case, it is the author's judgment that you have sufficient additional information to understand the main idea.

The Characteristics and Functions of Supporting Material

Define:
supporting material

_____

_____

Supporting material is used by authors to further clarify main ideas and subideas and also to make them interesting and memorable. Supporting material is usually the easiest matter to understand in a text because it is familiar, close to, or even a part of the experience you bring to your reading. It is also usually easy to imagine, visualize, or sense. Supporting material is indicated at the *1* or *a* level on an outline. Types of supporting material are as follows:

Define:
compar-ison

_____

Define:
analogy

_____

Define:
voracious

_____

Define:
metaphor

_____

Define:
simile

_____

Define:
validate

_____

Define:
contrast

_____

Define:
manipulate

_____

1. The *example* or *specific instance* is the most frequently used type of supporting material. It may be brief or long, real or made-up.

2. *Comparisons* show how two ideas, events, or objects are alike. Sometimes they show how difficult, unfamiliar ideas or objects are similar to familiar ideas and objects. The comparison of the unfamiliar with the familiar helps you understand the unfamiliar better. One type of comparison is the analogy. When two items in the same general category of things, such as two under-developed countries are compared, the comparison is called a literal analogy. When two objects from different categories are compared (a Third-World country and a voracious animal, for example), the comparison is called a figurative analogy. Other types of comparison are the metaphor and the simile. Metaphors link two unlike objects so closely that there is an implication that one object is the same as the other object (the camel is the ship of the desert). Similes show how two unlike objects are actually alike ("my love is like a red, red rose"). All of these types of comparison are used to clarify objects and ideas and thereby aid your understanding of them. They may also be used at times to emphasize or validate an object or idea.

3. *Contrasts* are the opposite of comparison. They are used to further explain or clarify by showing how one object or idea is *different* from another, often more familiar, object or idea. Comparison and contrast are sometimes used together to show both similarities and differences.

4. *Vivid description* is a type of supporting material that appeals to your senses. A writer who describes a rock concert in a vivid way can make you imagine not only sights but also sounds, smells, tastes, and even the shove of the crowd. Such description makes the main ideas more interesting, memorable, and clear.

5. *Personal anecdotes* and *stories* are used by writers to illustrate ideas and to catch your interest and help you remember the ideas.

6. *Statistics* and other *facts* are usually included by authors to prove main ideas. They can also be used to clarify. Read statistics and facts carefully to see if they seem true or if they have been manipulated to say what the author wants them to say.

7. *Quotations* from authorities are usually used to prove or emphasize a main idea by giving it extra weight. Authors who, through quotes, show that Abraham Lincoln, Golda Meir, Winston Churchill, or Margaret Mead agree with them thereby make their own ideas more believable and more easily acceptable.

8. *Graphs, pictures, drawings,* and all other *visual materials* help you understand main ideas and make them easier to remember.

Because supporting material is usually familiar and interesting to you, it is easier to notice, read, and remember than the more general main ideas and subideas. Do not make the common error of reading only the supporting material without determining what ideas it supports. You need to understand main ideas, subideas, and supporting material and their relation to each other for adequate comprehension of a text.

In-Chapter Exercise 2

The following is a list of four bits of material that have been scrambled into an illogical order. One is a main idea, one is a subidea, and two are items of supporting material. Unscramble them and write them in the outline below.

The Scrambled List

1. For example, they might use the SQ3R method for reading textbooks. The Q stands for Question.
2. They ask questions as they read.
3. Professor Robinson, who devised this method, says asking questions "will bring to mind information already known, thus helping you to understand that section more quickly."[3]
4. Good readers follow conscious reading strategies.

The Outline

Main Idea   I. _____

    Subidea   A. _____

        Supporting Material   1. _____

                                  _____

                                    _____

        Supporting Material   2. _____

                                    _____

                                    _____

[3] Francis P. Robinson, "Survey Q3R Method of Reading," in *SR/SE Resource Book,* Frank L. Christ, Ed. (Chicago: Science Research Associates, 1969), p. 36.

Now go back and read the material as you have placed it on the outline. It should make much better sense than it did in its scrambled form.

The Characteristics and Functions of Transitions

Define:
transition
or signal
word

Transitions, which are also sometimes called **signal words,** are used by authors for several purposes. Transitions can show relationships between ideas, change the subject by moving from one idea to another, or emphasize main ideas and make them stand out. Some types of transitions are as follows:

Define:
preoutline
or advance
organizer

1. *Transitions that name at the outset the main ideas to be discussed.* These are also called **preoutlines** or **advance organizers.** An author might, for example, state: *"This chapter or section will deal with. . . ."* and then name the main ideas that will be discussed. Read such transitions carefully and form a mental outline of the ideas in your mind before you begin to read. Then read to fill in the details.

2. *Transitions that separate and emphasize a list or series of ideas.* Many authors make the ideas in a list stand out by numbering the items *first, second, third,* or by using other words that can substitute for numbering such as *one, another, finally,* and *last.* When you encounter these words, ask yourself, "first and second what." Then find the main idea that should head the list. For example:

Main Idea	I. There are several types of transitions.
Subideas	A. Advance organizers
	B. Numbering

   Make certain that you know the main idea, because the list, by itself, will not make sense without a main idea heading.

Define:
Internal
summary

3. *Transitions that separate major sections of material in a book or chapter.* Headings and subheadings in boldface type, such as those used in this book and most other textbooks, both separate main ideas and announce what the next main idea will be. Read them to help you see the main chunks that make up the whole. Get the main idea of each chunk in mind so that you can then read to fill in details. Writers also sometimes separate major sections of material with **internal summaries** that restate what has just been said and then introduce the next topic. Some phrases that signal internal summaries are: *We have just. . . ; Next we will. . . .* or *In the last chapter. . . . ; In the next. . . .* or *Let us look back over. . . . ; Let us now turn to. . . .* Read such transitional material carefully. It functions something like a road sign that tells you where you have been and where you are going next. Here is an example from a computer science textbook:

   > In previous sections we have studied many aspects of data processing including various types of hardware, the concept of system software, programming languages, and computer applications. We will now turn our attention to integrating many of these concepts while gaining an insight into the management and use of a computer system via another case study. The important concepts which you will learn in this chapter include the following.[4]

[4] From *Data Processing: The Fundamentals* by Wilson T. Price (New York: Holt, Rinehart and Winston, 1982), p. 139. Underlining added. Copyright © 1982 by CBS College Publishing. Reprinted by permission of CBS College Publishing.

4. *Transitions that signal a change in time or place.* Usually brief words or phrases only are necessary to signal a change in time or place. Examples of these signals are: *next, soon, after, later, after a time,* or *much later.* Examples of place signals are: *at another place, near, above, beneath,* or *on the other side.* Notice such transitions as you read and move mentally with the author to another time or another place.

5. *Transitions that lead you from a main idea to a subidea or to supporting material.* Examples are: *for instance, for example, to quote, in comparison, in contrast, on the other hand, specifically, to illustrate.* Use these signals to help you mentally hook subideas and supporting material to the main ideas.

6. *Transitions that signal the end is in sight.* Examples are: *to conclude, in summary, finally, in brief,* or *let me end with.* Read material that follows these signals carefully. It will usually be an important concluding point or a summary of all the main ideas explained so far. Read to check whether or not you located all important material successfully.

7. *Transitions that change the point of view.* There are many transitional words and phrases that are used to change the point of view and to state relationships among ideas. Examples are: (a) *Those are the problems; let's look at the solutions.* (b) *Now that we understand the cause of the problem, let's study its effects.* (c) *Let's look at this from another angle (or point of view).* (d) *Not only . . . but also.* (e) *If (such is the case), then (this will happen).* (f) *Let's look at some similar cases (or some different ones).* (g) *however, nevertheless,* and *but.* Such transitional words and phrases help you follow author's thoughts as they move from idea to idea. They also show how ideas are related to each other.

Improve your understanding of the important ideas in the material you read by recognizing and analyzing the functions of main ideas, subideas, supporting material, and transitions. Remember that the function of main ideas is to present the author's major ideas. The function of subideas is to tell more about those ideas. The functions of supporting material are to make the ideas clear and interesting, to prove or emphasize them, to aid the reader's memory, and to connect the ideas to the reader's own experience. Finally, the function of transitions is to lead the reader from one idea to another, to show relationships among ideas, and to make ideas stand out.

In-Chapter Exercise 3

Read the following paragraph and notice how it has been constructed with a main idea (MI), subideas (SI), and supporting material (SM). Read it once to get a sense of the whole, and then re-read it to analyze the parts. Underline the main idea, box the transitions, and, finally, outline it on the blank outline below.

Physical "Noise"
The physical world in which we live often presents distractions that make it hard to pay attention to others. The sound of traffic, music, others' speech,

and the like interfere with our ability to hear well. Also, fatigue or other forms of discomfort can distract us from paying attention to a speaker's remarks. Consider, for example, how the efficiency of your listening decreases when you are seated in a crowded, hot, stuffy room that is surrounded by traffic and other noises. In such circumstances even the best intentions aren't enough to ensure clear understanding.[5]

Outline of Physical "Noise"

MI I. _____

   SI A. _____

   SI B. _____

      SM 1. _____

   SI C. _____

Identify two transitions:

1. _____

2. _____

In-Chapter Exercise 4

Now read another paragraph that comes from an article in *Change* magazine. It describes some of the changes that have taken place in college life in the past twenty years. Read it first to get a sense of the whole. Then re-read it to see how the parts contribute. Underline the main idea, box the transitions, and visualize the relationships among the parts by filling in the blank outline.

Sexuality and College Life
In the early 1960's a woman student at a distinguished university in Massachusetts fell sick in her boyfriend's apartment and stayed there overnight instead of returning to her dormitory; she was subject to disciplinary procedures even though she had slept in a separate bed. About the same time a young Stanford woman was similarly dismissed when a dean of women discovered that she had had sexual relations with a married man. Sometime later there

[5] From *Understanding Human Communication* by Ronald Adler and George Rodman (New York: Holt, Rinehart and Winston, 1982), p. 97. Copyright © 1982 by CBS College Publishing. Reprinted by permission of CBS College Publishing.

was much publicity about a Barnard student who had shared an apartment with her boyfriend while officially occupying a dormitory room. She too was punished for her offense. All three cases were from the most liberal institutions in the nation. Everywhere penalties for sexual improprieties were severe; even legitimate pregnancies were considered embarrassing if the women continued to attend classes. A vast army of housemothers and other residential staff were hired expressly to watch over the sexual conduct of students. Elaborate security measures were devised to keep the sexes divided. Male and female dormitories often were built far apart to underline the separation of the sexes.[6]

Outline of Sexuality and College Life

SM 1. _____

SM 2. _____

SM 3. _____

SI A. _____

MI I. _____

SI B. _____

SI C. _____

SI D. _____

Identify three transitions:

1. _____

2. _____

3. _____

How To Follow the Author's Train of Thought: General and Specific Ideas

Notice that the two outlines you just completed are quite different from each other. The author of the first paragraph began with the main idea, and the author of the second began with supporting material.

[6] Joseph Katz and Denise M. Cronin, "Sexuality and College Life," *Change,* February–March, 1980, p. 44.

Define:
general
_____
_____

Define:
specific
_____
_____

You can expect, in every text you read, to find a repeated movement back and forth between the **general** (main ideas) and the **specific** (subideas and supporting material). An author may begin with a general idea and then become specific, as in the paragraph about listening, or begin with specific ideas and then generalize about them, as in the paragraph about college life in the 1960s. You will be able to follow the author's thoughts and thus comprehend them more easily if you can learn to perceive this repeated movement back and forth from general to specific. Look for this pattern in the material you read, the lectures you listen to, even in your conversations with your friends. Figure 3.1 provides a conversation to serve as an example:

Figure 3.1 Note movement from general to specific in a conversation.

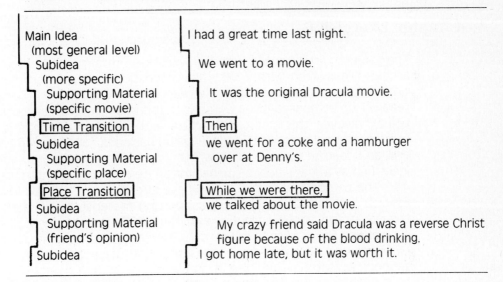

In-Chapter Exercise 5

Mark each of the following items as either *general* or *specific*. Remember that you need to know more about general ideas in order to understand them well. Specific material tells more *about* them. By itself, however, specific material does not make much sense either. To understand it, you must know what general ideas it describes or develops.

Label each item as *general* or *specific*.

1. It was round, blue, and comical looking. _____

2. College is a challenge to most people. _____

3. Reading can be rewarding. _____

4. All those frightened coeds prove the point. _____

5. You can compare it to a spinning top. _____

6. Automobiles can be dangerous. _____

7. I like most animals. _____

8. Twenty-five percent of them agree. _____

9. Physicians recommend it more often than other brands. _____

10. It is difficult to pick my favorite sport. _____

In-Chapter Exercise 6

The following article about American violence comes from a newspaper. News articles are written with a very characteristic paragraph structure. Sometimes each paragraph is only one sentence long. Most of the other texts you read will be composed of paragraphs that contain several sentences. At this point, however, this newspaper article, with its special format, is ideal for some additional practice of following the back and forth movement of general and specific material in a written text. Each brief paragraph can be identified as a main idea, a subidea, or an item of supporting material.

The paragraphs in this article have already been laid out in a pattern for you. The author begins with supporting material, as did the author of the paragraph about college life in the 1960s. As you read, identify the subject and focus as soon as you can. Then read each paragraph and label it MI (main idea), SI (subidea), or SM (supporting material). Label the types of supporting material used also (example, quote, statistics, etc.). The first two have been done for you. Underline the purpose or thesis sentence when you find it and box all transitions.

Subject:

_____

Focus:

_____

American Violence: Worse than Ever Before?

by JANE SEE WHITE

1. SM _____
example _____

1. A San Francisco bus driver took a sandwich break. As he walked from a coffee shop back to his bus, two men attacked, shooting him repeatedly, killing him. There was no clear motive for the attack.

2. SM _____
example _____

2. In Atlanta, moved by the slaying and disappearances of 17 black children, the City Council approved a new ordinance making it illegal for children 14 years old and younger to be outside, unaccompanied by an adult, between 7 p.m. and 6 a.m.

3. _____

3. In San Jose, California, sniper fire shattered a window in a fire truck as it raced to a blaze. A fireman was injured by flying glass.

4. _____
_____

4. On Staten Island in New York, a man shot his father-in-law through the head. He shot his mother-in-law and slit her throat. He shot his brother-in-law. Then he drowned his own 22-month-old son in the bathtub.

5. _____

5. All this, and more violence, occurred last week. But it might have been the week before—or the week to come.

6. _____
_____
_____

6. The weeks stretch into months. The violence seems never to abate. The blood-splashed headlines, the photographs of grieving kinfolk, the images of broken and twisted bodies seem to multiply.

7. —

7. Are we so violent? Have we somehow evolved into a more bestial, brutal society than once we were?

8. _____
_____

8. "No one knows. We don't have very good statistics to compare the violence now to years ago. But I'll tell you this: For all the lousy, heinous crimes you see in the press today, I can go back 20 years and match them," said Leonard Tropin, vice president of the National Council on Crime and Delinquency.

9. _____
_____

9. "Nobody is really sure whether violence is going up or down," said Murray Strauss, a University of New Hampshire sociologist who specializes in the study of violence. He added:

10. _____
_____

10. "There have been periods of U.S. history that were fully as violent—or more violent—than now. For instance, right after the Civil War."

11. _____

11. Most experts agree that though we may seem increasingly violent as a society, evidence neither exists to prove or disprove the contention.

12. _____
_____

12. Consider: The Federal Bureau of Investigation's widely watched crime statistics say that in recent years Fire Island—a 31-mile-long barrier reef off Long Island's south shore—had the highest crime rate in New York state.

13. _____
_____

13. Fire Island has no roads. About 230 people live there year-round. Officials say there has not been a murder, rape, robbery or an aggravated assault there in at least three years.

14. _____
_____

14. Yet, the FBI reports that in 1979 there were 648 crimes per 1,000 residents of the Fire Island village of Saltaire; in New York City, the rate was 119 per 1,000.

15. _____
_____

15. How? Partly because FBI statistics give the same weight to a toy wagon theft as to a murder; also, in an isolated village like Saltaire, the theft of a toy wagon is more likely to be reported to police than in New York City.

16. _____

16. Walter Menninger, a psychiatrist at the Menninger Foundation in Topeka, Kan., believes that, statistics aside, the key question is: Are we as much more violent as we believe?

17. _____
_____

17. "The answer is probably not. We have always been violent. The media have made our violence more evident—and I mean both real and fictional violence," he said. "So our perception is that there's much more violent crime and that's especially true among heavy television viewers."

18. _____
_____

18. "Violent fact is reinforced by violent television fiction," he said. "Grisly headlines increase our sense that we are surrounded by violence, but so, too, do the bloody fist fights and gleeful machine-gunning we see on television."

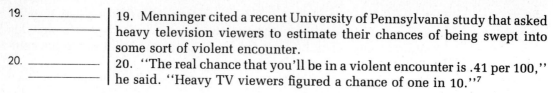

19. _____
    _____

20. _____
    _____

19. Menninger cited a recent University of Pennsylvania study that asked heavy television viewers to estimate their chances of being swept into some sort of violent encounter.

20. "The real chance that you'll be in a violent encounter is .41 per 100," he said. "Heavy TV viewers figured a chance of one in 10."[7]

Glance back through the article and then write a brief summary of it in outline form.

What is the subject?

What did the author say about it?

Continue to practice the skills that you used in the above exercise as you read your textbooks and other college assignments. You will find that some writers use many transitions while others use almost none. Some writers use a great deal of supporting material, while still others write mainly at the main idea and subidea levels. Whatever the nature of the text, you will have read well if, when you finish, you can state the subject and main ideas in summary form.

What If the Author Breaks the Rules?

You may, from time to time, look for what you have come to expect will be in the text, including difficult vocabulary, a subject and focus, main ideas, subideas, supporting material, and transitions. But you will still have trouble understanding it. Authors themselves sometimes create barriers to comprehension. They do so either by deliberately breaking the rules to create certain effects or by doing a poor job of writing.

Some of the most famous rule-breakers have been poetry and fiction writers. The works of such writers are usually studied in literature classes. The poet, e.e. cummings, for example, does not capitalize the letters in his name nor does he capitalize or otherwise punctuate his poetry according to the usual rules. The punctuation he does use may at first look like typographical errors. More careful reading,

---

[7] The Associated Press, February 8, 1981. Reprinted with permission.

however, shows that he uses punctuation in special ways to add meaning to his poems. For example, in one poem he tells how he slammed on the brakes and brought his car

>to a : dead.
>
>stand—
>
>; Still) [8]

The punctuation, even more than the words, creates a sense of a stopped car. James Joyce, the novelist, is another well-known rule-breaker. To capture the random stream-of-consciousness thoughts that pass through his characters' minds, he wrote long passages of rambling, disconnected, and unpunctuated material that includes images, associations, and bits of conversation. His novels are even difficult for scholars who understand his intentions and have read and re-read his works.

When writers break familiar rules, as in the two examples just cited, you will need to put aside your usual expectations of the text and try to determine why the author has broken the rules and what effect this has had on the text's meaning.

A more difficult reading problem is created by careless or unskilled authors who produce texts that can be nearly impossible to comprehend. Here is a list of some of the problems that can interfere with effective communication between you and the author. They are listed here to remind you that when comprehension is difficult, the fault may not always be entirely yours, and also to include in your new expectation of the text, the realization that authors can make errors.

Barriers to Communication Caused by Careless and Unskilled Writing

Define:
ambiguity
_____

_____

1. *Ambiguity.* Ideas are unclear. Possible cause: Ideas were never clearly and completely thought out by the author in the first place. Or, author thought about ideas but could not express them clearly.

2. *Incomplete idea.* The author does not tell you enough. Possible cause: Author assumes you will supply information you cannot reasonably be expected to supply.

Define:
jargon
_____

_____

3. *Insufficient emphasis on subject and main ideas.* Author does not clearly state, restate, or use transitions, supporting material, or other means to emphasize and clarify subject and main ideas. Reader finishes reading with no clear idea of what author was trying to say. Possible cause: The author fails to outline and plan ideas and then keep them in mind and make them clear while writing.

Define:
pretentious
diction
_____

4. *Jargon* and *pretentious diction.* The author uses language that is *pompous,* overused, or unnecessarily formal and complicated. Possible cause: The author is either trying to show off or is too lazy to think of fresh ways to say things.

Define:
pompous
_____

_____

5. *Quotations and citations from research and authorities are misleading or inaccurate.* Secondary source material is twisted and distorted to make it fit what the author wants it to say. Possible cause: Author did not read or understand the source material well enough, or deliberately misrepresented it to advance his or her own argument.

[8] From *Collected Poems* by e. e. cummings (New York: Harcourt, Brace, and Co., 1938), poem no. 134

6. *Inconsistent use of key terminology.* Author establishes and defines key terms to represent key concepts and then fails to use them consistently, and may even substitute other terms throughout the text. Possible cause: Author does not remember the established terms and then misses the errors in final editing or proofreading.

When you encounter the above problems in a text, do your best to comprehend the author's meaning in spite of the problems. Sometimes being aware of the problems and their possible causes can help you read for meaning without letting them distract you too much. You can also, of course, vow never to create such problems for readers of material you write yourself.

Now, as at the end of the first two chapters, complete your summary of this chapter.

Chapter Summary

As a reader you can expect authors to follow certain established language rules. Specifically, you can expect everything you read to have a subject and a focus; to be made up of main ideas, subideas, supporting material, and transitions; and to have a logical order of ideas that you can follow. Read the title and introductory paragraphs to find the subject and focus. Then read to find the main ideas that set forth the author's main line of thought. Analyze how they have been developed with subideas and supporting material. Supporting material is used by authors to clarify, to emphasize, to prove, to make ideas interesting and memorable, and to link main ideas to the reader's experience. Transitions help you follow the author's thoughts and discover the main ideas since their purpose is to state relationships, change ideas, and emphasize ideas. You can expect everything you read to move from the general to the specific over and over again. Follow this pattern of thought to help you improve your comprehension. When you finish reading, state the subject and the major points in summary form. Writers may interfere with your successful comprehension by breaking the usual rules or by doing a poor job of writing. When the author breaks the rules, try to understand why and see what effect it has on meaning.

Your Summary

What is the subject of this chapter?

What does the author say about it?

What You Can Expect of a Text

How To Find the Subject and Focus

How To Discover the Important Ideas

How To Follow the Author's Train of Thought

What If the Author Breaks the Rules?

END-CHAPTER EXERCISES

I. **Practice**
A. Read the following essay through to the end to get a sense of the whole. Then re-read it and analyze it. Use the following marking symbols to help you do this:
   1. Underline the sentence in the first paragraph that best states the subject and focus.
   2. Find the three main ideas in this essay, underline them, and label them *MI* in the margin. Now go back and break this essay into the three chunks of material that explain these three main ideas. Make the chunks obvious by drawing a line across the page to show where the author stops discussing one main idea and begins to discuss another. Number the chunks.
   3. Re-read each of the three chunks of material and analyze and mark them as follows:
      a. in the margin, label the subideas as *SI*
      b. in the margin, label the supporting material as *SM*
      c. Box the transitions

4. As you re-read, circle all (general vocabulary words) you do not understand and would like to learn, underline **specialized terms** twice, and mark all allusions you do not understand with a wavy line.

5. If any ideas of your own occur to you as you read, write them in the margin in[square brackets].

6. Write a very brief summary, in phrases only, at the end.

7. Answer the questions at the end.

Of Reading Books

by JOHN LIVINGSTON LOWES

1. I mean to talk for a little while, most informally and most unacademically, about reading—a subject which, partly through our fault, I fear, some of you have come to think of in terms of courses and degrees, but which is infinitely bigger than all that. It is not even scholarship that I shall have in mind. It is simply reading, as men and women have always read, for the delight of it, and for the consequent enriching and enhancement of one's life. I have put delight deliberately first, for the rest, I believe, is contingent upon that. "In general," said Goethe once, "we learn from what we love." And I propose first of all to exhibit some lovable readers—not a Professor or even a Doctor in the lot, I think—and allow them to speak for themselves. And first, then, reading for the sheer delight of it.

2. "In anything fit to be called by the name of reading," says Stevenson in his delectable *Gossip on Romance,*

   the process itself should be absorbing and voluptuous; we should gloat over a book, be rapt clean out of ourselves, and rise from the perusal, our mind filled with the busiest, kaleidoscopic dance of images, incapable of sleep or of continuous thought. It was for this . . . that we read so closely, and loved our books so dearly, in the bright, troubled period of boyhood. . . . For my part, I liked a story to begin with an old wayside inn where, toward the close of the 'year 17—,' several gentlemen in three-cocked hats were playing bowls. A friend of mine preferred the Malabar coast in a storm, with a ship beating to windward, and a scowling fellow of Herculean proportions striding along the beach—"

   and so on delightfully. . . .

3. Well, that is the meat upon which your inveterate readers are apt to have fed in childhood, and happy are you, if you have been caught at it young. For romances, and stories of giants, magicians, and genii, read with a child's quick and plastic imagination, are stepping-stones to later, deeper, if no more enduring loves. . . .

4. "But," you will say to me, "we haven't time." I know it; very few of us these days have time—those least, I sometimes think, who have it most. But even if, being modern, and ambitious, and efficient, and all that, we are whirled along with our fellow atoms in the rush, we shall not be

losing time if now and then we pause, and loaf (I wish the fine phrase had not been worn so trite), loaf, and invite our souls. And if you worship in the temple of efficiency, don't forget—and again I am drawing on the wise humanity of William James—that "just as a bicycle chain may be too tight, so may one's carefulness and conscientiousness be so tense as to hinder the running of one's mind." And after all, the smooth, free running of one's mind is fairly important to the precious efficiency of whatever machinery it be that your particular intelligence helps to run. Even as a business proposition (to fall again into the jargon of the day), time spent in unclamping our mental processes is time won, and not time lost.

5. And the thing is possible. Here is part of a letter which Matthew Arnold wrote to his sister. And Arnold, being a hard-driven public official, knew whereof he spoke.

> If I were you, my dear Fan, I should now take to some regular reading, if it were only an hour a day. It is the best thing in the world to have something of this sort as a point in the day, and far too few people know and use this secret. You would have your district still, and all your business as usual, but you would have this hour in your day in the midst of it all, and it would soon become of the greatest solace to you.

6. I am not, as you see, submitting a bibliography, or suggesting learned apparatus. For the moment we are concerned with reading for the sheer delight of it, when the world is all before us where to choose. But with delight there may be coupled something else. For one also reads to learn. And about that and one thing more, I shall be very brief.

7. Let me begin with a remark of Oliver Wendell Holmes:

> There are about as many twins in the births of thought as of children. For the first time in your lives you learn some fact or come across some idea. Within an hour, a day, a week, that same fact or idea strikes you from another quarter. . . . Yet no possible connection exists between the two channels by which the thought or the act arrived. . . . And so it has happened to me and to every person, often and often, to be hit in rapid succession by these twinned facts or thoughts, as if they were linked like chain-shot.

Now all of us have had that experience, and it is apt to give us a curious sensation. "Here," we say, "we've gone all our life without seeing that, and now all at once we see it at every turn. What does it mean?" Not long ago, for example, my attention was called for the first time, in a letter, to an international society of writers; two days later my eye caught a reference to it in a daily paper. Soon afterward I heard, for the first time to my knowledge, the name of a certain breed of terriers. Within a week I had come across the name in two different novels I was reading. What had happened? Simply this. I had doubtless seen both names time and again before, but nothing had ever stamped them on my memory, and so when they turned up again, they wakened no response. Then, all at once, something did fix them in my mind, and when they met my eye once more, they were there behind it, so to speak, to recognize themselves when they appeared. There had been set up in my brain, as it were, by each of them, a magnetic centre, ready to catch and attract its like.

8. Now one of the things which the process we call education ought to do, and by no means always does, is to establish in the mind as many as possible of these magnetic centres—live spots, which thrust out tentacles of association and catch and draw to themselves their kind. For there are few joys in reading like the joy of the chase. And the joy of the chase comes largely through the action of these centres of association in your brain. . . . I cannot lay too strong an emphasis upon the sort of pleasure which results from the constant recognition in what one reads of things which link themselves, often in endlessly suggestive fashion, with things one has already read, till old friends with new faces meet us at every turn, and flash sudden light, and waken old associations, and quicken the zest for fresh adventures. To read with alert intellectual curiosity is one of the keenest joys of life, and it is a pleasure which too many of us needlessly forgo.

9. And that leads me to say two things. In the first place, one cannot begin too soon to buy one's own books, if for no other reason (and there are many more) than the freedom which they give you to use their fly-leaves for your own private index of those matters in their pages which are particularly yours, whether for interest, or information, or what not— those things which the index-makers never by any possibility include. To be able to turn at will, in a book of your own, to those passages which count for *you*, is to have your wealth at instant command, and your books become a record of your intellectual adventures, and a source of endless pleasure when you want, as you will, to turn back to the things which have given delight, or stirred imagination, or opened windows, in the past.

10. That is one point. The other is this. Goethe observed to Eckermann one day, in those *Conversations* which constitute one of the most thought-provoking volumes in the world: "You know, Saul the son of Kish went out one day to find his father's asses, and found a kingdom." Which is a parable. For it is when you are looking for one thing as you read—it may be some utterly trivial affair—that ten to one you come upon the unexpected thing, the big or thrilling thing, which opens up new worlds of possibilities. Most of our discoveries—even if, as usually happens, they are discoveries only to us—are made when we are hot on the trail of something else. For because we are looking, we see, and we see more than we look for, because the eye which scans the page is actively alert to everything. And the more you *have*—the more live cluster-points of association there are in your brain—the more you see, and reading becomes a *cumulative* delight. "The dear good people," said Goethe once, "don't know how long it takes to learn to read. I've been at it eighty years, and can't say yet that I've reached the goal." One never does. There are always, as one goes on reading, unpath'd waters, undream'd shores ahead. And that is the secret of its perennial delight.

11. One reads for the sheer enjoyment of it; one reads to learn; and there is a yet more excellent way. "You don't *learn* anything," said Goethe of Winckelmann, "when you read him, but you *become* something." That

strikes to the very root of things, for it puts into one pregnant phrase the supreme creative influence in the world—the contagious touch of great personalities. And if a good book is, in truth, as Milton in a noble passage once declared, "the precious life-blood of a master-spirit, embalmed and treasured up on purpose to a life beyond life," then that creative influence of life on life is in the book, and as we read, our spirit is enriched and grows, and we *become* something. We are just a little ashamed these days, I know, in our reaction from a certain sort of cant, to read for our soul's sake, or our spirit's sake, or for edification, in the fine old sense of a sadly misused word. We feel, somehow, that it isn't quite the thing. Well, I don't care at all what terms you use; but we are more than intellect, and more than sense, and the deepest-lying springs of life are touched by life alone. And the men who have lived, and learned through living, and won through life a wide and luminous view—these men have the imperishable creative power of broadening, deepening, and enhancing life. They are the true humanists, and humanism, as I take it, is the development, not of scholars, not of philosophers, or scientists, or specialists in this or that, but of human beings. Goethe was such a humanist, and Goethe, by practice, not by precept, has pointed out the way.

12. "I read every year," he said, "a few plays of Molière, just as I also, from time to time, look over the engravings of the great Italian masters. For we little men aren't capable of maintaining within us the greatness of such things, and we have always to keep turning back to them from time to time, in order to quicken within us our impressions." "Today after dinner," wrote Eckermann—and this sort of thing happened again and again—"Goethe went through the portfolio of Raphael with me. He busies himself with Raphael very often, in order to keep himself always in touch with the best, and to exercise himself continually in thinking the thoughts of a great spirit after him." And this, mind you, was not a preacher, or a teacher, or a reformer, but the most puissant, richly endowed spirit of the modern world. Beyond delight, and beyond intellectual adventure, there is the spiritual contagion of great books.[9]

Write a brief summary in phrases only:

Subject: _____

Main idea 1. _____

Main idea 2. _____

Main idea 3. _____

---

[9] From *Of Reading Books* by John Livingston Lowes. Copyright 1929 by John Livingston Lowes. Copyright renewed © 1957 by John Wilber Lowes. Reprinted by permission of Houghton Mifflin Company.

Questions

1. What type of text is this? Classify it. _____

2. Who wrote it? _____
   a. What did you learn about the author's personal interests and values

      from reading this? _____

3. What was the author's purpose for writing this? _____

   _____

4. What type of audience did the author write this for? _____

   _____

5. What is this about? _____

6. How difficult was this for you to read? _____

7. How will reading this benefit you? _____

   _____

II. Application to Your Other Reading

   A. Select the first two or three pages of a chapter that you have been assigned to read in one of your textbooks. Use the identical marking symbols (explained in steps 1–6 on pp. 57–58) that you just used to mark "Of Reading Books." Then answer the same seven questions you just answered about that essay. Display your marked text in class and submit the answers to your questions.

III. Discussion and Class Activities

   A. Identify and analyze the supporting material used by one of your instructors in a lecture. Describe what effect this supporting material had on you as you listened.
   B. Reconstruct a recent conversation with a friend, and analyze the levels of generality and specificity in it as was done in the example on page 51.
   C. Watch a television documentary and state the subject, the focus, and the main ideas. Write them in brief summary form.
   D. Discuss how you can use the theory in this chapter to improve your note taking in lecture classes and your composition of essay exam answers.

IV. Vocabulary Review

Write brief definitions from memory of the specialized terms and general vocabulary words in this chapter. When you cannot remember a meaning, check the margins, and then write it.

A. Specialized Terms

1. subject _____

2. focus _____

3. purpose or thesis sentence _____

4. outline _____

5. main idea _____

6. subidea _____

7. supporting material _____

8. comparison _____

9. contrast _____

10. transition or signal word _____

11. preoutline or advance organizer _____

12. internal summary _____

13. general _____

14. specific _____

B. General Vocabulary

1. assume _____

2. conventional _____

3. component _____

4. restrict _____

5. analogy _____

6. voracious _____

7. metaphor _____

8. simile _____

9. validate _____

10. manipulate _____

11. ambiguity _____

12. jargon _____

13. pretentious diction _____

14. pompous _____

C. Allusions
Go back through the essay "Of Reading Books" and select five allusions you did not understand, look them up, and write their meaning below. Discuss what you have learned from this exercise in class.

1. _____

2. _____

3. _____

4. _____

5. _____

Write five general vocabulary words from the essay "Of Reading Books" that you selected to learn along with their meanings.

1. _____

2. _____

3. _____

4. _____

5. _____

Further Reading

The following works provide further information about some of the ideas discussed in Part I of this book.

Adler, Mortimer J. and Charles Van Doren. *How To Read a Book,* revised ed. New York: Simon & Schuster, 1972.

Algozzine, Jane. "Comprehension: The Key to Learning," *Publishers Weekly,* October 29, 1979, pp. 38–40.

Goodman, Kenneth S. and Olive S. Niles. *Reading: Process and Program.* Champaign, Ill.: National Council of Teachers of English, 1970.

Iser, Wolfgang. *The Act of Reading.* Baltimore: Johns Hopkins University Press, 1978.

Kinneavy, James L. *A Theory of Discourse: The Aims of Discourse.* Englewood Cliffs, N. J.: Prentice-Hall, 1971.

Shuy, Roger W., Ed. *Linguistic Theory: What Can It Say About Reading?* Newark, Del.: International Reading Assn., 1977.

Smith, Frank. *Reading without Nonsense.* New York: Columbia Teachers College Press, 1978.

Smith, Frank. *Understanding Reading,* 3d ed. New York: Holt, Rinehart and Winston, 1982.

Suleiman, Susan R. and Inge Crosman. *The Reader in the Text.* Princeton, N. J.: Princeton University Press, 1980.

Wood, Nancy V. *College Reading and Study Skills,* 2d ed. New York: Holt, Rinehart and Winston, 1982.

PART II
The Rapid-Reading Process

Part II of this book will help you learn to vary your reading speed to suit the type of material you are reading and your purpose for reading it. The following ideas will receive special emphasis in the next three chapters:

1. You will always have too much to read. Consequently, you will need the skill and flexibility to read some texts rapidly and others slowly in order to finish.
2. You will read only enough of a text to satisfy your purpose for reading, and then you will put it aside.
3. You will need special skills to read rapidly, or you will revert to your old, slow reading habits. In this part of the book you will be taught skills for surveying, skimming, scanning, selective reading, and speed reading.
4. You will have to be willing to take some risks while you are learning to read rapidly. Avoid worrying about what you are missing. Remember, you can always go back and read the text again.

Prepare for your reading by trying to answer the following questions:

1. Do you know what a flexible reader is?
2. Do you possess a variety of reading speeds and techniques or do you read everything the same way?
3. How do you decide when to read rapidly, when to read slowly, and when to put the text aside because you have learned enough to satisfy your present reading purpose?
4. Can you give examples of reading situations when you might survey? skim? scan? read selectively? use speed-reading techniques?
5. Do you know step-by-step procedures for using these rapid-reading techniques? If you do, can they be improved, or are you satisfied with them?

CHAPTER 4
Surveying Books, Chapters, and Articles

In this chapter you will learn:

How to discover the important ideas, organization, and features of a book by surveying.
How to find the main ideas and how they are organized in a chapter or article by surveying.

Define:
surveying

The intent of this chapter, like Chapter 3, is to widen further your expectations of the text by introducing you to some of the special features of books and articles and by teaching you an organized procedure for examining them. This procedure, which will enable you to become acquainted with a book or article in a short period of time, is called **surveying.**

Most authors begin with ideas that they arrange in a logical order before they write. Surveying enables you to form a mental outline of these ideas and to speculate about why the author has arranged them in a particular way. In surveying, you examine certain features of the text until you are able to state (1) the subject, (2) three or four main ideas, and (3) some of the supporting material. When you finish surveying, it will be as though someone had already told you about the text and what to expect from it. Surveying can be effectively practiced on all types of texts, including your textbooks and the most difficult books in the library. You can even survey a novel, although it is unlikely that you would want to very often.

Some Purposes for Surveying

All techniques that speed up your reading or change your usual reading habits demand active, concentrated effort, and it is impossible to put such effort into any task unless you know why you are doing it. Some purposes of surveying, then, are:

Define:
preview

1. *To* **preview** *a text before you read it.* Surveying to preview helps you understand the whole before you read the parts. You will locate the main ideas, understand their order, decide what additional reading will be necessary, and how you will do it most effectively. It is a valuable preliminary step for close reading.

Define:
review

2. *To* **review** *a text after you have read it.* Surveying for review helps you go back over material you have just read that may still be somewhat jumbled in your mind. This type of review helps you locate the pattern of ideas and arrange

them in your mind so that you can remember them for a discussion or examination.

3. *To obtain a quick estimate of a text.* There will be times when you will want to know something about a book or article quickly, without reading it. Within ten or fifteen minutes, surveying can help you form an opinion that will help you decide whether or not you want to read further.

4. *To create a context for research.* Surveying enables you to learn enough about a text so that you can take paraphrased or quoted material from it without misrepresenting the author. It would be unwise, for example, to quote an author on nuclear energy without knowing when the book was written or what the author's opinions, research experience, or approach to the subject is. Surveying enables you to learn about these matters before you quote so that you quote more intelligently.

5. *To learn something about a text when you do not have time to read it.* Surveying is never a substitute for close reading. Surveying is much more effective than reading when time is short, however. You could probably read only three or four paragraphs in the time it would take you to survey. Furthermore, surveying would enable you to state the subject and main ideas of the entire text instead of the subject of the first three or four paragraphs.

You will survey more effectively if you have one of these purposes in mind each time you use this skill.

Preparing to Survey

Besides setting a purpose, there are other mental preparations that you can make to help you survey effectively. You should try to determine at the outset what you have in common with the author. Draw on what you already know about the subject, and link it to the familiar material you encounter in the text. Try to predict the direction the author will take with the ideas. Make a few mental guesses and then look to see if you were correct.

Get set to look at each page differently from the way you do when you are reading. Remind yourself that you will be searching for certain things you expect will be there. You will also be predicting, guessing, and taking some chances. You will not be reading word-by-word and sentence-by-sentence.

In order to survey successfully, determine to learn the steps for surveying and follow them exactly. Failing to do so will cause you to slip back to your old habits and begin to read. Finally, prepare yourself to survey by setting a time limit. Do this for two reasons: to help you meet your purpose for getting certain information quickly and to help you avoid the tendency to slow down and read.

The Six Steps for Surveying a Book

To survey a book, set a time limit of no more than 20 to 30 minutes. Survey actively, using a pencil to mark what you are looking for. Proceed through the following steps:

STEP 1. *Read the title of the book*. Stop and think about what the title suggests to you. What do you already know about the subject?

In-Chapter Exercise 1

Here are some book titles to practice on.

	Do You Know Anything About the Subject?	
	Yes	**NO**

Define:
Vladi-
vostok

Improving Reading
Biology
Criminal Justice: Situations & Decisions
Vladivostok under Red & White Rule
The Last Generation of the Roman Republic
Physics in Your World

If the title communicates nothing to you, look up the words that you do not know before proceeding further. Then concentrate on the subject of the book as you continue with the other surveying steps.

Define:
front matter

Define:
back matter

STEP 2. *Locate the customary features and the special features of the book*. The customary features of a book, unless it is fiction, are the *title*, the *table of contents*, the *introduction* or *preface*, and the *chapters*. In addition, you may discover that a book has other special features such as an *index*, a *glossary*, an *answer key*, and special aids for reading such as *key terms in boldface*, *pictures*, *diagrams* and *graphs*, and *marginal notes* or markings to help you locate important ideas. There may be special *tables of information* about the book on the inside covers and on the outside back cover as well. Chapters may begin with *objectives or learning goals* and end with *summaries*, *quizzes*, *discussion questions*, and/or *references* and *suggestions for further reading*. Locate the features of a book by looking through the **front matter** (that which precedes the chapters) and the **back matter** (that which follows the chapters), by studying the inside and outside covers of the book, and by looking through a sample chapter.

In-Chapter Exercise 2

Locate the features of this book that you are now reading.

1. Look through the front matter and make a list of its contents:

   1. _____

   2. _____

3. _____

4. _____

5. _____

2. Look through the back matter and make a list of its contents:

1. _____

2. _____

3. _____

4. _____

3. Study the inside and outside covers of the book and make a list of their contents:

1. _____

2. _____

3. _____

4. _____

4. Look through a sample chapter and make a list of its special features:

1. _____

2. _____

3. _____

4. _____

5. _____

6. _____

7. _____

8. _____

STEP 3. *Read the Table of Contents.* The Table of Contents lists the topics that will be covered in the book and shows the order in which they will appear. Read it for a quick idea of the contents and organization of a book. Read it also to help you divide a book into meaningful chunks of material. Some

Tables of Contents list only the titles of the chapters. Others, as in this book, list both chapter titles and main headings.

In-Chapter Exercise 3

Practice reading the Table of Contents to this book. In the blanks below write the titles of the four main sections of this book. Then, in your own words, list at least two topics that you can expect to learn about in each section.

1. _____

_____

_____

2. _____

_____

_____

3. _____

_____

_____

4. _____

_____

_____

STEP 4. *Read the Introduction or Preface.* Usually you will come into closer personal contact with an author by reading the introduction or preface than in any other place in the book. Take time to get acquainted. The author may tell you what prompted the writing of the book; what its special features are; how it should be read or studied; what background you will need to read it effectively; what biases are present; why the book is organized as it is; and how special terminology is handled.

In-Chapter Exercise 4

Read both the *Preface* and *To The Student* located at the front of this book. List some of the useful information included in this material.

1. _____

2. _____

3. _____

4. _____

5. _____

When you have finished reading the introduction, look at the outside back cover of the book. Frequently, there is another brief explanation there of the main points and special features of the book.

Define:
**Intro-
duction**
_____
_____

STEP 5. *Read the titles and the first and last paragraphs of the first and last chapters.* Look to see how the author begins and ends the book. Almost without exception you can count on everything you read to have three distinct divisions:

Define:
main body
_____
_____

Define:
summary
_____
_____

> an **introduction** (where the author tells you what will be said);
> a **main body** (where the author says it);
> a **summary** or conclusion (where the author either tells you what was said, or, in the case of a **conclusion,** emphasizes one or more important ideas).

You can usually expect books to have these divisions and each chapter to have them also.

Define:
conclusion
_____
_____

By looking at the beginning and end of the first and last chapters of a book, you often encounter some of the most important ideas that will be developed.

In-Chapter Exercise 5

Look, for example, at the titles and the first and last paragraphs in Chapters 1 and 13 of this book and answer the following questions about them.

1. What is the title of Chapter 1?_____
2. Read only the first and last paragraphs of Chapter 1. What is this chapter

   about?_____

   _____

3. What is the title of Chapter 13?_____
4. Read only the first and last paragraphs of Chapter 13. What is this chapter

   about?_____

   _____

5. Why do you think the author began and ended this book with these

particular topics?_____

_____

Define:
synthesize
_____
_____

STEP 6. *Look through the main body of the book.* Stop only to read the chapter title and the learning objectives (like those at the beginning of each chapter in this book). If there are none, read the first paragraph of each chapter. Compare your impression of the topics and their sequence in the book with the information you got from reading the Table of Contents. (Synthesize) this information into a mental outline of what you can expect the book to contain.

In-Chapter Exercise 6

Practice Step 6 by reading the learning objectives at the beginning of Chapters 2 through 12. What additional information do you now have about the contents of this book?

You have now completed the six steps for surveying a book, but the process is not complete. Stop now, look away from the book, and list in your mind or on paper what you now know about the book. Be certain to include in your list answers to the questions below. Since you have just finished surveying this book, practice answering these questions as they pertain to it.

In-Chapter Exercise 7

1. What is the subject of the book?_____

_____

2. What are three or four of the main ideas in the book?

    1. _____

    2. _____

    3. _____

    4. _____

3. What do you know about the author and the author's purpose?

    _____

4. What are some of the most important special features of the book?

    _____

    _____

    _____

5. What will you now do with the book? Abandon it? Read parts of it? Read it rapidly? Read it with care, marking it and looking up words as you go along?_____

    _____

    _____

6. How has surveying this book been useful to you?_____

    _____

    _____

You may at first have difficulty remembering the six steps for surveying. One way to remember such a list is to take off the first letter or two of the key words and make a nonsense word or phrase of them. Here is a pair of rhymed nonsense words. This is a memory or (mnemonic) device to help you remember the steps for surveying a book.

Define:
mnemonic
_____
_____

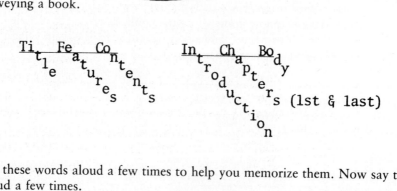

Say these words aloud a few times to help you memorize them. Now say the steps aloud a few times.

The Six Steps for Surveying a Chapter or Article

Surveying a chapter or article is very much like surveying a book. The purposes are the same. The main difference is that it is done on a smaller scale. In surveying a chapter, you pay special attention to the introduction, body, and summary or conclusion in an attempt to locate the most important ideas and to get an idea of the order in which they will be explained. Set a time limit of five to ten minutes, survey actively with a pencil in hand, and proceed as follows:

STEP 1. *Read the title.* What does it tell you about the subject? What do you already know about the subject? What do you predict the author might say about the subject?

STEP 2. *Read the introduction.* Read the learning goals or objectives, if there are any, and the introductory paragraph or section. Look for a purpose or thesis sentence that presents the subject and focus. Look for a listing of the main ideas that will be explained in the body. These features may not be present but, if they are, mark them and read them carefully.

STEP 3. *Read the summary or conclusion.* It is difficult at this point to stop reading and turn to the end of a chapter or article, but do it anyway. Remember you are trying to get a quick idea of the contents and organization. Read material marked summary or conclusion, or read the final paragraph. Look for a restatement of the main ideas or for one important idea that is given special emphasis by being stated at the end. Read through exercises, questions, and vocabulary lists to get additional clues to the main points the author wants to stress.

STEP 4. *Read the headings and subheadings in boldface type.* Turn back to the beginning of the chapter and read quickly through the boldface headings that name and separate the major topics. If there are no headings, read the first sentence, and no more, of each paragraph. These sentences will give you an indication of the main ideas and how much space is devoted to each of them.

STEP 5. *Study the visuals.* Look back through the text again and stop to examine all pictures, graphs, and diagrams. Read the captions under them. This material is usually included to clarify and emphasize major points. Find out what they are.

STEP 6. *Circle specialized vocabulary.* Look to see if specialized vocabulary is in boldface or italics and easy to spot. If it is not, you will still notice some of the important terms as you read introductions, summaries, headings, and picture captions. Circle these words now. They represent major concepts in the text.

Complete the surveying of a chapter or article in the same way you do a book. Stop and think about what you have learned from surveying. Ask questions that encourage you to think about the elements in the reading communication process: the *author* and the author's purpose; the *subject,* focus, and main ideas; special features of the *text* (such as specialized vocabulary or visuals); and the use you the *reader* will make of the text including its potential value to you.

In-Chapter Exercise 8

Take five minutes to survey the next chapter in this textbook. Follow exactly the six steps for surveying a chapter. When you have finished, answer the following questions:

1. What is the subject of Chapter 5?_____
2. List four main ideas.

   1. _____

   2. _____

   3. _____

   4. _____

3. What was the author's purpose in writing it? _____

   _____

4. What are some special features of the chapter that will help you read and

   learn from it? _____

   _____

5. How will it be useful to you? _____

   _____

   _____

Here is another mnemonic device to help you remember the steps in surveying a chapter or article.

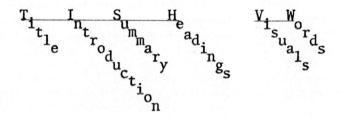

Use it to help you remember the steps until they become habitual.

Chapter Summary

The object of surveying is to get a quick idea about the author, the subject, the main ideas, and the organization of a book or article. Some of the purposes you might have for surveying are to preview, review, form a quick estimate of a text, create a context for research, or get some information in a short period of time. Prepare to survey by setting a purpose and figuring out what you already know about the subject. Then, prepare to break your usual reading patterns and habits. Finally, learn the steps for surveying and follow them exactly within a set time limit. The steps for surveying a book are: Read the title, locate the special features, study the Table of Contents, read the introduction, read the first and last paragraphs of the first and last chapters, and read the chapter objectives or the first paragraph of all the other chapters. The steps for surveying a chapter or article are: Read the title, read the introduction, read the summary, read the headings, study the visuals, and note specialized words. Ask questions when you finish surveying about the author and purpose, the subject and focus, the main ideas, and the special features. Consider also how much more work you want to do with the text as well as its value to you.

Your Summary

Write a brief summary in outline form. Use the headings and subheadings to help you organize your notes.

What is the subject of this chapter?

What did the author say about it?

END-CHAPTER EXERCISES

I. Practice

A. How good is your memory? Write the two mnemonics and the six words each of them represents that were included in this chapter to help you remember the steps for surveying books and articles.

1. Surveying a Book

mnemonic _____

Steps: 1. _____ 4. _____

2. _____ 5. _____

3. _____ 6. _____

2. Surveying an Article

mnemonic _____

Steps: 1. _____ 4. _____

2. _____ 5. _____

3. _____ 6. _____

B. The following are excerpts from the Preface to a biology book. Read and underline all of the special information that the author has included to help you read it. Then answer the questions in the margin.

Preface

What was the author's motivation for writing this book?

_____

_____

How is this book different from other biology books?

_____

This book grew out of two different introductory biology courses that we taught at Cornell University. Dissatisfied with existing texts, we wrote our own materials to produce a comprehensive, up-to-date introduction to all areas of biology. Like many biology teachers, we wished to expose the students to the scientific method in action and to share the excitement of biology by examining both historical background and modern research.

Modern biology books place heavy emphasis on molecular biology, since this was the area with the most rapid accumulation of knowledge in the 1960s. We have balanced the traditional emphasis on cells and molecules with more than the usual amount of material on plants, physiological adaptations, and ecology. Today there is a great deal of exciting research tying molecular and cellular biology to evolution and ecology. For example, the cells of some *Acacia* plants store cyanogenic compounds within their vacuoles and enzymes that can release cyanide from these compounds in the cytoplasm. When animals eat these cells, the vacuolar membranes are destroyed, the enzymes and their substrates come together, and cyanide is released. This cellular adaptation protects the leaves against herbivores without harming the intact plant. Examples such as this tie the different levels of biology together in this book. They also form the basis for a treatment of ecology and evolution that reviewers say is unrivalled among general biology texts. . . .

What is the advantage of short chapters to students and teachers?

This book is divided into many short chapters because our students report that it is more satisfying to master all of one short chapter than only part of a long chapter in an evening's work. More importantly, short chapters permit instructors to rearrange the sequence of topics to suit their own preferences. . . .

How should you read and study this book?

We have listed objectives at the beginning of each chapter. In studying each chapter, the student should first skim through the objectives and then read the chapter. Next, the student should study the figures in some detail and read the summary to consolidate the main points. At this point the student should review each objective carefully and answer it fully, referring back to the chapter when in doubt, and then complete the self-quiz.

What should you do with the discussion questions?

The questions for discussion should not be treated as part of the self-quiz. They are just what their name implies: questions to be batted about in discussion groups or over lunch. The student should be able to work out the answers to some of them from the information in the chapter. However, many of them are unanswerable—questions which research workers are addressing today, questions which have puzzled people for centuries, or questions raised but not yet answered by the modern explosion in biological knowledge.

What types of references are included?

The references are a mixed bag. They include original work referred to in the text or figures, reference books that we have found reliable, bedtime reading with a biological slant, and works that approach difficult material from a different viewpoint.

What are some of the aids for reading?

The text, running glossary, and cross references to sections in other chapters are aids for locating relevant information quickly. These will be particularly useful if the chapters are taught in an order different from that in the book. Chapters are divided into short, numbered sections with boldface type for easy identification. The asterisks throughout the text refer to words defined in the running glossary at the bottom of the page and can be ignored by the student with a good vocabulary, biological and otherwise. We find a good index easily the fastest way to find something, whether we are reading a book thoroughly or using it for reference. We have prepared an extensive index to be used in both ways since we anticipate that this book will become the general-purpose biology reference book on many a shelf.[1]

---

[1] From *Biology* by Karen Arms and Pamela S. Camp (New York: Holt, Rinehart and Winston, 1979), pp. v–vi. Copyright © 1979 by Holt, Rinehart and Winston. Reprinted by permission of Holt, Rinehart and Winston, CBS College Publishing.

II. Application to Your Other Reading

A. Take 20 to 30 minutes to survey one of your textbooks. Answer the following questions to demonstrate what you learned and submit your answers.

1. What is the title and subject of the book? How much do you already know about the subject?
2. What are three or four of the main ideas in the book?
3. What do you know about the author and the author's purpose?
4. What are some of the most important special features of the book?
5. Is the book easy or difficult for you? How fast will you read it?
6. How has surveying this book been useful to you?
7. Write a 50-word summary that might appear on the back of the book.

B. Survey a chapter in a textbook or an article that you have been assigned to read. When you have finished surveying, write out answers to the following questions:

a. What is the subject and focus?
b. What are three or four main ideas?
c. Write a three-sentence summary.

III. Discussion and Class Activities

A. Does it bother or frustrate you to survey? Why? What can you do about it?
B. What can you expect from surveying? What are its strengths? What are its limitations?
C. How can you use what you have learned in this chapter to help you with the reading you will do this year?
D. Do a class surveying project. Stop at the end of each step to see if there is general agreement on the information located.

IV. Vocabulary Review
A. Specialized Terms

1. surveying _____

2. preview _____

3. review _____

4. front matter _____

5. back matter _____

6. introduction _____

7. main body _____

8. summary _____

9. conclusion _____

B. (General Vocabulary)

1. estimate _____

2. paraphrase _____

3. synthesize _____

4. mnemonic _____

C. Allusions

1. Vladivostok _____

CHAPTER 5
Skimming, Scanning, and Selective Reading

In this chapter you will learn:

How to draw on your expectations of the text to help you read it rapidly.
How to use three more rapid reading techniques: skimming, scanning, and selective reading.

In the last chapter you learned that twenty or thirty minutes of surveying can help you gain preliminary information about a book, including its main subject, focus, major ideas, and organization. You also learned that surveying a chapter or article can help you locate the main subject and the three or four most important ideas. Surveying can be used with varying degrees of success on all types of texts, but it is especially useful for textbooks, textbook chapters, and all articles in which the author has used boldface headings and subheadings to announce the main ideas and thereby make the organization clear.

As useful as surveying is, it will not serve all of the possible purposes you will have for reading rapidly, nor will it be ideally adapted for all types of texts. This chapter will introduce you to three more rapid reading techniques—skimming, scanning, and selective reading. Knowing how to use these techniques will help you gain the (flexibility) that will yield the reading results you want at particular times. All three of these techniques will help you break out of the word-by-word, sentence-by-sentence reading pattern that untrained readers rely on. The advantage of these techniques is that they allow you to see the big picture quickly—the subject, the focus, and the main ideas. The (limitation) of these techniques is that they do not yield 100 percent comprehension. You will miss many details that would give a better understanding of the text if you were to read it closely. Skimming, if done skillfully and with concentration, will enable you to comprehend roughly half of the text. Scanning and selective reading yield smaller comprehension percentages, but they are adequate for certain purposes.

Before you use any rapid-reading techniques, take a few seconds to size up the text. Classify it, notice who wrote it, and judge its level of difficulty for you. Then establish your own purpose for reading. Finally, decide which rapid reading technique or combination of techniques would best suit the text and your purpose for reading it. Follow the procedures for using the techniques exactly. Such preliminary judgments will help you concentrate and keep you moving through the material rapidly.

Define: flexibility

Define: limitation

Rely on Your Expectations of the Text When Reading Rapidly

Each time you use a rapid-reading technique you should actively look for what you can normally assume will be in the text. As you learned in Chapter 3, you can usually expect:

a title
a subject
a focus
an introduction with a purpose sentence
a body with some major divisions
a summary or conclusion
main ideas
supporting material
transitions
a repeated movement from the general to the specific throughout

Locate these special features quickly when you skim, scan, or read selectively. Use a pencil to help you do so.

How To Skim

Define:
skimming

Skimming is a useful skill for library research, getting quick information from magazines and newspapers, re-reading difficult texts you have already read closely, getting some information from textbooks when you are pressed for time, moving through a stack of mail in a hurry, and finding out how a good novel ends. When done effectively, skimming enables you to understand the subject and focus of a text as well as its main ideas, their organization, and some of the details. Skimming is a more thorough method of rapid reading than surveying. In many cases, you will survey first and then, if you do not know enough to meet your purpose, you will skim. There are two methods of skimming: (1) skimming for the main ideas and organization and (2) skimming key words.

Method 1 Skimming for the Main Ideas and Organization

There are six steps in skimming to locate the main ideas and their organization.

STEP 1. *Read the title, the author's name, and the introduction to locate the subject, the focus, and possibly the main ideas.* Look for a purpose sentence in the introduction. Look also for a list of the main ideas. Consider what you do and do not know about the author.

STEP 2. *Read only headings and subheadings or the first and last sentence of each paragraph.* Headings and subheadings obviously label the main ideas. By reading them you will find the main ideas and see how much space is devoted

Define:
**topic
sentence**

_____

to each of them. You will also pick up a few details. The first sentence of most paragraphs, the **topic sentence**, introduces the main idea. The last sentence either summarizes the main idea or leads into the subject of the next paragraph. When there are no headings and subheadings, read the first and last sentences of all paragraphs to get an idea of the main ideas and their organization.

STEP 3.   *Actively look for transitions.* As you read topic sentences, look also for all transitional materials that show where the author is concluding one main idea and introducing another. Such transitions help you locate the major chunks of material in a text. Draw lines across the page each time a new main idea is introduced so that you can visualize these chunks. Number them in the margin to help with later reading or review.

STEP 4.   *Look for changes in key vocabulary to signal a change to a new topic.* Transitional material is not always obvious in a text. When transitions are used frequently and obviously, they help you find the main ideas and the divisions between them. When there is no obvious transitional material, identify the first main idea by reading a few sentences past the introduction and establishing the first topic in your mind. Then look for a repetition of this first idea and the vocabulary associated with it. When the vocabulary suddenly changes and the author seems to have switched to a new idea, stop at that point and locate exactly where the change occurs. Draw a line to establish the first chunk of material. Then locate the next topic and its vocabulary, and continue in this manner throughout the rest of the text.

STEP 5.   *Read the last paragraph of the text.* See how the author ends the text material. You can expect either a summary or a concluding idea. Read a summary as a check of your understanding of the main ideas. Read a conclusion to see what idea the author wants to emphasize by placing it last.

Define:
recapitulate

_____

STEP 6.   *Recapitulate the main ideas and their organization in your mind or on paper.* Finish skimming by answering questions that force you to state the subject and focus, the most important idea, the other main ideas, what you want to remember, and what use you will make of it.

In-Chapter Exercise 1

Before you read any further, practice using the six steps just listed to skim Chapter 6 for its main ideas and organization. Answer the questions as they relate to the chapter.

What is this about in general? (State the subject and focus.)

What is the most important point made about the subject? (State the concluding or most important point.)

How is the subject developed? (List the main ideas.)

What do you want to remember from this text?

What use will you make of it?

Method 2 Skimming Key Words

Skimming key words is a more thorough method of rapid reading than either surveying or skimming for main ideas and organization. Use it when the other methods do not permit you to learn enough, when the text is too difficult, or when you want to get to the end of a good novel. Here are the steps for skimming key words:

STEP 1. *Read the title, author's name, and the first paragraph, if necessary, to get the subject and focus.* Concentrate on what you already know about the subject and author.

STEP 2. *Read only the nouns, verbs, and other words that carry most of the meaning through the remainder of the text.* Move your eyes across each line of print several times faster than you ordinarily do, and your eyes will select the words that carry most of the meaning. Do not worry about what you leave out, and do not try to mentally fill in what you do not read. You will be reading 50 percent or less of the total number of words in the text. As you skim, concentrate on locating main ideas, watch for transitions, and analyze how and why supporting material is used. If you are using this method to skim fiction, concentrate on getting the plot straight.

STEP 3. *Slow down and read the last paragraph to see how the author ends.*

STEP 4. *Recapitulate in your mind or in writing, the subject, the main ideas, the most important point, what you want to remember, and what use you will make of the text.*

Define:
delete

It is more satisfactory to demonstrate skimming key words than it is to describe this method. The passage in Figure 5.1 has had everything but the major nouns and verbs (deleted.) Read the passage quickly, jot in the margin the points mentioned in Step 4 above, and finally, compare the deleted text with the full text in Figure 5.2.

Figure 5.1 Skimming key words

Who is
Dickens?

Dickens Excites Him

by TAMARA CHAPMAN

7:45 on Friday morning,	before	Bledsoe's class.
Bleary-eyed scholars,		, stagger into
class. have papers due, quiz		class discussion
. Assignments snowball		, at

Subject:
_____

_____

Main ideas:
_____

_____

Most
important
point:
_____

_____

Use to me:
_____

8 a.m.,   another hour in bed   inviting.
      "He's hard,"   student tells another,   compare stories   Bled-
soe's exams.   cringe.
      Enter   villain—   taskmaster   expects   students
understand   Wordsworth   iambic
hexameter.
            students really describe   hard? Bledsoe—
      professor   English, Dickens enthusiast   opera buff, balks at
idea. Hard?   really   ?
      Yep.
                  mean hard?   obstinately difficult?
      Not quite.   hard   challenging.
      Bledsoe says   tough   thought-provoking assignments.
            ,   not uncompromising.
            Bledsoe's approach to   . Answers,   ,   followed
by "but . . ."
            will not tell   his "favorite" book,   "best" effort   his
"most" exciting experience. Things aren't that simple,
            won't say much about himself—
admit   two passions   music   literature.
            look at Bledsoe's interest in Dickens.   studying at the
Dickens House   London, Bledsoe founded   Dickens Society,
                  celebrate   Dickens Christmas   Dickens'
birthday.   members   meet   discuss readings.
      Dickens,   ,   inspirational. People   enjoy
writer   everybody finds   satisfaction   writings.
      "Dickens   not   tedious   impossible.
      basic.   appeals   people   read for   basic things:
laugh,   cry,"
      When   speaks about Dickens, Bledsoe's   rapid speed increases.
      words tumble out   -   ,   jumps from his chair
      find   volume   book-lined office   ,   says, "   like
paradise."
      Bledsoe's interest   Dickens stretches   other activities.   ex-
ample,   composed songs set   Dickens' text. Some
      programmed   recital. Bledsoe, pleased with

      compositions,   ,   perfect outlet   creativity. Lit-
erature satisfies   analytical, research side   ,   music gives
      chance to create.
      Music,   "   perspective on literature,"
      literature   ideas.
      Bledsoe,   close to heaven.   job   loves,
      inspirational hobby.
      "I really have found exactly what   want to do in life."

Figure 5.2   Complete text.

Dickens Excites Him

by TAMARA CHAPMAN

It's 7:45 on a Friday morning, 15 minutes before Robert Bledsoe's first class.

Bleary-eyed scholars, loaded down with books and papers, stagger into class. They have papers due, a quiz in another week and a class discussion on Shelley. Assignments snowball like bills at the end of the month, and at 8 a.m., nothing short of another hour in bed sounds inviting.

"He's hard," one student tells another, as they compare stories on Bledsoe's exams. They both cringe.

Enter the villain—the merciless taskmaster who expects his students to understand the complexities of Wordsworth and the intricacies of the iambic hexameter.

Did students really describe him as hard? Bledsoe—37-year-old UTEP associate professor of English, Dickens enthusiast and opera buff, balks at the idea. Hard? Was that really the word they used?

Yep.

But did they mean hard? Hard as in obstinately difficult?

Not quite. Maybe hard as in challenging.

Bledsoe says he is tough in giving thought-provoking assignments. On the other hand, he's not uncompromising.

Such is Bledsoe's approach to questions. Answers, yes or no, are followed by "but . . ."

He will not tell you about his "favorite" book, his "best" effort or his "most" exciting experience. Things aren't that simple, he says.

In fact, he won't say much about himself—at most, he'll apologetically admit that his two passions in life are music and literature.

Take a look at Bledsoe's interest in Dickens. Besides studying at the Dickens House in London, Bledsoe founded the El Paso Dickens Society, which meets at least twice a year to celebrate a Dickens Christmas and Dickens' birthday. Group members also meet to discuss readings.

Dickens, Bledsoe says, is inspirational. People of all nations enjoy the writer and everybody finds personal satisfaction from the Victorian's writings.

"Dickens could not write a tedious book. That's just impossible. He's very basic. He appeals to people who read for very basic things: I want to laugh, I want to cry," Bledsoe says.

When he speaks about Dickens, Bledsoe's already-rapid speed increases. His words tumble out like machine-gun shells, and he jumps from his chair to find a particular volume in his book-lined office that, he says, "is just like a paradise."

Bledsoe's interest in Dickens stretches into his other activities. For example, he has composed songs set to Dickens' text. Some of his songs have been programmed in a recital. Bledsoe, pleased with his success, plans other compositons.

His compositions, he says, are the perfect outlet for his creativity. Literature satisfies the analytical, research side of Bledsoe, while music gives him the chance to create.

Music, Bledsoe says, "gives me an outsider's perspective on literature," while literature fuels his mind with ideas.

To Bledsoe, that comes pretty close to heaven. He has a job he loves, as well as an inspirational hobby.

"I really have found exactly what I want to do in life."

From Tamara Chapman, "UTEP Professor Gives El Paso the 'Dickens' ", *The El Paso Times,* El Paso, Texas, February 24, 1982, p. 10.

How To Scan

Define:
scanning
————

Scanning is used to locate a bit of information that you know is on a page as quickly as possible. You would not read a whole page in a dictionary to find the meaning of one word. Instead, you would use your knowledge of the alphabet and scan until you had located the word. Similarly, if you had consulted the index to a book to discover which pages contained needed information, you would then turn to those pages and scan to find the information. Use the following advice to help you scan rapidly and successfully.

1. *Concentrate on the bit of information you seek.* Have the name, the word, the date, the latest divorce statistics, how long Tennyson was engaged, the main thrust of the New Deal—or whatever it is you are looking for—in the front of your mind. Repeat it over and over to yourself as you look. Then the information you seek will have a tendency to leap off the page almost like magic.

Define:
**eye move-
ments**
————
————

2. *Use different* **eye movements** *than you would to read.* Above all, when you scan, you want to avoid slowing down to read. Consequently, you should not move your eyes from left to right across the page, line by line, or you may find yourself reading. Instead, cover the page by using one of the eye movement patterns diagrammed in Figure 5.3. One of them will work best for you. Always use it when you scan.

In-Chapter Exercise 2

Experiment with these eye movements by scanning the passage below. Assume that you are writing a paper on reading speed. Give yourself only three to five seconds to find out the minimum speed for adequate comprehension.

There is no one best reading rate; that depends on the difficulty of the passage and the skill of the reader. The best rate also varies with the task itself—on whether the reader is trying to identify every word, for example, in order to read aloud, or whether the reading is "for meaning" only. The rate must be different if extensive memorization is being attempted, because rote learning

Figure 5.3 Eye movement patterns for scanning.

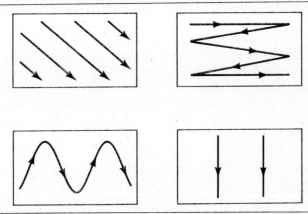

cannot be accomplished quickly. Word-perfect reading aloud and extensive deliberate memorization often require that a passage should be read more than once. A reader is unlikely to comprehend while reading *slower* than 200 words a minute, because a lesser rate would imply that words were being read as isolated units rather than as meaningful sequences. As we shall see in the next chapter, limitations of memory prevent sense being built up from isolated words.

Thus, while comprehension demands relatively fast reading, memorization slows the reader down. As a consequence, comprehension may be impaired and memorization becomes pointless in any case. If the brain already has a good idea of what is on the page, then slower reading is more tolerable and more time can be spared for memorization. But heavy memory burdens should be avoided when one is learning to read or unfamiliar with the language or subject matter.[1]

The minimum speed for adequate comprehension ———————————————

How To Read Selectively

Define:
**selective
reading**
———————
———————

Selective reading involves locating particularly important passages, slowing down to read them closely, and then either abandoning the text or moving on to another passage to read closely.

To do selective reading well, you need to know exactly what you are looking for and how to locate it as quickly as possible. You also need to believe that it is always acceptable to read only parts of a book. Most scholars who do research in

[1] From *Understanding Reading,* 3d ed., by Frank Smith (New York: Holt, Rinehart and Winston, 1982), p. 37.

many books and journals rarely read entire books. Let them be your model. Remind yourself regularly that you only need to read the parts of a book that are immediately useful for satisfying your present reading purpose.

Selective reading is a useful skill for library research and also for certain types of study-reading. When doing research, you will need to locate the passages that will contribute to your project and then read them. When doing study-reading, you might begin by reading or surveying a chapter before class, listening to the lecture on the chapter, marking the passages the instructor emphasizes, and then skimming the chapter again, slowing down to read selectively and closely the passages that were emphasized.

Locate the passages you want to read closely in a text by using the following *tips for selective reading.*

1. When surveying or skimming you will often encounter passages that you want to go back to and read closely. Mark them with a straight line in the margin, or, if it is a library book, a dot that you can erase later. Complete your surveying or skimming and then return to the passage to read it closely.

2. Consult the index to locate the material you want to read closely. The index is especially useful when you are looking for research materials. Avoid copying such material without familiarizing yourself with the book itself, however. Survey it for a few minutes before you quote so that you do not misrepresent the author. Imagine, for a moment, that you are writing a paper in favor of capital punishment. You locate a book on capital punishment, consult the index, and copy a sentence or two to further your argument without finding out that the author you have quoted is opposed to capital punishment. You need to know something about every book from which you take research material in order to appear knowledgeable and responsible when you quote. Use what you have learned from surveying to make your quote fit into your paper. You might write, for example, "Allen Smith, who in his preface frankly admits his bias against capital punishment, still concedes that the opposition has a few good arguments which he lists as follows, etc."

Define: misrepresent

Define: concede

Define: opposition

Chapter Summary

To read rapidly, first make preliminary judgments about the type of text, the author, your reason for reading, and the difficulty of the text for you. Then select the rapid-reading technique that is best suited to the text and your purpose for reading. Rely on your expectations of the text. Expect and look for a title, subject, focus, introduction, purpose sentence, body with major divisions, summary or conclusion, main ideas, supporting material, transitions, and a repeated movement from the general to the specific.

Skimming is more thorough than surveying. Skimming for main ideas and organization involves six steps: (1) Read the title, author's name, and introduction; (2) read the headings and subheadings, or the first and last sentence in the paragraphs; (3) look for transitions; (4) look for changes in vocabulary to find major divisions; (5) read the last paragraph; (6) recapitulate in your mind or on paper the subject, main ideas, and the use you will make of the text. Skimming key words involves four steps: (1) Read the title, author's name, and introduction; (2) read nouns and verbs only—skip 50 percent of the words; (3) read the last paragraph; (4) recapitulate the subject, the main ideas, and the use you will make of the text. Scan to find bits of information you know are there. Concentrate on what you are looking for, and use different eye movements than you would to read normally. Read selectively for research or study-reading. Survey, skim, or use the index to find the parts you want to read. Always survey or skim before you read selectively and before you quote.

Your Summary

To help you write the summary of this chapter, first survey the chapter, and then organize your notes according to the topics set up by the headings and subheadings.

What is the subject of this chapter?

What did the author say about it?

END-CHAPTER EXERCISES

I. Practice

A. Skim the following essay for its main ideas and organization. Before you begin, review the steps on pages 85–86. Then follow them exactly. Use the reading cues in the left-hand margin to remind you of what you should read and what you should skip.

Title:

How We Listen

Author's name:
Who is Copland?

by AARON COPLAND

Introduction:
underline subject,
focus, and main
ideas

> 1.   We all listen to music according to our separate capacities. But, for the sake of analysis, the whole listening process may become clearer if we break it up into its component parts, so to speak. In a certain sense we all listen to music on three separate planes. For lack of a better terminology, one might name these: (1) the sensuous plane, (2) the expressive plane, (3) the sheerly musical plane. The only advantage to be gained from mechanically splitting up the listening process into these hypothetical planes is the clearer view to be had of the way in which we listen.

Read:
Scan other material and circle words associated with each topic.

> 2.   The simplest way of listening to music is to listen for the sheer pleasure of the musical sound itself. That is the sensuous plane. It is the plane on which we hear music without thinking, without considering it in any way. One turns on the radio while doing something else and absent-mindedly bathes in the sound. A kind of brainless but attractive state of mind is engendered by the mere sound appeal of the music. . . .

Read:
Box transitions.
Draw lines to show major topic changes or "chunks."

> 3.   The surprising thing is that many people who consider themselves qualified music lovers abuse that plane in listening. They go to concerts in order to lose themselves. They use music as a consolation or an escape. They enter an ideal world where one doesn't have to think of the realities of everyday life. Of course they aren't thinking about the music either. Music allows them to leave it, and they go off to a place to dream, dreaming because of and apropos of the music yet never quite listening to it.

Read:

> 4.   Yes, the sound appeal of music is a potent and primitive force, but you must not allow it to usurp a disproportionate share of your interest. The sensuous plane is an important one in music, a very important one, but it does not constitute the whole story. . . .

Read:

> 5.   The second plane on which music exists is what I have called the expressive one. Here, immediately, we tread on controversial ground. Composers have a way of shying away from any discussion of music's expressive side. . . .

Read:

> 6.   My own belief is that all music has an expressive power, some more and some less, but that all music has a certain meaning behind the notes and that that meaning behind the notes constitutes, after all, what the piece is saying, what the piece is about. This whole problem can be stated quite simply by asking, "Is there a meaning to music?" My answer to that would be, "Yes." And "Can you state in so many words what the meaning is?" My answer to that would be, "No." Therein lies the difficulty.

Read:

> 7.   Simple-minded souls will never be satisfied with the answer to the second of these questions. They always want music to have a meaning, and the more concrete it is the better they like it. The more the music

reminds them of a train, a storm, a funeral, or any other familiar concep-
tion the more expressive it appears to be to them. This popular idea of
music's meaning—stimulated and abetted by the usual run of musical
commentator—should be discouraged wherever and whenever it is met.
One timid lady once confessed to me that she suspected something seriously lacking in her appreciation of music because of her inability to
connect it with anything definite. That is getting the whole thing back-
ward, of course.

Read:

8.   Still, the question remains, How close should the intelligent music
lover wish to come to pinning a definite meaning to any particular work?
No closer than a general concept, I should say. Music expresses, at different moments, serenity or exuberance, regret or triumph, fury or delight. It expresses each of these moods, and many others, in a numberless
variety of subtle shadings and differences. It may even express a state of
meaning for which there exists no adequate word in any language. In
that case, musicians often like to say that it has only a purely musical
meaning. They sometimes go farther and say that *all* music has only a
purely musical meaning. What they really mean is that no appropriate
word can be found to express the music's meaning and that, even if it
could, they do not feel the need of finding it.

Read:

9.   But whatever the professional musician may hold, most musical
novices still search for specific words with which to pin down their musical reactions. That is why they always find Tschaikovsky easier to "understand" than Beethoven. In the first place, it is easier to pin a meaning-
word on a Tschaikovsky piece than on a Beethoven one. Much easier.
Moreover, with the Russian composer, every time you come back to a
piece of his it almost always says the same thing to you, whereas with
Beethoven it is often quite difficult to put your finger right on what he is
saying. Any musician will tell you that that is why Beethoven is the
greater composer. Because music which always says the same thing to
you will necessarily soon become dull music, but music whose meaning
is slightly different with each hearing has a greater chance of remaining
alive. . . .

Read:

10.   Themes or pieces need not express only one emotion, of course.
Take such a theme as the first main one of the *Ninth Symphony*, for
example. It is clearly made up of different elements. It does not say only
one thing. Yet anyone hearing it immediately gets a feeling of strength,
a feeling of power. It isn't a power that comes simply because the theme
is played loudly. It is a power inherent in the theme itself. The extraor-
dinary strength and vigor of the theme results in the listener's receiving
an impression that a forceful statement has been made. But one should
never try to boil it down to "the fateful hammer of life," etc. That is
where the trouble begins. The musician, in his exasperation, says it means
nothing but the notes themselves, whereas the nonprofessional is only
too anxious to hang on to any explanation that gives him the illusion of
getting closer to the music's meaning.

Read:

11.   Now, perhaps, the reader will know better what I mean when I say that music does have an expressive meaning but that we cannot say in so many words what that meaning is.

Read:

12.   The third plane on which music exists is the sheerly musical plane. Besides the pleasurable sound of music and the expressive feeling that it gives off, music does exist in terms of the notes themselves and of their manipulation. Most listeners are not sufficiently conscious of this third plane. It will be largely the business of this book to make them more aware of music on this plane.

Read:

13.   Professional musicians, on the other hand, are, if anything, too conscious of the mere notes themselves. They often fall into the error of becoming so engrossed with their arpeggios and staccatos that they forget the deeper aspects of the music they are performing. But from the layman's standpoint, it is not so much a matter of getting over bad habits on the sheerly musical plane as of increasing one's awareness of what is going on, in so far as the notes are concerned.

Read:

14.   When the man in the street listens to the "notes themselves" with any degree of concentration, he is most likely to make some mention of the melody. Either he hears a pretty melody or he does not, and he generally lets it go at that. Rhythm is likely to gain his attention next, particularly if it seems exciting. But harmony and tone color are generally taken for granted, if they are thought of consciously at all. As for music's having a definite form of some kind, that idea seems never to have occurred to him.

Read:

15.   It is very important for all of us to become more alive to music on its sheerly musical plane. After all, an actual musical material is being used. The intelligent listener must be prepared to increase his awareness of the musical material and what happens to it. He must hear the melodies, the rhythms, the harmonies, the tone colors in a more conscious fashion. But above all he must, in order to follow the line of the composer's thought, know something of the principles of musical form. Listening to all of these elements is listening on the sheerly musical plane.

Read:

16.   Let me repeat that I have split up mechanically the three separate planes on which we listen merely for the sake of greater clarity. Actually, we never listen on one or the other of these planes. What we do is to correlate them—listening in all three ways at the same time. It takes no mental effort, for we do it instinctively.

Read:

17.   Perhaps an analogy with what happens to us when we visit the theater will make this instinctive correlation clearer. In the theater, you are aware of the actors and actresses, costumes and sets, sounds and movements. All these give one the sense that the theater is a pleasant place to be in. They constitute the sensuous plane of our theatrical reactions.

Read:

18.   The expressive plane in the theater would be derived from the feeling that you get from what is happening on the stage. You are moved to pity, excitement, or gayety. It is this general feeling, generated aside from the particular words being spoken, a certain emotional something which exists on the stage, that is analogous to the expressive quality in music.

Read:

{ 19.   The plot and plot development is equivalent to our sheerly musical plane. The playwright creates and develops a character in just the same way that a composer creates and develops a theme. According to the degree of your awareness of the way in which the artist in either field handles his material will you become a more intelligent listener.

Read:

{ 20.   It is easy enough to see that the theatergoer never is conscious of any of these elements separately. He is aware of them all at the same time. The same is true of music listening. We simultaneously and without thinking listen on all three planes.

Read:

{ 21.   In a sense, the ideal listener is both inside and outside the music at the same moment, judging it and enjoying it, wishing it would go one way and watching it go another—almost like the composer at the moment he composes it; because in order to write his music, the composer must also be inside and outside his music, carried away by it and yet coldly critical of it. A subjective and objective attitude is implied in both creating and listening to music.

Read:

{ 22.   What the reader should strive for, then, is a more *active* kind of listening. Whether you listen to Mozart or Duke Ellington, you can deepen your understanding of music only by being a more conscious and aware listener—not someone who is just listening, but someone who is listening for something.[2]

B. Skim the same essay again, only this time use the key word method of skimming. Review the steps on page 87 before you begin.

C. Using two different methods, you have skimmed the "How We Listen" article twice. See now if you can answer the skimming questions.

Questions

1. What is this article about in general? (State the subject and focus.)

_____

2. How is the subject developed? (Refer to the chunks, and list the main

ideas.) _____

_____

_____

3. What is the most important point made about the subject? (State the

concluding or most important idea.) _____

_____

---

[2] Aaron Copland, *What to Listen for in Music*, revised ed. (New York: McGraw-Hill, 1957), pp. 9–19. Copyright © 1957 McGraw-Hill Book Company. Reprinted by permission.

4. What do you want to remember from this text? _____

_____

5. How will you use what you have learned? _____

_____

    D. Practice scanning by first reviewing the eye movements for scanning on page 91. Now turn back to page 95 and experiment, using one of these methods to look for the answer to this question: Which composer do most people find easier to understand, Beethoven or Tschaikovsky? Remember to concentrate on the information you are looking for while you scan. Write your answer: _____

    E. Since you have now skimmed the "How We Listen" article twice, you are in a good position to do some selective reading. Turn back to the essay and locate the two paragraphs that answer the question: How can the expressive meaning of the *Ninth Symphony* be described? Scan to find the paragraphs, and then slow down and read them.

        Write your answer: _____

_____

II. Application to Your Other Reading
    A. Bring one of your textbooks to class. Scan the index to locate a topic that interests you. Turn to the pages where this topic is discussed and read selectively about it for five minutes. Write a paragraph about what you have learned.
    B. Take no more than three to five minutes to skim a magazine or journal article for its main ideas and organization. Write a three-sentence summary of the article and submit it.

III. Questions for Discussion and Class Activities
    A. Name at least three reading purposes for which skimming would be an appropriate technique. Do the same for scanning and selective reading.
    B. Bring your unread school newspaper or local newspaper to class. Practice the key word method of skimming on pages 87–88 twice. Then use this method to skim the newspaper for five minutes. Make a list of what you learned in that time.
    C. Use scanning to locate a name in a phone book, a word in a dictionary, and a fact on a page found through the index. Scan, for example, to locate the date and location of the Battle of Hastings in a history textbook.

IV. Vocabulary Review
A. Specialized Terms

1. skimming _____

2. topic sentence _____

3. scanning _____

4. eye movements _____

5. selective reading _____

B. General Vocabulary

1. flexibility _____

2. limitation _____

3. recapitulate _____

4. delete _____

5. misrepresent _____

6. concede _____

7. opposition _____

C. Allusions

1. Charles Dickens _____

2. Aaron Copland _____

CHAPTER 6
Increasing Reading Speed

In this chapter you will learn:

How and when to use speed-reading.
How to determine your present reading rate.
How to increase your present reading speed.

You have now been presented with five different methods of rapid reading in Part II of this book, and each is valuable for different reading purposes. The first method, surveying, permits you to get the subject and three or four of the important ideas in only a few minutes. Scanning and selective reading are useful for finding specific information in a hurry. Both techniques for skimming permit more comprehension than the other methods, as much, in fact, as 50 percent of the text. They are useful when you need to get some idea about the contents of a text in a short period of time. None of these methods is a substitute for careful close reading.

The purpose of this chapter is to present ways to increase your present reading speed. Increased speed will be most useful to you when you are reading easy material that you already know something about. If you read difficult material rapidly, you will have to settle for less comprehension than you would at a slower rate. Unlike the methods discussed in Chapters 4 and 5, **speed-reading**, as it is described here, involves seeing most of the words, as opposed to skipping over large chunks of material or even many of the words. With training, both your eyes and your mind can learn to move faster to keep up with faster eye movements.

Define:
speed-reading
_____
_____

When To Use Speed-Reading

Use your judgment to determine when to read fast and when to slow down. Speed-reading is not appropriate for all types of material. You may at times want to use your fastest speeds to hurry and find out what happens at the end of a novel. If, on the other hand, you read fiction mainly to relax and forget your other responsibilities, you may never want to read it rapidly. Speed-reading can be an extremely useful skill when you want to achieve any of the following purposes:

Define:
supple-
mentary
_____
_____

1. To get some information from a long reading assignment when you are pressed for time.

2. To read journal articles in the library when you are doing research or a supplementary reading assignment.

3. To get quick information from the newspaper and news magazines, such as *Time* and *Newsweek.*
4. To do the first reading of a difficult book that you will later reread in whole or in parts.
5. To read correspondence, papers, and do other on-the-job reading.
6. To read professional magazines and journals to keep informed about your career field.

Note that the above list does not include reading difficult textbooks, library materials, supplementary readings, or literature that you judge are worthy of being read closely, critically, and with as close to 100 percent comprehension as possible.

Developing Realistic Expectations about Reading Speed

Most people with no special training read everything at about the same rate. As a consequence, they waste time and read less than they would if they varied their rates to adjust to the type of text and their purpose for reading it. Your final object in working to improve your reading speed will be to develop a range of reading speeds. You will also work to develop the judgment to select the appropriate speed for the text and your purpose. High speeds will be used to meet those purposes just listed above. Medium speeds will be used for relatively difficult materials that do not have to be read with perfect comprehension. Your slowest speeds will be reserved for material you judge worthy of the time and effort required to read them closely and carefully.

Define:
oral reading rate

_____

_____

Define:
silent reading rate

_____

_____

Reading rates are measured in words read per minute. The average **oral reading rate,** or the rate at which you would read this book aloud, is for most people around 150 words per minute. Your top **silent reading rate** can, with training and practice, extend to about 800 words per minute. It is physically possible to see 800 words per minute and still comprehend them. Speeds above 800 words per minute are skimming speeds. Reading programs that claim to be able to teach you to "read" at several thousand words per minute are actually teaching you techniques for skimming and surveying. You might have noticed that such programs usually promise also to double or even triple your present reading rate. This is a more reasonable promise. The speed at which the average beginning college student reads an easy text is usually within the range of 150 to 240 words per minute. It is both possible and desirable to double or even triple that rate in order to establish the range of speeds you will need. The remainder of this chapter will provide you with techniques and practice to help you accomplish this.

In-Chapter Exercise 1

How Fast Do You Read Right Now?

You can easily measure how fast you read right now. Put a stop watch or a watch with a sweep second-hand in front of you. Then read the following passage at a comfortable rate. Do not try to speed up now—read, instead, as you usually do. When you have finished, look at your watch to see how long you took and record your time in minutes and seconds in the space provided. Then, to test your comprehension, answer the questions.

You *Can* Go Home Again

Astronaut Buzz Aldrin once wrote, "I traveled to the moon, but the most significant voyage of my life began when I returned from where no man had been before." Coming home from an extended overseas voyage can throw you for a similar loop. Often, you must deal with culture shock, incompatibility with and alienation from friends, and attacks of acute boredom.

The three years Brenda Barnabe spent in Southeast Asia accustomed her to the sight of extreme poverty and the daily struggle for survival. When she returned to North America, she experienced a retroactive culture shock. "I couldn't believe the wastefulness of our way of life and how many things we take for granted."

Jonathan Lachnit was studying in Cairo when the Iranian hostage issue broke. He kept hearing rumors about how Americans were changing, becoming more insular and militaristic. The rumors, he says, were slightly exaggerated, but his year away was enough to show a change in American attitudes. "Nobody wanted to hear about how people in the Third World really live. They were too wrapped up in themselves and assumed things ran as smoothly over there as they do here. I felt this urgency to tell people about the poverty and suffering in the Middle East, but nobody really cared."

For Jean Coury, who spent a year abroad, it wasn't the culture shock or problems of communication with her friends that bothered her, but sheer boredom. "Traveling is addicting, and it's difficult to readjust to school life. I can't sit down very long anymore. I have an urge to explore."

But readjusting doesn't have to be too difficult—if you're as patient and tolerant with your friends as you were with the foreigners you met. All of these students agreed that the benefits of traveling and living abroad outweigh any problems they had in readjusting to American life.[1]

Time: Minutes _____ seconds _____

Answer the following questions by circling the best answer:

1. Buzz Aldrin is: (a) an astronaut, (b) a student, (c) a professor, (d) an Iranian hostage.
2. Coming home from an extended overseas voyage can cause: (a) culture shock, (b) incompatibility with your friends, (c) acute boredom, (d) all of the above.
3. After spending three years in Southeast Asia, Brenda Barnabe became accustomed to: (a) the novelty of foreign travel, (b) the sight of extreme poverty and the daily struggle for survival, (c) the shock of being where few people she knew had ever been before, (d) the boredom of spending such a long time in a foreign country.
4. According to the text, when Brenda Barnabe returned to her home in North America she experienced: (a) great joy at seeing her friends and

[1] Reprinted by permission from the 1981 issue of *Insider*. © 1981, by 13-30 Corporation.

family again, (b) a feeling of relief from being in familiar surroundings, (c) sadness from leaving new friends behind, (d) shock from the wastefulness in American society.

5. Where was Jonathan Lachnit studying when the Iranian hostage issue broke? (a) Cairo, (b) Bankok, (c) Tokyo, (d) Calcutta.

6. When Jonathan came home, he found that people were: (a) interested in his experiences, (b) interested in the Third World, (c) disinterested in his experiences, (d) disinterested in the Third World.

7. Jonathan was quoted as saying Americans are: (a) too wrapped up in themselves to care about others in other countries, (b) extremely generous with foreign aid, (c) eager to travel and experience for themselves, (d) wasteful.

8. Jonathan also said that Americans: (a) should travel more, (b) find it difficult to readjust after traveling, (c) assume things run as smoothly in other countries as they do in their own, (d) were upset about the Iranian crisis.

9. Jean Coury, after a year abroad, had trouble with: (a) culture shock, (b) communicating, (c) her friends, (d) boredom.

10. All of the students quoted agreed that foreign travel: (a) was a mistake for them, (b) was a great benefit and created no problems, (c) was a benefit that outweighed the problems it temporarily created, (d) should be a part of their parents' experience.

Check your answers: (1) a; (2) d; (3) b; (4) d; (5) a; (6) d; (7) a; (8) c; (9) d; (10) c. Give yourself a comprehension score by subtracting ten points from 100 points for each wrong answer.

Your comprehension score: _____ %

Now calculate your speed in words per minute by consulting the table below. The article contained 310 words.

Time	Words per Minute
30 seconds	620
45 seconds	413
1 minute	310
1 minute 15 seconds	248
1 minute 30 seconds	207
1 minute 45 seconds	177
2 minutes	155
2 minutes 15 seconds	138
2 minutes 30 seconds	124
2 minutes 45 seconds	113
3 minutes	103
3 minutes 15 seconds	98
3 minutes 30 seconds	89
4 minutes	77

Your speed: _____ words per minute

A comprehension score of 80 to 100 percent is excellent. A score of 60 to 70 percent is also satisfactory, however, since you have just answered very detailed questions on a very short reading passage. If your speed was in the range of 155 to 248, you are within the average range for beginning college readers. Incidentally, the higher your beginning speed, the easier it will be to increase it significantly when you do the exercises for increasing speed at the end of this chapter.

Nine Suggestions for Increasing Reading Speed

To improve your reading speed, you must change some of your present reading habits. Here are nine suggestions for change that will result in faster reading speed with adequate comprehension:

1. *Decide to concentrate.* Get mentally and physically set to keep your mind on the text. Assume an alert physical attitude by sitting up straight. This will help you to become mentally alert as well. Then, put everything else out of your mind and focus your attention on the material you are about to read. Actually say to yourself, "I will concentrate and understand as much of this text as possible."

2. *Set a purpose.* Consider before you begin to read what you want to get from the text. Then actively read to achieve your purpose.

3. *Size up the text.* Read the title and enough of the first paragraph to make a judgment about the type and level of difficulty of the text for you. Try to place the text in a category such as history, philosophy, poetry, fiction, or essay. Then decide whether it will be difficult, relatively difficult, or easy for you to read.

4. *Decide on a speed.* If your initial judgment of the text and your purpose for reading permit the use of your highest reading rate, then make a conscious decision to use that rate. By neglecting to make such a decision you run the risk of slowing down.

5. *Form some questions.* Ask three questions about the text before you begin to read. Read the title and ask the usual question words, *who, what, where, when, why, how,* and *how much,* if no other questions occur to you. Questions help

Define: predict

you bring what you know about the subject of the text to the front of your mind. This mental activity, in turn, helps you predict or anticipate what the author may say about the subject. You will, as a result of questioning, concentrate better because you will read to see if your predictions were correct.

6. *Plan to write some notes when you finish reading.* Knowing that you will be jotting down the main points will help you concentrate and look for them.

Define: **vocalization**

7. *Cut down on **vocalization**.* Vocalization is word-by-word reading. Vocalizers either whisper, move their lips, or mentally pronounce each word as they read. Vocalization is a carry-over from the reading out loud that you did in primary school. Even though you eventually stopped reading aloud most of the time, you may be continuing to read as though you were pronouncing each word. If your beginning speed was 150 words per minutes or less, you are vocalizing.

Rather /than/ focusing /on/ individual /words/, try reading / in meaningful phrases./ Your speed/will increase immediately./ You will never/eliminate vocalization entirely/because some words/are difficult/and/demand/individual/ attention. Work toward the goal/of vocalizing/only part of the time/and reading in phrases/most of the time. The last four sentences were marked to give you the sense of reading word/by/word and/in phrases./ Read through them again and then continue to read in phrases.

Phrase reading will improve your comprehension of most texts. At times, however, especially if the text is difficult for you, you may find yourself staring at phrases rather than comprehending ideas. At such times, it will sometimes improve your comprehension of difficult material to read it aloud. Such deliberate vocalization is a close reading technique that does, of course, interfere with reading speed. The results, however, are often worth the time and effort. Then, once you begin to concentrate and comprehend again, you can go back to phrase reading.

Define: compulsive

_____

_____

Define: **regression**

_____

_____

8. *Eliminate* (compulsive) *regressions.* You may have developed the bad reading habit of aimlessly going back to reread what you have just read because you feel that you have missed something. Such regressing obviously interferes with speed. Break this habit by reading to the end without backtracking even if you have to cover up what you have just read in order to do so. If you must regress at times, do so deliberately, looking for material that you know is there.

Define: **eye fixations**

_____

_____

9. *Look for ideas when you read.* Reading occurs when the eyes see words, and meaning is registered in the brain. Even though it is impossible to observe what happens in the brain, it is possible to observe how the eyes operate while reading. Punch a hole in a newspaper, hold it up close to your face so that you can look through it, and ask someone to read. Note that the eyes move and stop, move and stop across the page in short, jerky motions. These are called **eye fixations.** Now put down the newspaper and move your head quickly from side to side. You will see only a blur. The eyes see sharp images only when they stop and fix on a point. All readers, slow or fast, read by moving from one eye fixation to another. Fast readers' eye fixations are different from those of slow readers, because they are able to grasp ideas more rapidly. Consequently, they spend less time staring at individual words and more time actively searching for ideas. To aid their search, fast readers stop for less time on each eye fixation. They also spend less time in moving from fixation to fixation and in snapping the eyes from the end of one line to the beginning of the next. Fast readers also take in as many as two and a half to three words per eye fixation as compared with the one or even fewer words per eye fixation of the slow reader. Fast readers, finally, skip some words, like *a, an,* and *the,* that they know from habit are there but that actually carry no meaning. They also read many familiar words and phrases in very brief fixations, recognizing them by overall shape instead of actually seeing all of the letters. As your speed improves, your eye fixations will automatically become more like those of fast readers because your mind will be working faster. You can speed up this process by using one of several mechanical means that can force both your mind and your eyes to move faster than usual. If your mind does not keep up with your eyes, slow down. Work for a speed that promotes maximum speed in both eyes and brain.

Three Mechanical Ways To Improve Your Speed

The ways of improving speed just listed in the section above are designed mainly to speed up your mind and to help you concentrate. Here are three mechanical suggestions that should also speed up both your mental activity and your eye movements. Use the suggestion that works best for you. All of them will force you to read faster than your current reading rate. As you read, your brain will grasp the important words and phrases that carry the meaning.

1. Move a 3 × 5 card down the page at an uncomfortably rapid speed, forcing your eyes and brain to move faster than usual to keep ahead of it. Or, place the card under the line you are reading and drag it down the page. Read to keep up with the card.

Define:
**peripheral
vision**

_____

_____

2. Place your open hand on the page and drag it down the page at a steady, rapid pace. Move your eyes rapidly enough to keep your hand in your **peripheral vision** as you read. You may trail a pencil down the page instead of your hand and have the same effect.

3. Rapidly underscore each line you read with either your finger or a pencil. Do not mark the page with the pencil. Your eyes will move rapidly as they try to keep pace with the rapidly moving finger or pencil.

The Importance of Practice

Once you develop some faster reading speeds, you should then practice using them as often as possible. There are various ways you can do this. One way is to make predictions about what will be in the text and then read rapidly to see whether or not you were right. Another way is to count the number of pages you can read in 15 minutes and then to count off the same number of pages, plus one or two additional ones, and see if you can read the new total in the same amount of time. A third way of practicing for speed is to decide how many pages you should be able to read in a particular book in an hour and then to check the clock frequently while you read to make certain you are meeting your time schedule.

You can check to see if you are maintaining your top reading speeds by calculating your reading speed occasionally. This can be done in any book you are reading by following the steps in the next exercise.

In-Chapter Exercise 2

Practice calculating your reading speed.

Step 1. Determine the words per page. Practice by determining the words on page 105 of this book. First, count the number of letters in the first line and divide it by five to get the average number of words per line. Write the words per line ____ . Then count all of the lines down the page on a full, printed page and subtract two to compensate for the short lines. Write the lines per page: ____ . Multiply words per line (the first figure) by lines per page (the second figure) to establish the number of words on a typical page in the book. Write the words per page: ____ . Now that you know the words per page for this book, you can calculate how fast you are reading it at any time by following Steps 2 through 4.

Step 2. Read for 10 minutes and then count the total number of full pages and fraction of a page that you read in that time.

Step 3. Multiply the number of words per page times the pages and fraction of a page read.

Step 4. Divide this number by the number of minutes you read (10 in this case.)

The method for making these calculations may be summarized as follows:

words per page × number of pages read = total number of words read
total number of words read ÷ minutes spent reading = words per minute

Work through the exercises at the end of this chapter to get a start on improving your speed. Then continue to practice the new techniques you have developed in an interesting novel or in a book of light nonfiction that is on a subject you want to read about. Push your speeds uncomfortably high. Later, when you drop back to what seems a comfortable speed, you will still be reading faster than you did before.

Chapter Summary

Speed-reading, the most thorough of the rapid-reading techniques described in Part II of this book, involves seeing most of the words at a rapid speed rather than skipping and only reading selected sections of the material. Speed-reading can be used for a variety of purposes including getting quick information from news sources, processing mail and office reports quickly, doing the first reading of a difficult text, getting quick research information in the library, or gaining some information from a reading assignment when time is short. Most readers can expect to double or triple their present reading speeds and perhaps even to achieve speeds up to 800 words per minute. Speeds higher than 800 words per minute are skimming speeds. The average college student with no training in speed-reading reads between 150 and 240 words per minute. This average speed may be improved by deciding to concentrate, setting a purpose, sizing up the text, deciding on a speed, forming questions, planning to write some notes, cutting down on vocalization, eliminating compulsive regression, and making the eyes and brain work more efficiently by moving a card, a pencil, or the open hand down the page. Finally, for maximum improvement, practice newly developed speeds until they become habitual by setting goals for pages to be read, timing against the clock, and occasionally calculating speed in words per minute in various books currently being read.

Your Summary

What is this chapter about?

What did the author say about it?

END-CHAPTER EXERCISES

I. Practice

A. The following exercises are designed to increase your reading speed. You will be reading against the clock, so you will need an instructor or a friend who is equipped with a stop watch or a watch with a sweep second-hand to time you. Mentally prepare yourself to read rapidly by reviewing the nine suggestions for rapid reading on pages 104 to 105, and then experiment with the mechanical ways to improve your speed on page 106 until you find the one that works best for you.

1. This first article is divided into segments that are each 200 words in length. When the person timing you says "start," you will have a minute and a half to read the first segment. When your timer says "stop," if you have just completed the segment, you will have read at 150 words per minute. You will be given a few seconds less time to read each succeeding segment. You will gradually increase your speed on each segment until, at the end, you will be reading 450 words per minute. Notice that the time allowed for each segment and the corresponding words per minute are written in the margin next to each 200-word segment. Review some of the "timer commands" before you begin. Note that the timer will say, "Start. You have one minute 30 seconds to read at 150 words per minute." When the time has elapsed, the timer will say, "Time. Start. You have one minute 15 seconds to read at 175 words per minute," and so on throughout the exercise until you are finally reading 450 words per minute.

Be prepared to take a few chances with this text. If you are so rushed that you do not finish a segment when your timer says "time," skip the rest of it and go on to the next segment. You will find that you have not missed that much by having to skip a bit and that you will be able to pick up much of what you missed from context. Be prepared also to be uncomfortable during this exercise. You will have to push yourself to read at these new speeds just as you would push yourself to swim or run faster. Finally, when you have finished reading, answer the questions at the end to check your comprehension. Before you begin, take one minute to survey the article. Then follow the timer's commands as you read. When you finish, compare the study formula preferred by this author to that taught in this book. You will find it on the inside front cover or on page 280.

Magical Memory Tour: The Unending Quest for a Study Formula That Works

by PATRICIA WESTFALL*

Thought, not memorization, is the soul of learning. Every professor says this. What teacher would claim not to be teaching students to think?

But just try and pass a test by thinking. Every student who has forgotten the year Thomas Aquinas died knows that thinking ability is not what gets tested. Memorization—dictaphone style—is the ability in question. Thinking won't derive the seven phyla or reveal the eighth wonder of the world. Only memorization counts in the crunch, and students who wish to survive had better master the skill. But how?

"Perhaps the most basic thing that can be said about human memory, after a century of research, is that unless detail is placed in a structural pattern it is rapidly forgotten," said Jerome Bruner in *Process of Education* in 1960. Bruner's concept, the importance of structure, lies in one form or another at the root of all how-to-study methods.

In the Beginning . . . Was SQ3R
The first and most famous of the foolproof, try-it-you-can't-fail study formulas was Frank Robinson's SQ3R method published in 1946. The acronym stands for "Survey, Question, Read, Recite, Review." The method, still taught today in a great many college how-to-study courses, works this way. First, **survey** the structure of the chapter, reading paragraph headings and summaries; this helps your mind get a firm grasp of the whole assignment before you read.

Timer Commands
Start
You have 1 minute 30 seconds to read at 150 words per minute (w.p.m.).

Time
Start
You have 1 minute 15 seconds to read at 175 w.p.m.

* Patricia Westfall, a contributing editor for *Insider*, spends snowed-in Iowa winters searching for the ultimate in study methods.

Next, turn those paragraph headings into **questions** which must be answered by the text. Then **read** (the first R) to find those answers. Robinson stresses that reading must be an active process; you should be searching for answers, not just passing your eyes over the type.

Every so often (every other page, in fact) you should stop, close the book and try to **recite** what you have just read. This is the step that is supposed to fix the information in your memory. Finally, after you have read and recited the complete assignment, take a few minutes to **review** what you've just learned before calling it a night.

The Confession

Robinson's sure-fire thoroughly tested formula was preached passionately by academic counselors until the student population boom of the 1960's. That's when new how-to-study formulas began to pop into print at a rate second only to sex manuals—and volumes ahead of diet books. Most of these were variations on SQ3R.

OK4R by Walter Pauk—meaning Overview, Key ideas (find them he meant), Read, Recall, Reflect and Review—was published in 1962. Next came Spache & Berg's 1966 PQRST (Preview, Question, Read, Summarize, Test), followed by OARWET in 1968 (Overview, Ask, Read, Write, Evaluate, Test). The champion entry was the 1973 PANORAMA which stands for "Purpose (think about why you are reading your text); Adaptability (adapt your reading speed to the difficulty of the material): Need to question (an obvious and painful stretch for the acronym); Overview; Read and relate (that is, relate the main ideas to personal experience); Annotate; Memorize; and (if you still care at this point) Assess."

Walter Pauk—the OK4R man—finally called for an end to this acronym olympics by daring to put into print what everybody had known all along: despite proof that these formulas work, no sane student ever bothers to use one. In an article knocking PANORAMA as silly ("you're reading your text because your professor told you to"), Pauk wrote, "There is no question about the value of converting a title into a question, but I can honestly say that I have never met a single student who has ever used the technique even though he knew about the textbook system incorporating this step."

A shocking confession from a man who has been teaching how-to-study courses most of his academic career.

Student indifference hardly stifled the acrolympics, however. REAP was published in 1976. REAP was different though. REAP looked as if it might have something to do with how people actually study.

Undaunted, Our Heroes Press On

How students actually study is something few researchers have bothered to study. How one *should* study, yes—advice abounds. But *do* study? No. In 1976 Robert Szabo published a sketchy survey (not study) of practices followed by successful students on his campus. Even that survey—incomplete as it was—showed how far from students the acrolympics have been.

Timer Commands

Time
Start
You have 1 minute to read at 200 w.p.m.

Time
Start
You have 53 seconds to read at 225 w.p.m.

For example, most of the top students preferred studying in cycles—working hard for three or four days, then goofing off entirely for the next three or four days. So much for the "study a little bit each day" platitudes vouchsafed by the formulas.

Students also preferred to work in four- and five-hour stretches, kayoing the formula emphasis on one-hour study sessions. All the formulas stress the importance of frequent rest breaks, but good students say the breaks interrupt concentration.

Like Pauk, Szabo found no student using a formula. He found this meant students rarely remembered the main ideas in a text, remembering instead trivial details and facts. Yet, noted the rueful Szabo, "They manage to obtain acceptable grades."

Did Szabo and colleagues consider this a hint that maybe they should abandon the quest for a perfect formula? Never. Szabo concluded his article with a ringing cry to press on to new acronyms. "We must find a method that reaches students where they are," he said.

R Is for Read

REAP might be the method Szabo was calling for. Published by two University of Missouri professors, it is, first, simpler than all the others. The R stands for read. That's it. No Survey, Question, Preview or Overview. Just sit down and read. That's what students do anyway, so for the first time in a generation the first step of a formula makes sense in human terms.

The next step, E—Encode, is equally simple. Using any method you want, simply close the book and try to phrase what you've read into your own words. Section by section? Chapter by chapter? Book by book? That's your choice. The only requirement of the method is that you actively rephrase the material *immediately*. The other two steps, Annotate and Ponder (upon which the authors elaborate at length) are just refinements of Encode: write down your encoding (for later review?) and then think (think?) about it, they say.

When one examines REAP, it's not so different from earlier formulas in that it calls for an active engagement with the material to be memorized. It is different in that it throws away the hoopla and rigid rulesiness of earlier formulas and states the meat of the matter: *Successful study requires taking time to put things in your own words immediately.* Repeat, *immediately.*

The Forgetting Curve

Why does study require an immediate Encoding (or Recalling or Reciting or Evaluation or Call It What You Will)? The answer to that is suggested in some classic early research on memorization, such as the 1913 nonsense syllables study by Ebbinghaus (ah yes, the one you had to memorize for Introductory Psych, remember?). In the Ebbinghaus study, subjects studied a list of nonsense syllables and then were tested repeatedly. After

Timer Commands

Time
Start
You have 48 seconds to read at 250 w.p.m.

Time
Start
You have 44 seconds to read at 275 w.p.m.

Time
Start
You have 40 seconds to read at 300 w.p.m.

20 minutes they had forgotten 47 percent—almost half. After a day, 62 percent were forgotten; two days, 69 percent; 31 days, 78 percent. The results were clear: the bulk of forgetting takes place within minutes after study and then tapers off.

A similar study by Spitzer in 1939 which used meaningful material came up with similar numbers—46 percent of the material was forgotten after a day: 79 percent after 14 days. Forgetting is an immediate thing. By tonight you will have forgotten almost 50 percent of this article—unless you try to encode it or put it in your own words the minute you finish.

Spitzer proved that encoding works to counter the brain's awesome and instant forgetting power. In another study he conducted, some subjects merely studied (i.e. read) materials while others recited the information in their own words immediately after reading it. Seven days afterwards, those who had recited remembered 83 percent of what they had read. The others only remembered 33 percent. This shows that encoding works, but for the why of that working you'll have to return to Bruner's concept about structural patterns. Encoding apparently makes you create memorable patterns. It works.

Time
Start
You have 37 seconds to read at 325 w.p.m.

Note-taking, Like Love, Requires You Listen Dearly

Assigned readings are not the only material you must commit to memory. You will also be tested on lectures. Studying lecture notes is a lot like studying a text. First you read, then you encode. But before you can read or encode you must take notes, and that requires listening.

It is a subtle skill, perhaps because it's so human a skill. Professors are not textbooks; they're humans who do not organize themselves into easy-to-grasp chapters and headings and who often talk rapidly, slowly or monotonously.

But listeners are fallible, too. They listen in monotone, racing like a dictaphone to capture every word. Most students listen to a lecture as if every idea had equal weight. Not so. In an hour-long lecture, there will be at most only six or seven main points that you are expected to remember.

Time
Start
You have 34 seconds to read at 350 w.p.m.

The rest of the information is detail, colorful anecdotes, relevant tangents or side dressings of opinion which the professor has included to clarify the main points for you. He hopes the extra information will tease you into greater awareness of those main points. He would be horrified to realize that most of his students *miss* those main points and remember the details instead.

You can pick out the main points by listening for cue phrases. Sometimes cues are very simple: "Our topic for today is. . ." the professor will say. But other times he will bury his cue in elaborate rhetoric, and you will have to figure out where the rhetoric ends and the main point begins: "Picture the day Lincoln arrived at Gettysburg in his dark top hat and cape, his shoulders stooped," the professor intones, and you wonder if this lecture is about Gettysburg, Civil War fashion, or curvature of the spine. Keep listening. He'll drop a cue eventually.

Cues for related subpoints can be very brief and are easily missed if you're not listening hard. Phrases like "on the other hand," "another way of looking at that," "next in importance," "turning now to," can signal a new point. Sometimes a single word—"however," "therefore,"

Timer Commands

Time
Start
You have 32 seconds to read at 375 w.p.m.

"but"—may introduce a point. You have to think as you listen, learning to differentiate the trivial from the important.

Encoding Follows Naturally
Once listening is mastered, notetaking becomes absurdly simple. All you have to do is write down the main points, adding just as much detail as you care to for your own entertainment or clarification. Studies have been made of different notetaking styles, and the studies are, frankly, inconclusive. One study comparing four notetaking styles—a formal outline method, a two-column format, the "Cornell three-column format" and "no special method"—revealed that none of the methods had any merit over the others. There were no differences in student grades attributable to notetaking methods.

But a study that compared students who did not take notes with those who did, revealed that note-takers always make better grades. It's not "how" but "whether" you take notes that counts. Why? None of the researchers ventured any answers, but it may be that notetaking is a form of encoding. Lectures make you select what's important (because you don't have time to get *everything* down), and they make you put the

Time
Start
You have 30 seconds to read at 400 w.p.m.

information down in your own words (because you don't have time to put it down in the professor's words). In lecture you become an encoder in spite of yourself. You're forced to do there what you should do for texts. No wonder so many students feel they learn more in lectures. A text ought to be more valuable than a lecture because it's better organized, more comprehensive and less likely to mumble. Yet a text can't force you to encode.

Ah, But What Of It?
One autumn when students returned to campus, a professor named E. B. Greene gave them the same exams they had taken the spring before. Even "A" students had forgotten 50 percent of all they had successfully memorized the term before. Another professor, E. T. Layton, found that students lost two-thirds of their algebraic knowledge after a year.

What's the use? Even with the best study habits, you will eventually forget what you've learned. You will get through tests, but what of it if it's all gone by next term? Memorizing, dictaphone style, seems to all students a pointless exercise.

In a 1932 book called *The Psychology of Study*, Cecil Mace wrote, "If the student has any compensating merit, it lies in being something

Time
Start
You have 28 seconds to read at 425 w.p.m.

more than a mere recording machine." That something, he argued, was thinking ability. You are doomed to forget most of what you learn; the only merit in all this is that somehow because of it, or at worst in spite of it, you learn to think.

But what is thinking? The best Mace could do in 30-odd pages of essay was suggest that free association might be involved. Hundreds of other thinkers have struggled with the question, and among them the most honest might be Walter (OK4R) Pauk who has said that thinking, despite all the thinking done about it, remains largely a private matter.

So how is memorization related to this private skill? For an insight into that we can go all the way back to a letter the not-yet Saint Thomas Aquinas wrote to a Brother John: "Since you have asked me how one should set about to acquire the treasure of knowledge, this is my advice to you concerning it: namely, that you should choose to enter, not straightway into the ocean, but by way of the little streams; for difficult things ought to be reached by way of easy ones. . . . Do not heed by *whom* a thing is said, but rather *what* is said you should commit to your memory. . . ."

Victor White, commenting on this letter, has written: "Note how careful St. Thomas is. Brother John is to commit what is said to his *memory*; he is not straightway to commit his *intellect* to it. He is not at once to swallow everything that is said; let him remember it in order to test and examine it, but not at once to assent to it. Suspension of judgment is one of the first things a learner has to learn: we have to learn how to entertain ideas without promptly either affirming them or denying them. Here again it is a matter of that difficult business of restraining the mind's own native impetuosity, the natural desire of the reason to be unreasonable. We want to jump to conclusions before we have reached them; to take sides, make a stand, vehemently affirm or deny before we have considered, examined, tested, proved."

St. Thomas Died in 1274

Memorization may seem more worthwhile to you if you perceive it, like Victor White does, as a tool of dispassion. Memorization is not commitment. It's just a way to hold onto thoughts as you sift through sometimes frightening new ideas looking for the ones you will come to live by. Remember that—even if you can't remember when St. Thomas died. Meanwhile, you can be sure researchers will press on, looking for a memorizing formula you can live with.[2]

Timer Commands

Time

Start
You have 27 seconds to read at 450 w.p.m.

Time

Start
Continue reading at this speed.

Comprehension Questions on "Magical Memory Tour"

Circle the correct answers.
1. The author claims that the main thing tested in college examinations is the student's ability to: (a) think, (b) memorize, (c) write rapidly, (d) play the academic game.
2. The first and most famous study formula was the: (a) OK4R, (b) OARWET, (c) SQ3R, (d) PQRST.
3. The study formula preferred by this author is: (a) PANORAMA, (b) OK4R, (c) SQ3R, (d) REAP.

[2] Reprinted by permission from the 1978 issue of *Insider*. © 1978, by Patricia Westfall.

4. The main criticism made of most of the study formulas mentioned in this article is: (a) students do not use them, (b) they do not work, (c) they are psychologically unsound, (d) they are a product of the 1960s.
5. The author claims that when most students sit down to read, they begin by: (a) surveying, (b) asking questions, (c) reviewing, (d) reading.
6. The author concludes that the most important feature of the study formulas is: (a) to take good lecture notes, (b) to put material in your own words immediately, (c) to listen more carefully, (d) to overview before you read.
7. Research on memorization shows that most people forget: (a) all of what they have learned within a week, (b) roughly half of what they have learned within 24 hours, (c) nothing during the first day, (d) roughly a fourth of what they have learned in the first two days.
8. The method used to help students retard the rate of forgetting is called: (a) encoding, (b) decoding, (c) previewing, (d) repeating.
9. To help you identify the main points in a lecture, the author advises that you: (a) tape the lecture, (b) ask the professor for the main points after class, (c) check a friend's notes, (d) listen for cue words and phrases.
10. The students who make the best grades: (a) take no lecture notes at all, (b) take lecture notes using the three-column method, (c) take lecture notes using the two-column method, (d) take lecture notes, but the method is unimportant.

Answers:
(1) b; (2) c; (3) d; (4) a; (5) d; (6) b; (7) b; (8) a; (9) d; (10) d.

Subtract ten points for each incorrect answer and record your score:
_____ %
You have read well if your score is 70 percent or better.

2. This second article is set up exactly like the first one, only you will begin reading at 200 words per minute and finish reading at 600 words per minute. Take one minute to survey the article and then follow the timer's commands. Use your hand or a pencil to set your pace. Finally, answer the comprehension questions at the end.

Your First Job: What To Look For, What To Expect

by DON AKCHIN*

Timer Commands
Start
You have 1 minute to read at 200 w.p.m.

An industrial relations specialist once compared entering the work world to being an immigrant in a new country. In both cases, you must cope with a new language, a new environment, and different customs, rules and mores. The challenge of a first job, then, is as much handling the culture shock as it is mastering the particular work task.

* Don Akchin, a survivor of First-Job Shock, is now a senior writer for 13-30 Corporation.

The more forays you make into the work world before graduation—through part-time jobs or internships—the easier the transition will be. Though there will still be surprises, nearly everyone who's new to working faces similar adjustment problems, as career experts and recent graduates can tell you.

Your First Job Means Starting Over

No matter how brilliant your professors thought you were, your first job means starting over—from the first grade. "As a senior in college, you're at the top of the scale," says Becky Troth, a 1978 graduate who works as a research analyst for a small San Francisco firm that leases railroad cars. "I was an R.A., and sophomores came to me for advice. I felt old and wise. Now at work I'm back to being on the bottom. Everyone thinks I'm extremely young and extremely naive. In college, people told me I looked older. Now I have people telling me I look 16."

Time

Start
You have 53 seconds to read at 225 w.p.m.

Some recent graduates react with the "I'm a genius" attitude. They know they're brilliant, and people who don't see that must be incredibly stupid. Consciously or unconsciously, many new graduates come across to others as elitist, smug, superior. These traits aren't becoming to beginners, and in the eyes of your co-workers, you are a beginner.

Another common reaction is the opposite, the "I'm an idiot" feeling. You thought you knew a good bit, but suddenly you're overwhelmed with new data, new ways of doing things, and you can't possibly make sense of it all. That's more the attitude your co-workers were expecting you to show—but only till you've had a chance to settle in and gain confidence.

Perspective is the key. If you're humble enough to recognize that you have a lot to learn, but self-assured enough to know you can learn it eventually, you can steer a middle path toward making your job a success. You can't possibly know everything the day you walk in. If you did, you'd be bored the second day. So admit it, and let the pieces gradually fall into place.

Time

Start
You have 48 seconds to read at 250 w.p.m.

Suddenly, You're a Member of a Team

You can't take too long to figure out what you're doing, however. People are depending on you and on the way you do your job. That makes it important that you master your work as soon as you can.

Being depended upon is not a typical part of the student experience. "As a student, if you screw up you're hurting no one but yourself," says Troth. "In a business situation, you're affecting everyone else by what you do." Until she started working, Troth didn't realize how much independence students have. Most can pursue their own interests without worrying about other people.

You are, in other words, a member of a team (the most junior member, remember), and the team's success depends in part upon you. That adds a weighty new responsibility, one that calls for more discipline than studentdom demands.

"If I woke up and didn't feel like going to class, I didn't," says Susan Archer, a personnel trainee with a major national retailer headquartered in New York City. "It's an adjustment just to go to a job every day. And I still find muself thinking, 'Well, I've got Christmas vacation coming.' But then I realize that I don't."

"I guess what I'm saying is, you're faced with a lot more responsibility at work than you ever were before, and you have to start taking things a lot more seriously. That in itself is an adjustment."

Performance Is the Only Measure of Success

The first and foremost goal of any company is its own financial success. In college the fact that your term paper is in on time and reasonably good is important to you, perhaps, but makes not a whit of difference to the university. In the business world (and to a lesser extent in government and nonprofit agencies), your work affects the organization's survival. You can cost the company money if you do poor work that must be done again by someone else. You can bring money into the company or save it money by your efforts, too.

In this environment, there can be only one measure of success—performance. "Once you're in the door, they don't care what your background is. Your performance is all that counts," says Gordon Tucker of his employer, Procter & Gamble. "They want to see results."

This means pressure. There's more pressure at Procter & Gamble than at many companies because it is company policy to dish out heavy responsibility right away. "You're thrown into the fire and expected to hold your own alongside some of the most brilliant marketing people in the country," says Tucker, whose first job, as a brand assistant, made him responsible for a budget of several million dollars. "There's an extreme amount of pressure and a lot of competition between peers. But it's not like a bitter rivalry. It's very performance-related."

Some students can earn top grades with a bare-minimum effort, and in school that's all it takes for an automatic annual promotion to the next grade. In the business world, promotions are neither so regular nor so automatic, and sliding by is not enough.

Office Politics Can't Be Ignored

Even doing a good job may not be enough. Success often means both performing well and making sure the right people *know* about your performance. In other words, you have to use politics to your advantage.

Many discussions about office politics, or any politics, start from the assumption that politics is negative—at best, a necessary evil—and something that ought to be avoided if possible. That's an unrealistic view.

Politics is simply dealing with people to get things done, and wherever there are people, there is politics. The job that's free of politics does not exist.

Says Chuck Sundberg, dean of the Placement and Career Planning

Timer Commands

Time

Start
You have 44 seconds to read at 275 w.p.m.

Time

Start
You have 40 seconds to read at 300 w.p.m.

Time

Start
You have 34 seconds to read at 350 w.p.m.

Center at the University of California at Los Angeles, ''Your supervisor *Timer Commands*
has his own needs, wants, desires and aspirations, and those are going
to affect the way he deals with you and the projects he's supervising.
You've got to be aware of that. And if anybody suggests that's wrong,
then they'll never adjust to life, because that's life, friend!''

Once you understand that office politics is a factor, you must deal
with it constructively. ''If you're going to move in an organization, you
need to find what are the political pathways,'' says Dr. Harry Levinson,
a clinical psychologist who heads the Levinson Institute. ''You cannot
assume that just by doing a good job, you're going to make it. You won't.
People have to know who you are and what you can do.

''That doesn't mean you have to be manipulative,'' continues Levinson. ''But it does mean you have to take the time to get acquainted   *Time*

with people in an organization. Find out what different people do, what   Start
different departments do, and let people find out what you do—your   You have 30 sec-
skills and competencies. If you ignore that, you may find yourself getting onds to read at
the short end of the stick—not because people are malicious, but because   400 w.p.m.
they don't know you.''

There's A Lot Less Feedback
Many recent graduates find it hard to get an idea of just how they're
doing. Feedback tends to come less frequently in the business world than
in college, and some new employees find this frustrating.

''You don't have grades, so you have no way to gauge how good
they really think you are,'' says Troth. ''You want something to latch
onto, and there's nothing really tangible to say that you're doing all right,
or that you should improve.''

On most jobs, there is some formal evaluation of your performance
after six months—or certainly within one year. But a lot of feedback is
informal, and you must be attuned to it to pick it up. ''You have to be
sensitive to the cues you're getting in hallway conversations, such as
comments about the paper this person did or the job that one did,'' says   *Time*
Sundberg. ''Most evaluation is quite informal and appears to be off the   Start
cuff.''   You have 27
                                                                            seconds to read at
Troth says her supervisor seldom comments about good work, but   450 w.p.m.
gives negative feedback loudly and clearly. ''I've had to adjust my expectations of what I expect to get back from him,'' she says. But she has
also found that ''if you do one thing well, you're given other things to
do.'' That, too, is feedback. ''It's exciting to know someone has enough
faith in your abilities to keep handing you projects,'' she says.

Troth describes a lesson her first job has taught her: ''You can't think
you're worthless if you're not getting reinforcement from other people.
You've really got to rely more on your own self-confidence.''

You Have To Watch for Opportunities
Self-confidence may be in short supply those first few weeks on the job,
when you're trying to cope with all the adjustments this sudden dose of

culture shock requires. Your immediate goal will be simple survival. But once you're on your feet, don't forget what you came for.

Your first job is more than a simple entry into the world of work. It has an important long range effect: it starts your career in a direction. Ideally it will lay a solid foundation that your career can build on—and it will help you decide, early on, if the direction you're heading in is the right one.

But the job itself doesn't do these things for you. A great first job can offer you opportunities, but you have to act on them.

"You can't put yourself in the hands of the organization and say, 'Do something with me,' " says Levinson. "The organization can try, but it can't take responsibility for your life. You have to take your own initiative."

Here are some things you should gain from your first job:

–*Solid experience.* "What students ought to try to get most out of that first job is experience that is marketable for the next one—either in that organization or elsewhere," says Sundberg. The most useful experience comes out of jobs that offer real challenge and serious responsibilities.

Charles Guy Moore, executive director of the National Institute of Career Planning, suggests in his book *The Career Game* that you select a job you can grow into, then plan to grow out of it. A job that you can easily handle from day one doesn't stretch your mind or test your mettle. And once you've mastered a difficult job and learned all it can teach you, it makes sense to move on to a greater challenge.

–*Varied exposure.* Within your career field there are many different kinds of job possibilities. Your first job can be an opportunity to explore many of the options or at least observe them at close range. For starters, this means finding out what other people in your company do, and what their work offers them.

People who are hired as trainees have a head start. Susan Archer's job as a personnel trainee began with three months spent touring different divisions within the personnel operation at her employer's New York headquarters. "We got to see what happened in each one, and we were doing little mini-projects." Then the trainees were assigned to divisions. "I asked for training and development, and they asked for me, and here I am," she says. "I like this division. I like what they do here." One of her assignments will be to design next year's program for trainees.

–*Flexibility.* The foundation of career knowledge you lay should be as broad as possible. The world changes rapidly, and today's glamorous occupation may be obsolescent tomorrow. You should get exposure to all the work experiences you can and try to keep your options open. In the direction you've set, there are any number of interesting side roads.

–*Visibility.* As Levinson noted in discussing office politics, you must not only do good work, but also have your good work noticed by those who count. In many cases, you can make yourself visible both to key people in your company and to people in your field outside your company. (One good way is to attend conventions or trade shows.)

Timer Commands

Time
Start
You have 24 seconds to read at 500 w.p.m.

Time
Start
You have 22seconds to read at 550 w.p.m.

Time
Start
You have 20 seconds to read at 600 w.p.m.

–Personal satisfaction. This is what work ought to be all about.   *Timer Commands*
"That's the elusive goal—satisfaction with work," says Tucker of Procter
& Gamble. "With me it means satisfaction with my own personal performance. I like doing a good job in anything I do. In many cases, you
have to be able to derive satisfaction just from knowing you've done a
good job, not from any praise you receive."

Whatever Happens, You Learn From It
Despite all your efforts, you could find yourself in a company where you
don't belong, in a career you're not really interested in after all, in a job   Time
that isn't suited to your talents. These things happen.

Start
Continue reading
at this speed.

"No matter how thoroughly you research your own psyche and your
own interests and the world of work," says Sundberg, "when you take
a job you're going to plunge into something that remains fairly unknown.
You might find yourself in the wrong company or the wrong field. You
won't know that until you get your feet wet. Because of that, you might
not do well.

"One might call that failing. I wouldn't call it failure. I would call
it learning a lot."[3]

Comprehension Questions on "Your First Job"
Circle the correct answers.
1. New jobs are pleasant if you have been to college because your co-
   workers will immediately recognize your special capabilities.
   True   False
2. Which was *not* included as advice for the new person on the job? (a)
   recognize you have a lot to learn, (b) be self-assured enough to know
   you will learn, (c) show your co-workers how much you already know, (d)
   don't try to learn everything the first day.
3. How does this author suggest that working compares with going to
   school? (a) working is easier, (b) work and school are about the same, (c)
   working is harder because it requires more responsibility, (d) school is
   harder because it requires more responsibility.
4. Where does the author claim performance is most important, at work
   or at school? _____
5. Where is it easier to get promotions, at work or at school? _____
6. Which of the following would this author say you should *not* be doing
   if you are "using politics to your advantage" on the job? (a) manipulating
   people to get them to do what you want them to do, (b) figuring out
   what is important to your supervisor, (c) finding out what your co-workers do, (d) letting people know about your special skills and competencies.
7. How does the author suggest you can learn about how well you are doing
   on a job? (a) ask your co-workers, (b) ask your supervisor, (c) wait to see
   if you get a raise, (d) notice whether you are given extra things to do.

[3] Reprinted by permission from the 1979 issue of *Insider.* © 1979, by 13-30 Corporation.

8. Which does the author say should be the more important force in your life, the organization you work for or your own initiative? _____

9. Once you have mastered a difficult job, the author suggests you: (a) teach it to others, (b) move on to a greater challenge, (c) relax and enjoy the rewards of your hard work, (d) get an extra job on the side.

10. If you make a mistake and get into the wrong company or field, the author suggests that you: (a) consider yourself a failure, (b) learn to adjust, (c) consider it a learning experience, (d) aim for success no matter how difficult it might be to attain.

Answers:
1. false; 2. c; 3. c; 4. work; 5. school; 6. a; 7. d; 8. your initiative; 9. b; 10. c.

Subtract ten points for each incorrect answer and give yourself a score: ____ %
If you received 60 percent or better, you comprehended well, especially at the speed required by this exercise.

3. This last exercise is 600-words long. When you are told to start, try to read it at the speed you finished reading the last article. This means you will read it in one minute or less. Rapidly underscore each line or drag your hand down the page to keep your mind and eyes working at top efficiency. Take 15 seconds to survey this article before you begin. When you finish reading, take the comprehension test at the end.

The Art of Matching a Company's Personality with Your Own

Companies have personalities just like people. You'll probably enjoy your first job more—and you'll probably be more successful at it—if your company's personality matches your own.

Dr. Harry Levinson of the Levinson Institute says that business firms have structures similar to those of families. The company personality is set by the example of its top executives, by the way it is organized and by the kinds of people it attracts.

How do you determine whether your personality fits the company's? Levinson says there are a number of signs to look for, both in the company and in yourself:

–*Handling affection.* Some companies shower praise on employees daily or weekly; some project the image of the strong, silent, never-completely-satisfied father. "Some of us need to have a lot of close personal relationships, other people tend to be loners, still other people need a lot of applause," says Levinson. "Some people need to please other people."

–*Handling aggression.* A government bureau may be a comfortable niche for a cautious person, but stifling to an aggressive risk-taker—who would be quite at home in certain companies that share his head-on style.

Switch to two fixa-
tions per line.

"Some people do better vigorously attacking problems or undertaking projects by themselves," says Levinson. "Others don't want to take risks; they're more cautious. Some people bend over backwards trying not to be seen as aggressively hostile; they have difficulty taking charge. Some people need to compete and vanquish people."

–*Handling dependency.* "Some may do better in highly structured situations where someone tells them what to do. Other people can't lean on anyone else, they have to do it all themselves," says Levinson. "Some can work interdependently, on a team. If you need to depend on a highly structured organization, you might do fine in the Army but you'd have a hard time selling Fuller brushes door to door."

–*Ego ideal.* Levinson: "All of us have a picture in our own minds of how we would like to be. That's called the 'ego ideal'; it's what we're always striving toward. We need to know what things we do make us feel good about ourselves, give us a sense of moving toward our ego ideal; and what things make us feel less good about ourselves." Companies also have idealized images of themselves. A humanitarian may feel better about working for an organization that stresses the ideal of service over profit; a pragmatist might not.

Discovering the company's personality is a simple matter of on-the-scene observation and asking the right questions. "You can get a sense of a company just by walking in the front door," says Levinson. "You can tell by how people act toward you when you're being interviewed. You can look at the way the office is painted and decorated; whether it's congenial or uncomfortable; whether people are smiling or not; whether the place feels tense."

Talk to employees about what they do at work, what they like and don't like, and what the company likes and doesn't like them to do. Find out how long they've been there—and whether people generally stay or move on quickly. Read the bulletin boards. Listen to determine whether people are proud of the company or constantly complaining—and what they complain about.

After sifting through all this information about the company and matching it with what you know about yourself, you can decide whether you'll fit. Unlike the family you were born into, the company family gives you the choice of whether to join.[4]

Time spent reading: _____ Words per minute: _____
(Consult the chart below.)

Time	Speed
30 seconds	1200 w.p.m.
45 seconds	800 w.p.m.
1 minute	600 w.p.m.
1 minute 15 seconds	480 w.p.m.
1 minute 30 seconds	400 w.p.m.
1 minute 45 seconds	342 w.p.m.
2 minutes	300 w.p.m.

[4] Reprinted by permission from the 1979 issue of *Insider.* © 1979, by 13-30 Corporation.

2 minutes 15 seconds	266 w.p.m.
2 minutes 30 seconds	240 w.p.m.
2 minutes 45 seconds	218 w.p.m.
3 minutes	200 w.p.m.
3 minutes 15 seconds	184 w.p.m.
3 minutes 30 seconds	171 w.p.m.
3 minutes 45 seconds	160 w.p.m.
4 minutes	150 w.p.m.

Comprehension Questions on "The Art of Matching a Company's Personality with Your Own"

Circle the correct answers.

1. Which of the following was *not* mentioned as contributing to a company's personality? (a) the example of its top executives, (b) the way it is organized, (c) its location, (d) the people it attracts.
2. If a company's personality matches your own, you will: (a) probably enjoy your new job and be more successful, (b) become more like the people who work for the company, (c) rebel against the conformity imposed by the company, (d) have an easier time getting to know your co-workers.
3. Some people need more praise than others to do well on the job.   True   False
4. Which of the following was mentioned as a good place to work for a cautious person who does not like to take chances? (a) library, (b) government bureau, (c) utilities company, (d) newspaper corporation.
5. Aggressive risk-takers are characterized as people who: (a) can't get along with others, (b) are at home in aggressive companies, (c) have difficulty taking charge, (d) do not want to be seen as aggressively hostile.
6. If you like to work in a highly structured organization, the author says you might like working: (a) in a local government, (b) selling Fuller brushes door to door, (c) in the Army, (d) as a school teacher.
7. Which is the best definition of ego ideal? (a) the idealized image we have of a company, (b) the idealized image we have of ourselves, (c) the daily goals we set for ourselves, (d) the ideal way of relating to other people.
8. Which of the following was mentioned as a way to judge a company's personality? (a) read the bulletin boards, (b) interview the director, (c) write letters of inquiry, (d) read the annual reports.
9. When you talk to employees about the personality of their company, you should find out: (a) how much vacation time is allowed, (b) if there are insurance benefits, (c) if they travel a lot, (d) if they are complaining and, if so, what about.
10. How is the company family *unlike* the family you were born into? (a) there is no strong father figure, (b) there is no strong sense of security, (c) you can choose whether or not to join it, (d) you cannot really be yourself.

Answers:
1. c; 2. a; 3. true; 4. b; 5. b; 6. c; 7. b; 8. a; 9. d; 10. c

Subtract ten points for each incorrect answer and give yourself a score: _____ %

Since the questions are detailed and cover only a short passage, a score of 60 percent or better is excellent.

Now turn back to page 103 and compare your present speed and comprehension scores with your beginning scores.

Beginning speed _____   Beginning comprehension _____
Ending speed   _____   Ending comprehension   _____

II. Applications to Your Other Reading

A. Select a book that you can read rapidly. Read for 15 minutes, and then stop to count the pages you have read. Count off the same number of pages plus two and read them in the next 15-minute interval. Add a page each 15 minutes until you are reading a page a minute or 60 pages an hour. Reading at this rate, or faster, finish the book.

III. Class Discussion and Activities

A. Refer back to the analysis you did of your present reading responsibilities at the end of Chapter 2 (page 38). Label the items in your list as easy, relatively difficult, or difficult. Underline all items that, in your judgment, you could read rapidly either because they are easy for you or because you do not need a great deal of information from them. Compare your judgments with those made by other students in the class. Discuss why certain material is easy or difficult and why it might best be read rapidly or slowly and closely.

B. Observe the eye fixations of the student next to you in class by punching a hole through a newspaper and looking through it to watch the reader's eyes. Then switch so that your fellow student can watch your eyes as you read.

C. Bring a book to class that you want to read and can read rapidly. Show it in class and tell why you want to read it or why you liked reading it.

D. Listen to the other students discuss the books they bring to class. Make a list of the titles you would like to read yourself.

E. Devise a system for trading enjoyable books with your classmates.

IV. Vocabulary Review
A. Specialized Terms

1. speed-reading _____

2. oral reading rate _____

3. silent reading rate _____

4. vocalization _____

5. regression _____

6. eye fixations _____

7. peripheral vision _____

B. (General Vocabulary)

1. supplementary _____

2. predict _____

3. compulsive _____

Further Reading

The following works provide further information about some of the ideas discussed in Part II of this book.

Adler, Mortimer J. and Charles Van Doren. *How To Read a Book,* revised ed. New York: Simon & Schuster, 1972.

Maxwell, Martha J. *Improving Student Learning Skills.* San Francisco, Calif.: Jossey-Bass, 1979.

Maxwell, Martha J. *Skimming and Scanning Improvement.* New York: McGraw-Hill, 1969.

Smith, Frank. *Understanding Reading,* 3d ed. New York: Holt, Rinehart and Winston, 1982.

Tinker, M. A. "Recent Studies of Eye Movements in Reading," *Psychological Bulletin,* 55, 1958, pp. 215- 231.

Walker, Carolyn. "Teaching Reading Rate Improvement to College Students," paper delivered at *Western College Reading Association Conference,* March 1978.

Wood, Nancy V. "Ten Labs to Improve Your Reading Speed and Skimming Skills," *College Reading and Study Skills,* 2d ed. New York: Holt, Rinehart and Winston, 1982.

Conclusion: Develop a System for Leisure Reading

This book will help you develop the skills necessary to read a book to the end with comparative ease. When you have acquired these skills, commit yourself to a lifetime of leisure reading. Here are some suggestions to help you do so.

1. Think of yourself as a competent and flexible reader. Be willing to try to read anything.

2. Always have a book that you are currently reading and another one waiting to be read.

3. Read a few minutes every day: just before you go to sleep, at breaks during the day, or early in the morning.

4. Read to reward yourself. Do not read books that bore you. A book that has not caught your interest after 20 pages should be put aside.

5. Plan ways to acquire books to read—trade with friends; visit bookstores, used book sales, and book exchanges; browse in libraries; read book reviews and book lists.

6. Discuss what you read with others. This will fix it in your mind and demonstrate its value to you.

7. Be aware of the benefits of reading to you. Reading can help you escape problems and relax, give you new information to think about, and help you develop new interests. Regular reading can also improve your vocabulary, your writing skills, and your ability to think. Done habitually, it can make you an educated person for life.

PART III
The Close-Reading Process

Part III of this book will help you learn to do the close, thorough reading of material that you must not only understand but must also learn and remember. The following ideas will receive special emphasis in the next four chapters:

1. Study the whole text first to understand the organizational pattern.
2. Study the parts next to get meaning from the paragraphs and sections of material.
3. Study the smaller parts to get added meaning from the words and sentences.
4. Complete your reading by studying the organization of the whole text again. Reorganize the ideas into patterns that you can learn and remember.

Prepare for your reading by trying to answer the following questions:

1. Why do authors organize their ideas before they begin to write?
2. What is a pattern of organization? Can you name some types of patterns?
3. What can you expect when you read a paragraph?
4. How do you find the main ideas in paragraphs and sections of materials?
5. How do you read passages that are difficult because of unusual vocabulary and complicated sentence construction?
6. What is style? How can an awareness of style improve your reading?
7. How can you improve your memory of what you read?
8. What are some special activities to improve your memory?

CHAPTER 7

Discovering the Organization of Ideas

In this chapter you will learn:

> How to study the whole text and analyze the author's organization of ideas.
> How to identify some conventional forms and patterns of organization.
> How to read when the organization is not clear.

Define:
assumption

Define:
conventional forms

Define:
patterns of organization

In Chapter 4 you learned how to discover the important ideas, organization, and features of a book or article by surveying. This chapter deals with the same subject of discovering organization, but it does so on a more thorough and detailed level. The assumption is that you will survey to get a quick idea of the author's organization and then read closely to do a more thorough analysis of it. It is important to get an idea of how the whole text is organized as early as possible. This makes it easier to understand and remember the parts.

The purpose of this chapter will be to introduce you to a variety of **conventional forms** and **patterns of organization** to help you discover how material has been organized. This information will further widen your expectations of each text you read. It will also help you follow an author's thought processes more easily and make more accurate predictions. Understanding organization will, finally, provide you with a framework for remembering what you have read.

What You Already Know about Organization

Define:
category

Define:
structure

The human mind, psychologists tell us, has a natural tendency to see relationships among ideas, to group them in categories, and to relate them to previous knowledge and structures already present in the mind. We mentally manipulate ideas in these ways in order to understand them better and to remember them longer. Think for a moment what you would do if you were asked to go to the grocery store to buy lettuce, carrots, milk, oranges, hamburger, tomatoes, bread, watermelon, cheese, a roast, potatoes, and butter. One of the conditions is that you would not be permitted to write these twelve items on a list. Instead, you would have to rely on

129

your memory. Stop now and reorganize these items in an order that would help you remember them. Write your reorganized list in the space below:

Notice how your mind immediately began to reorder these items so that they could be remembered. You might have put them in basic food groups, taking advantage of a pattern for organizing food that is already present in your mind. Or you might have thought of the geographical layout of a grocery store and mentally pictured the location of each item as you walked through the store. Or you might have grouped them according to the meals and times at which they would be eaten: bread, butter, milk, and oranges for breakfast; cheese, hamburger, lettuce, and tomatoes for lunch; and roast, potatoes, carrots, and watermelon for dinner.

Most authors, when they begin to write, start with a hodgepodge of ideas like the original grocery list. The ideas do not remain in random order for long, however. The author sees that some of them may be grouped together, that one idea may seem to belong at the beginning, and that another should be saved for last. Before authors begin to write, they place their ideas in a preliminary order. During the process of writing, these ideas continue to be manipulated and moved around until they eventually assume what, in the author's judgment, is the best order for the reader to understand them. The reader, in turn, searches and tries to uncover the author's original outline in order to take advantage of the organizational help the author has provided.

The Causes for Patterns of Organization

A great many factors influence authors' thinking and the decisions they make about organization when they write. Some of these are as follows:

Define:
sophisti-
cated
_____
_____

1. *The Audience.* An uninformed audience may influence an author to use a clear and easily understood pattern of organization, such as a list, accompanied by a great deal of transitional material, such as numbers or headings, to make it clear. When writing for a (sophisticated) audience, an author may use a more complex pattern and few transitions to make it clear. The reader, consequently, will have to work harder to find the pattern.

2. *The Purpose.* An author with a persuasive purpose may save the most important point until last or may use a special persuasive pattern of organization. An author with an informative purpose will usually state the main point immedi-

Define:
chrono-
logical
_____
_____

ately, in the first paragraph. Material that is written to entertain is often written in narrative form, with events presented (chronologically.) Finally, authors who write to express personal feelings or values may select poetic or essay forms. These examples, even though oversimplified, suggest the main point. An author's purpose often influences the organizational pattern, and, from the reader's viewpoint, understanding this pattern can often, in turn, provide insight into the purpose.

3. *The Occasion.* The occasion for writing can also influence an author's pattern of organization. Certain patterns are by custom associated with certain occasions for writing. Imagine an author writing instructions for baking a cake, for example. A reader can expect on this occasion to find the instructions written in step-by-step recipe form.

Define:
convention
_____
_____

Who was
Aristotle?
_____
_____

4. *The Subject.* A subject may suggest an obvious and natural pattern of organization, or it may suggest several. In the latter case, the author will have to decide which pattern is best. An anecdote or story is usually most naturally related in a chronological pattern, as it happened in time. The grocery list that you have already thought about could be organized in at least three different ways: according to the basic food-group topics, according to the geographical layout of the store, or according to the times the food would be eaten.

What is
the
Rhetoric?
_____
_____

Define:
topoi
_____
_____

5. **Convention.** Authors are often influenced by forms and patterns of thought that are part of our culture and consequently cause them to think and write in established ways. Aristotle, in the second book of the *Rhetoric,* which was written more than 2000 years ago, lists ways speakers and writers can think about and invent ideas for developing their subjects. He calls these aids to thought **topoi.** One example, and there are many, is the question that asks if the subject is *greater than* or *less than* something else. We would designate such thinking now comparison and contrast thinking. The point is that for centuries people have been taught established patterns to help them think about what they want to say.

The next two sections of this chapter name and describe some of the conventional forms and patterns of organization that authors use to help them think and write. Learn to name and describe them in order to recognize them in the material you read.

Six Conventional Forms

Part of the challenge of reading is to discover the author's organization and then to reorganize the ideas in your own mind so that you can remember them. Since authors do not tell you exactly how they will organize their material, you have to recognize when they are using a conventional form, or a pattern of organization, or a combination of the two. Let us look first at some of the conventional forms with which authors expect you to be familiar. These forms are used for specific purposes and occasions. We have come to expect them and find reading difficult when authors violate our expectations. Here is a partial list of examples of such forms. You can probably add to it.

Define:
literary

1. *(Literary) forms.* There are established forms for many types of poems including sonnets, limmericks, and haikus. Plays have a traditional form and so do novels. These forms are taught in your literature classes.

2. *Newspaper-article form.* News articles are often written so that the first paragraph contains the most important information, which answers the questions Who, What, Where, When, Why, and How. Less important details follow. There are two practical reasons for this form: The reader in a hurry can get the essential information by reading the first paragraph or two of each story; and the editor putting the newspaper together can cut off a final paragraph to make a story fit a given space without deleting essential information.

Define:
hypothesis

3. *Scientific paper form.* Scientific papers are, by convention, usually organized according to the following set parts: (1) the introduction; (2) the statement of hypothesis; (3) a description of the experimental procedure; (4) an analysis of the data; and (5) conclusions, which often include recommendations for future research. Mathematical papers follow a similar form with some variation. They may start with a theorem instead of a hypothesis, and procede to a proof of the theorem.

4. *Letter forms.* Business letters contain traditional parts including the date, addresses of the sender and receiver, the salutation, the body, the closing and signature, and information about copies and enclosures. Personal letters, although not so rigidly formed, have a salutation and a closing, and are easily recognizable as letters.

5. *Textbook form.* Textbooks stand out from other books because they often include a variety of teaching aids, such as learning objectives, exercises, glossaries, answer keys, prefaces to students, and boldface headings and subheadings to emphasize main divisions.

6. *The introduction, body, conclusion form.* Probably the most commonly used form for both material you listen to or read includes the three parts: the introduction, where the author tells you what will be said; the body, where the author says it; and the conclusion or summary, where you find out what has been said. Furthermore, you can expect to find certain types of information and organization within these three parts. In the introduction, you can expect any or all of the following: an attention getter, a definition of terms, background information on the topic, background information on the author including special experience and education, motives for writing and personal biases, advice on how to read, a description of special features, a statement of subject and focus, a preoutline of ideas, and sometimes a description of the pattern of organization in the body of the text. In the main body itself, you can expect to find main ideas, subideas, and supporting material used to explain the subject. In a conclusion, you can expect a major idea to be featured. In a summary, you can expect a restatement of the major ideas in the main body of the text.

In-Chapter Exercise 1

Refer back to the article entitled "How We Listen" on page 94. Locate the introduction, body, and conclusion in this article, write their paragraph numbers below, and list the information included in each part:

I. Introduction: paragraph # _____
Special information included:

_____

_____

_____

II. Body: paragraph # _____ through # _____
Main ideas:

_____

_____

_____

_____

III. Conclusion: paragraph # _____
Major idea featured:

_____

Define:
**predo-
minant
and sub-
patterns of
organiza-
tion**

_____
_____
_____
_____

Now look at the ideas you just listed that make up the body of the essay. They have been arranged by the author in an order that will help you understand and remember them. You can expect the material in the body of any text to be arranged according to a **predominant pattern of organization** that organizes the entire body or according to a series of **subpatterns of organization** that overlap and intermix.

Thirteen Patterns of Organization

In the early stages of the composition process when authors list ideas, often in random order to begin with, and later according to various patterns, they often find themselves relying on some established ways to think about, develop, and order these ideas. Authors may find themselves, for instance, thinking in terms of causes and effects, problems and solutions, differences and similarities, topics and categories, actions and consequences, plans and results, or implications, major examples, or final significances. Or they might find it useful to trace the history of an idea or series of events and make projections for the future. At times it will seem best to lead up to a main point and at other times to state it immediately and then

Define:
exhaustive
_____

prove it. All of these ways of thinking—and this is not an (exhaustive) list—help authors: (1) come up with ideas to write about in the first place, (2) think in detail about them in order to generate supporting material, and (3) figure out the order for arranging or organizing the ideas in the final written product. It is this last function of these patterns of thought—to help with organization—that will be described here. Just as you were introduced to some conventional forms in the preceding section, here you will be introduced to some common patterns of organization. An understanding and ability to recognize both forms and patterns will help you locate the important ideas, concentrate and understand them, and commit them

Define:
conjunction
_____

to memory. Remember as you read through the patterns listed below that one of these patterns might organize an entire text or be used in (conjunction) with other patterns to organize a part of a text. It is useful to try to find the predominant patterns and then look for subpatterns. Notice also as you read this list that various types of transitions or signal words are used both to identify the pattern itself and also to make the ideas stand out.

Define:
**topical
pattern**
_____

1. **Topical Pattern.** The topical pattern is commonly used in college textbooks. In this pattern, material is grouped into logical categories like the food groups for the grocery list. Another simple example is the organization of a curriculum vitae or resumé. As a writer, you might start to write your resumé with a random list of details about yourself. Then, as you organize this material, you find that most items can be grouped under a few logical topic headings such as education, work experience, hobbies and interests, and special honors and awards. As a reader, you need to locate the major topics and analyze why they have been placed in a particular order.

   In textbooks the *transitional* or *signal device* most frequently used to make the ideas stand out in topical organization is *headings* and *subheadings*. This chapter that you are now reading is organized according to topics. Read through the headings and subheadings in boldface type to get a quick idea of the topics and their order. Notice how some topics prepare you for others. Locate and analyze the order of topics in all material organized topically.

Define:
**classifi-
cation
pattern**
_____

2. **Classification Pattern.** Classification is a specific type of topical organization in which a main topic is subdivided or classified into a list of its subtopics, types, or parts. Here is an introduction to a section of material that is organized this way:

   > Anthropology is traditionally divided into four branches: physical anthropology and the three branches of cultural anthropology: archeology, linguistics, and ethnology.[1]

[1] From *Anthropology*, 3rd Edition by William Haviland (New York: Holt, Rinehart and Winston, 1982), pp. 10–11. Copyright © 1982 by CBS College Publishing. Reprinted by permission of CBS College Publishing.

Following this introduction the author describes each of the four branches, or parts, of anthropology. Other examples of material arranged this way might be four types of thinking, five types of insects, three branches of government, or three types of senior citizens.

The transitional or signal devices used most often to make the ideas in a classification pattern stand out are enumeration (first, second, third) and a key term that identifies the topic (branches of government). Material can be made into a quick outline that is easy to visualize and remember.

In-Chapter Exercise 2

Reread the passage about anthropology again and complete the outline.

Branches of Anthropology

1. _____

2. _____

    a. _____

    b. _____

    c. _____

Define:
**chrono-
logical
pattern**

_____

_____

3. **Chronological Pattern.** Material arranged chronologically is explained as it occurs over a period of time. Think, for example, of the grocery list arranged according to when it would be eaten. Certain types of books are usually arranged this way including histories, biographies, autobiographies, diaries, and novels or stories. As a reader, you need to figure out how much time is covered, where the breaks in time are, and whether strict chronology is followed. There may be frequent flashbacks or sudden projections into the future, for instance. *Time transitions* or *signals (next, soon, after, later, much later)* are used to make the changes in time in chronological organization stand out.

Define:
**process
pattern**

_____

_____

4. **Process Pattern.** The process pattern of organization is a subtype of the chronological pattern. It is most commonly used to explain how to follow a process to accomplish a goal. Recipes, instructions for building and assembling, or directions and procedures to follow are arranged according to this pattern. The steps for surveying and skimming on pages 70–77 and 85–87 of this book follow the process pattern. Transitions or signals used to make the parts of a process stand out are *enumeration (first, second, third)* and words like *next, then,* and *finally.* As a reader, your task will usually be to get the steps straight, list them, and either learn them or follow them.

Define:
**spatial
pattern**

_____

_____

5. **Spatial Pattern.** Some material is best described according to its location in a geographical area or within a given space. Think of the grocery list, for ex-

Define:
**general
to
specific
pattern**

_____

_____

ample, arranged according to the location of each item in the store. Another example might be of a rock concert where the line outside is described, then the crowd inside, and, finally, the performers on the stage. *Place transitions or signals are used to make the parts of this scene stand out: over there, to the right, outside, inside, on the stage.* You will find it useful in reading material that is arranged this way either to visualize it in your mind or to draw a sketch of it.

Define:
**deductive
pattern**

_____

_____

6. **General to Specific Pattern.** Making a general statement at the outset and then supporting it with specific details is called the **general to specific** or the **deductive pattern of organization.**

In-Chapter Exercise 3

Locate the general statement in this paragraph and underline it. Notice how the rest of the paragraph presents details that clarify and explain the general statement.

Emerson estimated that a man might have, if he were fortunate, some hundreds of reasonable moments in a long life. He was thinking probably of moments of inspiration from sources less traceable than the book in one's hand. The great pages are the most constant and dependable sources of "reasonable moments," if we mean by them moments when we know more completely what we are, and why we are so, and thus "see into the life of things" more deeply than in our everyday routine of existence. Such reasonable moments are the highest aim of reading. In them we do more than communicate with our authors—in the humble sense of communicate. We partake with them of wisdom.[2]

1. What is the general point? _____

2. List at least three details that clarify and explain the general point.

    1. _____

    2. _____

    3. _____

When reading material arranged deductively, make certain that you locate and understand the general point first. Then read to see how the rest of the material clarifies, explains, or proves it.

[2] I.A. Richards, *How To Read a Page* (New York: W. W. Norton, 1942), pp. 15–16.

Define:
**specific
to
general
pattern**

_____

_____

Define:
**induc-
tive
pattern**

_____

_____

Define:
**compari-
son and
contrast
pattern**

_____

Transitions or *signals,* which lead from main ideas to subideas and supporting material *(for instance, for example, to clarify),* may be used to help you differentiate the general from the specific in this pattern.

7. **Specific to General Pattern.** Starting with details and ending with the general point is called specific to general or the **inductive pattern** of organization. For an example, look back at the paragraph about how college life has changed since the 1960s on page 49. Note that the author begins with a series of specific examples that lead up to the general point made toward the end of the paragraph. The same types of transitions or signals that you would find in the general to specific pattern *(for instance, for example)* can also be used for the specific to general to emphasize the levels of generality and to make the main point stand out.

8. **Comparison and Contrast Pattern.** In Chapter 3, comparison and contrast were listed as forms of supporting material (see page 45). When the comparison and contrast references are brief, we categorize them this way. At times, however, an author will develop an idea throughout an entire text by using predominantly comparison, contrast, or both. In this case the technique becomes an organizational pattern.

In-Chapter Exercise 4

Note how the following newspaper story about a Democratic and a Republican convention is organized according to contrasts.

GOP Convenes Smoothly but Demos Fight Discord

More than 400 Republicans at the party's county convention Saturday, like the diverse instruments in an orchestra performing in harmony under the direction of a skillful maestro, finished their business in about 3½ hours.

Almost 200 Democrats took the same amount of time finding someone to lead their band.

Delegates debated more than three hours before selecting a chairman to run their eight-hour convention, the first order of business before they really got down to business. Discordant notes struck again and again like the squeaks and squawks of a symphony tuning up in the orchestra pit.

Some delegates thought it was good old Democratic fun. Others found it frustrating. . . .

While Democrats spent about three hours getting started, Republicans used about the same amount of time to vote on 27 resolutions, approve delegates to the state convertion and listen to a speech. . . .

Democrats milled about in dimly lit, aging Liberty Hall. Delegates in the audience shouted to be heard when recognized by the chairman.

Republicans sat in orderly rows in a bright, modern auditorium. . . . Three microphones were available for audience members to use when addressing their fellow delegates. Potted plants decorated the stage. . . .

While Republicans say ironing out the politics *before* the convention is the way to run a meeting, some Democrats disagree. . . .[3]

To gain greater insight into the organization of this piece, outline it in the space provided below. There are at least seven differences mentioned. The first two have been listed for you. See if you can find the other five.

Outline: *Differences* **between the Republican and Democratic Conventions**

Republicans	Democrats
1. 400 attending	1. 200 attending
2. Finished in 3½ hours	2. Took eight hours
3.	3.
4.	4.
5.	5.
6.	6.
7.	7.

The *transitional* or *signal* words and *phrases—by contrast, in comparison, while, some, others*—are sometimes used to make ideas stand out in this pattern.

Define: **master example pattern**

9. **Master Example Pattern.** In Chapter 3, examples were also identified as a form of supporting material, particularly when they are used briefly at various points throughout a text. At times, however, an author may select a master example to use as the organizational feature of a text. Then the example becomes a pattern of organization. Imagine an article, for instance, about the long-term effects of the Vietnam War on its veterans. The main ideas might be the psychological effects, the physical effects, and the effects on the veteran's family. Rather than organizing the material for the article under these three topic headings, however, the author uses one example of one veteran whose personal life illustrates, throughout the article, all three topics. The example is the main organizing principle of the article. A transition or signal such as *"To return to our original example"* might be used to clarify this pattern. Or, you may find the single word *example* used at intervals to call your attention to the master example.

[3] From Ruthanne Brockway, "GOP Convenes Smoothly but Demos Fight Discord," *The El Paso Times*, El Paso, Texas, May 16, 1982, p. 1A.

Define:
**definition
pattern**
_____
_____

10. **Definition Pattern.** Definitions were listed as a form of supporting material in Chapter 3, and, like comparison/contrast and examples, the definition is a form of support when used briefly and on a small scale. When the purpose of an entire article, however, is to define an idea or a concept, definition can become an organizational pattern. The signal word *definition* is sometimes used to cue the reader that the author will define. Or the author may begin with a question, *What is* _____ *?* to signal an intent to define.

Define:
**cause–
effect
pattern**
_____
_____

11. **Cause–Effect Pattern.** The cause–effect pattern, which can be reversed as the effect–cause pattern, is used to explain the effects from certain ideas or events. For example, the causes of air pollution might be described followed by its effects on a select population, or the effects of defoliation in Vietnam might be

Define:
blunt
_____
_____

described followed by an explanation of the chemical cause. Authors may use *blunt* transitions or *signals* to make a cause–effect or effect–cause pattern clear, such as *"These are the causes of the problem. Now let's examine the effects."* You might not always have that much help from the author in identifying this pattern. Whenever you read a passage that describes a controversial subject or a problem, however, look to see if the author has thought and written about it in terms of what has caused it and what its effects are. Look for the signal words, *cause* and *effect*. Then make a mental or written list of the causes and effects.

Define:
**problem-
solution
pattern**
_____
_____

12. **Problem–Solution Pattern.** The problem–solution pattern may take more than one form. The problem or problems may be described and solution or solutions be proposed. Or, a problem or dilemma may be stated, all of the possible solutions examined, and a single best solution proposed with reasons to support it. In each case the author is inviting you to think about certain problems and solutions: how to vote, what to wear, how to heat your house, whether to make abortions legal, whether to send arms to another country, whether to change the quota for immigrants, whether or not hand-guns should be legal, whether to raise tuition. Blunt *transitions* or *signals* may be used, particularly to separate the problem section from the solution section: *"These are the problems President Lincoln faced. Let's look at how he solved them."* Or, if you are not given that much help, you will usually at least encounter the signal words *problem* and *solution* to help you identify this pattern. Because the problem–solution pattern is used to discuss subjects that may be controversial, this pattern is often associated with primarily persuasive purposes. When it is, the author's favorite solution, which is actually the main point of the text, may be saved until the end.

Define:
**motivated
sequence
pattern**
_____
_____

13. **Motivated Sequence Pattern.** The motivated sequence is a persuasive pattern used to get people to think of a solution to a problem and then to act on it. It is a favorite pattern of authors who write advertising copy. Material arranged according to this pattern usually is presented as follows:

1. *Attention.* The creation of interest and desire.
2. *Need.* The development of the problem, through an analysis of things wrong in the world and through a relating of those wrongs to individuals' interests, wants, or desires.

3. *Satisfaction.* The proposal of a plan of action that will alleviate the problem and satisfy the individual's interests, wants, or desires.
4. *Visualization.* The verbal depiction of the world as it will look if the plan is put into operation.
5. *Action.* The final call for personal commitments and deeds.[4]

In–Chapter Exercise 5

The following advertising letter follows the motivated sequence pattern of organization. The five parts have already been set off in chunks for you. Label them in the margin and underline the material in each chunk that satisfies the requirements of each step.

Dear Fellow Inhabitant of Earth:

1. _____

Imagine a world with an underground ocean and one with rivers of molten sulfur; imagine a planet where the winter temperatures would melt tin and lead.

Imagine a cloud-capped volcano almost three times as high as Everest against a clear red sky; imagine a frozen satellite covered with clouds of organic matter.

Imagine a place where the night sky is ablaze with a million moons; imagine a dark companion of a distant star on which creatures very different from us look up and wonder whether elsewhere there also are thinking beings.

2. _____

Every one of these places—except just possibly the last—is a real world. Space is filled with so many strange and exotic worlds that it would take countless lifetimes to satisfy my passion to know them.

I'm writing to you in the belief that you feel this passion, this characteristically human zest for high adventure and scientific knowledge; that you'd welcome opportunities to hear from scientists in the vanguard of planetary exploration, learn about astonishing discoveries as they happen, perhaps even influence the future course of discovery.

3. _____

I'd like to share with you my excitement over these possibilities and take you along—figuratively—on our voyages of discovery.

So my colleagues (scientists and nonscientists alike) and I have formed a nonprofit organization devoted to encouraging, supporting, participating in and perhaps even helping to underwrite the greatest adventure the human species may ever know—the exploration of the solar system, the search for planets around other stars, and the quest for extraterrestrial life.

This organization is called The Planetary Society, and this is your invitation to become a Member. . . .

[4] The motivated sequence pattern is explained in Douglas Ehninger, Bruce E. Gronbeck, Ray E. McKerrow, and Alan H. Monroe in *Principles and Types of Speech Communication,* 9th ed. (Glenview, Ill.: Scott, Foresman, 1982), p. 147.

4. _____ There is today a generation of men and women for whom, in their youth, the planets were unimaginably distant points of light, and the Moon was the paradigm of the unattainable. In middle life, these same people have seen their fellows walk on the Moon and make a preliminary reconnaissance of all the planets from Mercury to Saturn.

In old age, they will likely see humans wandering over the magnificent landscapes of Mars, their journey illuminated by the battered faces of the moons Phobos and Deimos.

Only *one* generation in the three-million-year history of humanity will live through such a transition. That generation is yours and mine; we are very lucky.

It may be up to you—and other like-minded people—to help ensure these efforts continue, because funding for planetary exploration has dwindled to less than one-tenth of one percent of the federal budget. . . .

5. _____ To accept this invitation, please return the enclosed acceptance form in the postage-paid envelope. Send no payment now unless you wish—we'll be happy to bill your $15 annual membership dues later. The temporary membership card enclosed will identify you as a member until you receive your permanent card.

Sincerely,

Carl Sagan
President[5]

Notice that the main point, the action step, is at the end of the letter, the most emphatic and persuasive location. Sometimes when you start to read a text that is organized this way and you recognize the pattern, you can go right to the end, to the action section, to see what the author wants of you. You can do this either to protect yourself from unsought persuasion or to save time.

Finding the Predominant Pattern and Subpattern

Open any of your textbooks and read a page or two, and you will find that there is usually a pattern of organization that predominates. Yet, within that pattern the author will have thought about the topic in more than one way so that subpatterns and various types of supporting material are also present. Here is an example drawn at random from an advertising textbook. Note that description is the predominant pattern of organization, as the title itself suggests. Note, also, that the authors forecast a topical organization for some of the future chapters, and then use both comparison and quotations from authorities to help define what is meant by advertising:

[5] Used with permission of The Planetary Society, Pasadena, California 91109.

Viewpoints on Advertising

Predom-
inant
pattern:
Definition

What is advertising? And what is it not? Although almost everyone uses the term freely, many people are not clear as to the size and scope of advertising. Advertising exists in numerous forms, each of which has as its primary purpose the persuasive presentation of the advertiser's story. Some people consider advertising a science, some an art—others define it as a profession or craft.

Topical
organization
promised
later

We shall examine briefly its role in communication, marketing, and our economic and social structure, all of which are considered in more detail in later chapters.

Compari-
son

Advertising Age editor Sidney R. Bernstein compares advertising to the salesman. It is, in essence, he says, "a substitute for the human salesman talking personally to an individual prospect or customer across a store counter or a desk or an open door. And as a substitute for the personal human salesman advertising has pretty much the same functions, abilities and attributes as the human salesman."*

Quota-
tions
from
authorities

Prominent politicians and business leaders have recognized the importance of advertising. According to Sir Winston Churchill, "Advertising nourishes the consuming power of men. It creates a better standard of living. It sets up before a man the goal of a better home, better clothing, better food for himself and his family." And President Franklin Delano Roosevelt said, "If I were starting my life over again I am inclined to think I would go into the advertising business in preference to almost any other."

Back to
predo-
minant
pattern:
Definition

Some people consider advertising an art and others consider it a science. It is not likely that these two groups will ever agree. In general, creative people (writers, artists, etc.) tend to regard it as an art and themselves as "artists" who use their creative ability to devise methods of communicating advertising ideas.[6]

How To Read When the Organization Is Not Clear

Unclear and confusing organization can be caused by careless writing or by careless reading. Whichever the cause, the result is the same: frustration because you cannot

[6] From *Advertising: Its Role in Modern Marketing,* 5th edition by S. Watson Dunn and Arnold M. Barban. (Hinsdale, Ill.: The Dryden Press, 1982), pp. 3–5. Copyright © 1982 by CBS College Publishing. Reprinted by permission of CBS College Publishing.

* S. R. Bernstein, "What is Advertising?" *Advertising Age,* April 30, 1980, p. 32.

easily locate the main ideas nor determine how they have been organized. In such a situation, try the following solutions:

1. Read the title to get a clue to the topic and how the author has thought about it.
2. Look for an introduction, a body, and a conclusion. Read the introduction to see if the author explains the topic and how it will be organized.
3. Start a list of main ideas. Each time the subject is changed, list the new idea.
4. Look for transitional words, phrases, and even sentences and paragraphs that make the main ideas stand out.

If the author makes no explanation of subject and organization and uses little transitional material, the task of sorting out the ideas and organizing them will be a bit more difficult. Try it anyway as you make your list of ideas. Label digressions and supporting material, but put only major ideas on your list. Then, finally, put the ideas you have isolated in an outline form that makes sense to you and that you can, consequently, learn and remember.

Chapter Summary

The most important reasons for analyzing an author's organization are to improve your understanding and memory of what you read. The advantages of learning a variety of conventional forms and patterns of organizations are to widen your expectations of the text and to help you follow and make predictions about the text. During the writing process, authors make random lists and organize these lists. They often use established forms and patterns to help the reader understand their ideas. The factors that may influence an author's organization of ideas include the audience, the purpose and occasion for writing, the subject, and convention. Six examples of conventional forms that authors might use to organize their material are literary forms; newspaper-article form; scientific paper form; letter forms; textbook form; and the introduction, body, and conclusion form. The body of a text may be arranged according to a predominant pattern of organization and/or a series of subpatterns that overlap and intermix. Thirteen examples of such patterns are topical, classification, chronological, process, spatial, general to specific (deductive), specific to general (inductive), comparison and contrast, master example, definition, cause–effect, problem–solution, and the motivated sequence. The reader should locate both the predominant pattern and the subpatterns. When this is difficult, read the title and introduction for clues to organization, list the main points, look for transitions, and impose your own order on the material.

Your Summary

Write your summary of this chapter in outline form using brief phrases only.

What is the subject of this chapter?

What did the author say about it?

_____

END-CHAPTER EXERCISES

I. Practice

A. Refer back to the following selections that you have already read and identify the predominant pattern of organization in each one. Justify your answer.

1. "American Violence: Worse Than Ever Before?" (pp. 52–54)
   Pattern: _____

   Why do you think so? _____

2. "Of Reading Books" (pp. 58–61)

   Pattern: _____

   Why do you think so? _____

3. "How We Listen" (pp. 94–97)

   Pattern: _____

   Why do you think so? _____

4. "Your First Job: What to Look For, What to Expect" (pp. 115–120)

Pattern: _____

Why do you think so? _____

5. "The Six Steps for Surveying a Chapter or Article" (p. 77)

Pattern: _____

Why do you think so? _____

B. Read the following excerpts from college textbooks, identify the predominant pattern in each, and justify your answer.

1. The Family

The family is a reference group that often exerts significant influence on consumer decisions. Hence, it is very important in the planning of advertising. The family can influence consumer behavior in two important ways: (1) through individual personality characteristics, attitudes, and beliefs, and (2) through assigned roles.

Personality is largely determined in the first several years of life when family contact is paramount. Hence, the purchase influences of personality in later life can be traced to family patterns. The fact that parents occupy most of a child's time and also provide a stabilizing force makes their beliefs and attitudes an important influence on those of the child. As children grow up and into new ways of life and new ideas, they tend to make certain shifts, but many studies support the idea that parent–child attitudes and beliefs are basically congruent.

Assigned roles is another area in which family influence on purchase decisions can be noted. Children may be allowed to make certain decisions, such as the brand of candy or breakfast cereal bought. In some households, the husband may be primarily responsible for certain buying decisions—for example, cars and life insurance—and the wife others, such as food, clothing, and appliances. And both husband and wife may share equally in yet other product choices.[7]

Pattern: _____

Why do you think so? _____

2. Microfilm

Overall, our society seems to be characterized by record keeping and preserving of printed records. For instance, colleges must store student transcript

---

[7] From *Advertising: Its Role in Modern Marketing,* 5th edition by S. Watson Dunn and Arnold M. Barban (Hinsdale, Ill.: The Dryden Press, 1982), p. 232. Copyright © 1982 by CBS College Publishing. Reprinted by permission of CBS Publishing.

information, businesses must store tax information, and so on. We are becoming engulfed in an ocean of paper. One means for combating this storage and handling problem is the use of *microfilm*.[8]

Pattern: _____

Why do you think so? _____

3. Assigning Time

The first task in learning to understand and use standard musical notation is to interpret rhythmic notation properly. Fundamentally, rhythmic notation deals with the assignment of time. Before we actually begin to consider traditional notation, let us perform some experiments in metrical time assignment.

Using your own pulse or a watch ticking for a beat, tap your finger lightly in time to it. Now begin counting 1, 2, 3, 4, 5, 6, 7, 8, 1, 2, 3, 4, 5, 6, 7, 8 with that beat. Continue to think 1 to 8, but say only the odd numbers 1, 3, 5, 7. Do that a few times. Next, think all the numbers but say only the even numbers 2, 4, 6, 8 a few times.

If you have established a beat that matches your pulse, it probably has a rather slow tempo, or speed. After you have practiced these exercises at a slow tempo, you should try them again at a faster tempo.

Experiment with the first letters of the alphabet. Count silently from 1 through 8, then as you come to 1 again, recite A—as you think 1, 2, 3, 4. Recite B—as you think 5, 6, 7, 8. In all of these experiments, you are dealing with assigned time.

In class, you can all participate in the performance of the following rhythmic composition utilizing body percussion sounds as your instructor directs you. In groups, perform your sounds when an X appears (Group I does a foot stomp, Group II a finger snap, and so on).[9]

Pattern: _____

Why do you think so? _____

4. Advantages of Active Listening

When we talked about active listening as a way of understanding others, we discussed two of its advantages. We saw then that it increases the chances that you're receiving a message accurately, and that it keeps you truly paying attention instead of carrying on an act. In addition to these benefits, listening reflectively also has advantages as a tool for helping others.

[8] From *Data Processing: The Fundamentals* by Wilson T. Price (New York: Holt, Rinehart and Winston, 1982), p. 57. Copyright © 1982 by CBS College Publishing. Reprinted by permission of CBS College Publishing.

[9] From *Music Fundamentals: A Performance Approach* by Phyllis A. Irwin (New York: Holt, Rinehart and Winston, 1982), p. 10. Copyright © 1982 by CBS College Publishing. Reprinted by permission of CBS College Publishing.

First, it takes the burden off you as a friend. Simply being there to understand what's on other peoples' minds often makes it possible for them to clarify their own problems. This means you don't have to know all the answers to help. Also, helping by active listening means you don't need to guess at reasons or solutions that might not be correct. Thus, both you and your friend are saved from going on a wild-goose chase after incorrect solutions.

A second advantage of active listening is that it's a great way to get through layers of hidden meanings. Often people express their ideas, problems, or feelings in strangely coded ways. Active listening can sometimes help cut through to the real message.

The third advantage of active listening is that it's usually the best way to encourage others to share more of themselves with you. Knowing that you're interested will encourage less feeling of threat, and leave them willing to let down some defenses. In this sense active listening is simply a good way to learn more about others and a good foundation on which to build a relationship.

Another benefit of active listening is the catharsis it provides for the person with a problem. Even when there's no apparent solution, simply having the chance to talk about what's wrong can be a tremendous relief. This sort of release often makes it easier to accept unchangeable situations rather than complaining about or resisting them.

Finally, at the very least active listening lets the other person know that you understand the problem. While this might seem true of other helping styles, understanding isn't always present. For instance, you've probably had well-intentioned helpers reassure you or offer advice in a way that left you certain they really didn't know what was upsetting you. Because it requires paraphrasing, active listening is the surest way to help you understand others' problems.[10]

Pattern: _____

Why do you think so? _____

5. Emergency Leader

In the spring of 1861, faced with the secession of a number of southern states and the imminent collapse of the Union, Abraham Lincoln ordered Fort Sumter to be provisioned and reinforced, knowing full well that his action would precipitate civil war. After Fort Sumter had been fired upon, Lincoln—on his own authority and without prior authorization from Congress—proclaimed a naval blockade of southern ports, summoned the South Carolina militia to active service, spent government money on war materiel, suspended the writ

---

[10] From *Understanding Human Communication* by Ronald Adler and George Rodman (New York: Holt, Rinehart and Winston, 1982), p. 184. Copyright © 1982 by CBS College Publishing. Reprinted by permission of CBS College Publishing.

of habeas corpus, and in general simply ignored constitutional restraints on his power.[11]

Pattern: _____

Why do you think so? _____

II. Application to Your Other Reading
A. Photocopy or reproduce a passage out of one of your own textbooks, identify the predominant pattern, justify your answer, and submit it.
B. Locate an article in your local or school newspaper that follows conventional news-article form as described on page 132. Clip and submit it.

III. Questions for Discussions and Class Activities
A. Name and describe three texts you have read this week that were organized according to conventional forms. What forms were used? How did identifying the form help you read?
B. Name and describe two texts you have read this week that were organized, wholly or in part, according to patterns of organization. What patterns were used? How did identifying the pattern help you read?
C. Make a list of the six conventional forms described in this chapter. Can you add at least two additional forms to the list?

1. _____

2. _____

3. _____

4. _____

5. _____

6. _____

7. _____

8. _____

[11] From *Governing: An Introduction to Political Science* 3rd edition by Austin Ranney (New York: Holt, Rinehart and Winston, 1982), pp. 339–340. Copyright © 1982 by CBS College Publishing. Reprinted by permission of CBS College Publishing.

D. To gain additional insight and understanding into organizational patterns, brainstorm the topic *stress* according to the patterns named
below. Write three or four items under each title listed below each
pattern and then number the items in the order you would follow if
you were going to write about them. The first one has been done
for you.

Ways To Think and Write about the General Topic: **Stress:**

1. *Chronological*

Title: *One Stressful Day*

   2. An impossible amount to do

   3. Worked hard all day

   1. Woke up feeling pressured

   4. Rewarded myself with a movie

2. *Description:*

Title: *How Stress Affects Me*

   _____

   _____

   _____

   _____

3. *Cause–effect:*

Title: *Stress: Causes and Effects*

   _____

   _____

   _____

   _____

  4. *General to Specific (Deductive):*

  Title: *Stress Can Be Harmful*

  _____

  _____

  _____

  _____

  5. *Specific to General (Inductive):*

  Title: *Stress Can Be Beneficial*

  _____

  _____

  _____

  _____

  6. *Classification:*

  Title: *Types of Stress*

  _____

  _____

  _____

  _____

  7. *Comparison and Contrast:*

  Title: *A Comparison of the Stress Levels of Modern Life and Turn-*

  of-the-Century Life

  Then   *Now*

  _____   _____

_____   _____

_____   _____

_____   _____

8. _Problem–Solution_

   Title: _Some Ways to Deal with a Stressful Day_

   _____

   _____

   _____

   _____

9. _Motivated Sequence_ (put in all five steps):

   Title: _Stress Pills Can Help!_

   1. Attention _____

   2. Need _____

   3. Satisfaction _____

   4. Visualization _____

   5. Action _____

IV. Vocabulary
   A. Specialized Terms

   1. conventional forms _____

   2. patterns of organization _____

   3. convention _____

   4. topoi _____

   5. predominant pattern of organization _____

   6. subpattern of organization _____

B. (General Vocabulary)

    1. assumption _____

    2. category _____

    3. structure _____

    4. sophisticated _____

    5. chronological _____

    6. literary _____

    7. hypothesis _____

    8. exhaustive _____

    9. conjunction _____

    10. blunt _____

C. Allusions

    1. Aristotle _____

    2. *Rhetoric* _____

D. Match the organizational pattern with its description. Locate the best description and write the number next to the pattern.

Patterns

    _____ 1. topical pattern

    _____ 2. classification pattern

    _____ 3. chronological pattern

    _____ 4. process pattern

    _____ 5. spatial pattern

    _____ 6. general to specific pattern

    _____ 7. deductive pattern

    _____ 8. specific to general pattern

_____ 9. inductive pattern

_____ 10. comparison and contrast pattern

_____ 11. master example pattern

_____ 12. definition pattern

_____ 13. cause–effect pattern

_____ 14. problem–solution pattern

_____ 15. motivated–sequence pattern

Descriptions

1. material arranged to show similarities and differences
2. a single example used throughout to illustrate all of the main ideas
3. material organized to define an idea or concept
4. material grouped in logical categories
5. material arranged to explain the effects of certain ideas or events
6. presents one or more problems and one or more solutions
7. main topic divided into subtopics, types, or parts
8. material arranged according to its location in an area or space
9. details arranged to lead up to a general statement
10. material arranged as it occurred in time
11. details arranged to lead up to a general statement
12. a general statement supported by details
13. a step-by-step sequence to describe how to accomplish a goal
14. a general statement supported by details
15. ideas arranged to motivate readers to find a solution and take action

CHAPTER 8
Reading Paragraphs and Sections of Material

In this chapter you will learn:

> How to study parts of the text to help you understand the organization of the whole.
> How to broaden your expectations of paragraphs to help you read them.
> How to read a paragraph.
> How to read a section of material.

In the last chapter you were told that in order to comprehend a text effectively you would need to look at the whole text and analyze the authors' organization. This task is not particularly difficult when authors use a sufficient amount of transitional material. Some texts, however, in spite of your best efforts, will seem particularly difficult to read either because the author has not helped you enough with transitional material or because you do not have sufficient background information on the subject. In these cases, the pattern of organization and even the ideas themselves may be difficult to perceive. You will get additional insight into the organization of the whole text as well as into the parts that make up the whole if you approach difficult texts paragraph-by-paragraph and then section-by-section. This approach can make texts seems less intimidating. You will also find that after having read the paragraph and section parts, you will then be able to reassemble the parts and understand the main ideas and organization of the whole message more easily.

Broadening Your Expectations of the Paragraph

There are conventions for paragraph construction that both you and the authors you read have either been taught or know from experience. For example, you and the authors you read know that paragraphs begin with an indented first line. A review of other information about paragraph construction will broaden your background and expectations about reading paragraphs.

Define:
unit

You have already learned some theory in Chapter 3 that will help you read paragraphs. The theory in that chapter applies not only to a chapter, book, or essay, but also to the paragraph unit. Here is a quick review of the theory in Chapter 3 that will help you read paragraphs:

1. You may expect to find main ideas, subideas, supporting material, and transitions in varying amounts and combinations in paragraphs.

Define:
function

2. You will find both general and specific material in paragraphs.
3. Each paragraph has a particular (function) in the overall text.

The Types and Functions of Paragraphs

Define:
unique

The following six types of paragraphs have (unique) characteristics and functions in the text. Learning to identify and understand them will help you understand the whole text.

Define:
**intro-
ductory
paragraph**

1. *The **introductory paragraph**.* Although the introductory paragraph typically is located at the beginning of a book or a chapter, an author may also include such paragraphs in the body of a text to introduce new sections of material. Some functions of the introductory paragraph are: to catch your interest, to introduce you to the subject and focus, to tell how the subject will be developed, to give necessary background information, and to define difficult terms. Introductory paragraphs may fulfill any or all of these functions.

In-Chapter Exercise 1

Here is an example of an introductory paragraph from an advertising text-book that includes at least three types of information one can expect to find in such paragraphs:

Attention-getting
material

Advertising people are fond of quoting a statement attributed to that successful nineteenth-century merchant, John Wanamaker, "I know half the money I spend on advertising is wasted; but I can never find out which half." Advertising agencies, advertisers, and media spend many millions of dollars each year in attempts to find out which advertising is wasted and which is successful. Specifically, they try to discover whether a particular advertisement or campaign accomplished what had been ex-

Background infor-
mation

pected of it. This feedback tells the advertising planner such things as how many persons received the message, how they interpreted it, which media were best, what sales resulted from the advertising, and the like. And as you will recall from Chapter 11, especially Figure 11.3, this feed-back serves as additional research input for successive phases of the plan.

Subject and focus

In this chapter, we will examine various methods of measuring the effectiveness of advertising and promotion.[1]

In your own words write brief answers to the following questions about the paragraph you just read.

[1] From *Advertising: Its Role in Modern Marketing,* 5th edition, by S. Watson Dunn and Arnold M. Barban. (Hinsdale, Ill: The Dryden Press, 1982) p. 273. Copyright © 1982 by CBS Publishing. Reprinted by permission of CBS College Publishing.

1. How does the author get your attention? _____

_____

2. What background information is included? _____

_____

3. What is the subject and focus of this chapter? _____

_____

Define:
**main idea
paragraph**
_____
_____

2. *The **main idea paragraph**.* The function of a main idea paragraph is to present a major idea on the author's original outline and then to tell more about it. There is usually one sentence, phrase, or part of a sentence in such a paragraph that introduces the main idea. It is called the *topic sentence*. When it is located at the *beginning* of the paragraph, as it is most of the time, it gives control and direction to the rest of the paragraph by promising the reader what it will be about. As a reader, you will hold the idea in the topic sentence in your mind while you read to see how the rest of the paragraph is related to it. The rest of the paragraph may be at the subidea level, the supporting material level, or both. One or several types of supporting material may be used to develop the idea.

Even though the topic sentence is at the beginning of the paragraph most of the time, it can also appear in the *middle* or, if the paragraph is organized inductively, at or near the *end*. Some paragraphs begin with a topic sentence, continue with a development of the main idea, and end with a summary that restates the main idea in the last sentence of the paragraph. More frequently, however, main idea paragraphs do not contain a final summary statement but are, instead, open-ended in order to lead into the next paragraph more effectively.

In-Chapter Exercises 2 through 5, which follow, illustrate some of these generalizations about main idea paragraphs.

In-Chapter Exercise 2

A main idea paragraph follows about an artist and his work, with the levels of generality indented to show relationships in the paragraph.

Main idea (most general)	It would be a mistake to think of Caravaggio's work as without tenderness.
Supporting material: specific example	In the *Madonna of Loretto* [105] he shows us not the remote grace of a Botticelli Virgin or the sweet, calm beauty of a Raphael Madonna but a simple Roman mother.

Supporting material:
description of the
example

As she stands gravely on the doorstep of her back-street house where the plaster is falling away from the walls, two humble pilgrims fall to their knees in confident prayer. They raise their loving faces to the Virgin and Christ Child while turning toward us their muddy, travel-stained feet.

Subideas

It is perhaps not surprising that some of Caravaggio's contemporaries, brought up on the elegant and well-nourished Madonnas and worshippers of the Renaissance and surrounded by the splendor of Counter-Reformation art, should have found pictures like these disrespectful and lacking in devotion. It should be equally unsurprising that once the initial shock wore off, the honesty and truth of Caravaggio's vision made a profound impact on both artists and the public.[2]

1. What is the main idea? _____

_____

2. What supporting material is used to illustrate the main idea? _____

_____

3. What is the subidea in this paragraph? _____

_____

In-Chapter Exercise 3

A main idea paragraph about computers follows, with the topic sentence at the beginning, a variety of types of supporting material, and a summary sentence at the end.

Topic sentence
(Hold this informa-
tion in your mind
as you read the
rest of the para-
graph.)

To say that the computer has had a broad and significant impact on our lives would be an understatement at the least.
                                                                    Microcomputers are currently available for $2000 or less which have computing powers in excess of large-scale machines costing a million or more dollars 25 years ago. If

---

[2] From *Culture and Values*, Vol. II, by Lawrence Cunningham and John Reich. (New York: Holt, Rinehart and Winston, 1982) p. 174. Copyright © 1982 by CBS College Publishing. Reprinted by permission of CBS College Publishing.

Supporting mate-
rial:
  example
  statistics
  comparisons
  series of exam-
  ples

progress in transportation had proceeded at the same pace as that in computing, a round-the-world airline flight would take 24 minutes and the average automobile would get 550 miles per gallon. Indeed, high-speed computational devices have been a primary factor in rapidly changing techniques used in many areas. For instance, with the computational and information manipulation capabilities of the computer, the office clerk sees many of the office procedures significantly change, the accountant must adjust to dramatically changing accounting techniques, the business manager must learn to use highly sophisticated market forecasting tools, the engineer must become reoriented to a whole new set of ground rules in problem solving, and most importantly, the average individual must adjust to the manner in which computers affect his or her life.

Summary
sentence

As a result, it seems important that every college student gain a basic knowledge about how this powerful tool affects our lives in so many ways and about how we can make it best serve our needs.[3]

1. What is the main idea of this paragraph? _____

   _____

2. List two bits of supporting material used to prove the main idea. _____

   _____

3. What is the summary idea expressed in the last sentence? _____

   _____

In-Chapter Exercise 4

A main idea paragraph about types of readers with the topic sentence at the end follows.

Supporting
material:
  comparison
  contrast
  specific
  examples

Of course, a given reader may be very tired or not at all, very young or very old, in a good mood or in a bad one; he may have a very good or a very deficient memory, a very great or very limited capacity for concentration, a considerable or moderate attention span; he may be a more or less experienced reader; he may be reading the text for the first, second, or tenth time; he may find the sentences and situations presented more or less familiar; he may want to read for fun or out of a sense of duty; he may show particular interest in the language, the plot, the characters, or the symbolism; he may hold one set of beliefs or another; and so on.

[3] From *Data Processing: The Fundamentals* by Wilson T. Price, (New York: Holt, Rinehart and Winston, 1982), p. vii. Copyright © 1982 by CBS College Publishing. Reprinted by permission of CBS College Publishing.

Topic sentence   In

other words, his physiological, psychological, and sociological condi-
tioning, his predispositions, feelings, and needs may vary greatly and so
may his reading; his knowledge, his interests, and his aims determine to
a certain extent the conventions, assumptions, and presuppositions he
takes to underlie the text, the kinds of connections he is particularly
interested in making, the questions he chooses to ask, and the answers
he brings to them.[4]

1. Write a restatement of the main idea of this paragraph in language you

   can easily understand. Make it brief. _____

   _____

In-Chapter Exercise 5

An open-ended main idea paragraph about divorce follows.

As with marriage, divorce in non-Western societies is a matter of great concern
to the families of the couple. Since marriage is primarily not a religious but
an economic matter, divorce arrangements can be made for a variety of reasons
and with varying degrees of difficulty.[5]

Define:
**open-
ended
paragraph**

_____

_____

   This final paragraph is classified as **open-ended** because it does not
introduce a topic, develop it in detail, or summarize it at the end. Rather it
introduces the topic of divorce and states that there are various reasons
and varying degrees of difficulty in divorce. There is the suggestion at the
end of this paragraph that more is to come.

1. What would you anticipate that the next paragraph in this chapter might

   be about? _____

   _____

Define:
**subidea
paragraph**

_____

_____

3. *The subidea paragraph.* The function of a subidea paragraph is to tell more
   about the main idea introduced in a preceding paragraph. On the author's original outline, material in subidea paragraphs would be indented under the main
   idea.

[4] Susan R. Suleiman and Inge Crosman, *The Reader in the Text*, Princeton, N.J.: Princeton University
Press, 1980, p. 229.

[5] From *Anthropology*, 3rd Edition by William Haviland, (New York: Holt, Rinehart and Winston,
1982), pp. 409–410. Copyright © 1982 by CBS College Publishing. Reprinted by permission of CBS
College Publishing.

In-Chapter Exercise 6

Now read the paragraph below, which follows the paragraph you just read (Exercise 5 above) in the anthropology text. It is a *subidea paragraph* because it develops the ideas in the preceding paragraph. It, however, does not have a topic sentence and main idea of its own.

Among the Gusii of Kenya, sterility or impotence were grounds for a divorce. Among the Chenchu of Hyderabad and the Caribou Indians of Canada, divorce was discouraged after children were born, and a couple was usually urged by their families to adjust their differences. A Zuni woman might divorce her husband by placing his belongings outside the door to indicate he was no longer welcome in the household. Divorce was fairly common among the Yahgan, who lived at the southernmost tip of South America, and was seen as justified if the husband was considered cruel or failed as a provider.[6]

1. What is this paragraph about? _____

_____

2. Did you correctly anticipate the subject matter of this paragraph? _____

_____

Define:
relative

_____

_____

   The exercises you have just completed demonstrate the importance of learning to understand the (relative) importance of the ideas in paragraphs and in the overall text. The chapter that contains the two paragraphs you just read has 65 paragraphs in it. If all of these were main idea paragraphs, you would be faced with the task of locating 65 ideas and learning them. Your task is easier than this. As you read, you will begin to notice that several paragraphs can be grouped together to form a section of material about a main idea. In your mind, you will (visualize) the relationships among such a group of paragraphs as follows:

Define:
visualize

_____

_____

Main idea paragraph 1.	States main idea that divorce practices differ from culture to culture
Subidea paragraph 2.	Gives a list of examples of how divorce is handled in various cultures
Subidea paragraph 3.	Gives additional examples of how divorce is managed in other cultures. Comparisons made to divorce in our culture.

[6] From *Anthropology*, 3rd Edition by William Haviland, (New York: Holt, Rinehart and Winston, 1982), p. 410. Copyright © 1982 by CBS College Publishing. Reprinted by permission of CBS College Publishing.

Subidea paragraph 4.	Gives a comparison of divorce rates in ours and other cultures and the implications. Some causes of divorce.

Subidea paragraph 5.	Gives more causes of divorce in ours and other cultures.

Subidea paragraph 6.	Gives additional causes of divorce and final observations about how common it is.

This section of material on "Divorce" is printed in full in the End-Chapter Exercise section of this chapter. You may read and analyze it there to see how paragraphs 2 through 6, as summarized above, support and develop the main idea in paragraph 1.

Define:
**transi-
tional
paragraph**

4. *The **transitional paragraph.*** The function of a transitional paragraph is to conclude the discussion of one main idea and then introduce the next one. These paragraphs usually do not have a topic sentence. Besides changing the subject, a transitional paragraph also emphasizes the subjects being discussed and sometimes states how they are related to each other. In-Chapter Exercise 7 provides an example.

In-Chapter Exercise 7

Summary of preceding paragraph	about the rococo style of art

Transitional paragraph	For all its importance, however, the rococo style was not the only one to influence 18th-century painters. The other principal artistic movement of the age was *neoclassicism*, which increased in popularity as the appeal of the rococo declined.[7]

Summary of next paragraph	about neoclassicism

1. This transitional paragraph changes the subject from the _____ style to

_____

Authors do not often use an entire paragraph to make a transition from one section of material to another. A more common way of changing the subject

[7] From *Culture and Values*, Vol. II, by Lawrence Cunningham and John Reich (New York: Holt, Rinehart and Winston, 1982), p. 231. Copyright © 1982 by CBS College Publishing. Reprinted by permission of CBS College Publishing.

is to start a paragraph with an opening transitional sentence or phrase that links the new paragraph to the preceding one. The second sentence in such a paragraph is usually the topic sentence. In-Chapter Exercise 8 provides an example.

In-Chapter Exercise 8

Transitional sentence that refers to earlier information

It was pointed out earlier that chromosomes usually come in pairs.

Topic sentence

At fertilization, one chromosome of a pair is contributed by the female, and one by the male.

Subideas developing idea in topic sentence

The two chromosomes constituting each pair are usually the same size and shape and therefore are referred to as **homologous** (Gk. "same proportion") chromosomes. One chromosome of a pair, then, is the **homologue** of the other. Two of the distinguishing events of meiosis are the pairing and separation of homologous chromosomes. [8]

1. What is the main idea that has been discussed in earlier paragraphs?

_____

2. What is the main idea of this paragraph? _____

_____

Define: **summary paragraph**

5. *The* **summary paragraph.** The function of the summary paragraph is to restate all of the main ideas that have been made previously. Summary paragraphs are usually found at the end of books or chapters. You may also find internal summaries, however, within the body of a chapter or essay. Read all summary paragraphs, whether they occur at the end or in the middle, as a final check on your understanding of the material you have just read. You may also turn to the end of a chapter before you begin and read the final summary paragraph first as an introduction to the ideas in the chapter.

Define: **concluding paragraph**

6. *The* **concluding paragraph.** The function of a concluding paragraph is to present an important key idea. This idea receives special emphasis and is thereby easy to remember because of its position at the end of the text.

[8] From *Biology: The Essential Principles* by Tom M. Graham (New York: Holt, Rinehart and Winston, 1982), p. 157. Copyright © 1982 by CBS College Publishing. Reprinted by permission by CBS College Publishing.

In-Chapter Exercise 9

Here is the last third of the concluding paragraph in *How to Read a Page* by I. A. Richards. Notice the special emphasis given the concluding idea both by its phrasing and its position in the text.

The greatest evil *is* injustice, things out of place and therefore against one another—in a mind, in a nation, and in the World State. Only in a state ruled by Reason can we be certain that freedom for Thought, in the only sense that matters, will not be withheld or destroyed. For Reason is what gives us that freedom, and that is why it must rule.[9]

1. What is the concluding idea in this book? _____

_____

Virtually all essays, chapters, articles, or books end either with a summary or a concluding paragraph. Read these paragraphs carefully to discover what the author considers particularly important.

How to Read a Paragraph

You will read paragraphs more effectively if you do the following:
1. Identify the kind of paragraph you are reading. It could be an introductory, main idea, subidea, transitional, summary, or concluding paragraph.
2. Locate and underline the topic sentence if there is one.
3. Notice and analyze the levels of generality in the paragraph. Pay particular attention to the subject of the paragraph (the main idea) and what the author says about it (the subideas and supporting material).
4. When you have finished reading the paragraph, summarize it in two or three words in the margin. This practice will help you concentrate on difficult material, and it will also help you when it is time to review.

How to Read a Section of Material

The following suggestions will help you read sections of material.
1. Identify sections either (1) by reading headings and subheadings that label the sections, or (2) by reading several paragraphs that explain one main idea and then by bracketing these sections or drawing lines across the page when the subject changes. Number the sections so that you will see how many you will need to read and understand.

[9] I. A. Richards, *How to Read a Page* (New York: W. W. Norton, 1942), p.242.

2. Notice that some texts begin with introductory sections of material instead of introductory paragraphs. Note that they may also end with a concluding section instead of a concluding paragraph.

3. Find the main idea of each section of material and underline it. A heading or a topic sentence may state it. Or, you may have to read part of the section to determine what most of it seems to be about, and then underline the main idea. Carry the main idea in your mind as you read to see how the rest of the section develops and supports it.

4. Analyze and visualize the levels of generality in a section of material as was done for you in the example on pages 160–161.

Define:
cluster

5. Write a brief summary at the end of each section or chunk of material to help you focus on the main idea. (Cluster) some supporting ideas around it. This practice will aid concentration, comprehension, and review.

Chapter Summary

When it is difficult to understand the ideas and their organization in a particular text, it helps to read first paragraph-by-paragraph and section-by-section. Later you can see how these parts contribute to the meaning of the whole. You can expect paragraphs to contain main ideas, subideas, supporting material, and transitions in varying amounts. You can also expect them to contain both general and specific material and to have a function in the overall text. There are six types of paragraphs, each of which functions in a specific way: They are introductory, main idea, sub-idea, transitional, summary, and concluding paragraphs. In reading a paragraph, notice its type and function, underline the topic sentence if there is one, notice and analyze the levels of generality, and jot a brief summary in the margin. In reading a section of material, first perceive it as a section, then find its main idea, analyze its levels of generality, and write a brief summary of it at the end.

Your Summary

Use the title, reading goals, headings, and subheadings in this chapter to help you write a summary in outline form.

What is the subject of this chapter?

What did the author say about it?

END-CHAPTER EXERCISES

I. Practice

A. Read the following paragraphs that are numbered one through nine, and complete the following activities:

1. Underline the topic sentence if there is one.
2. State the main idea of the paragraph.
3. List at least two supporting details.
4. Identify the type of paragraph (introductory, main idea, subidea, transitional, summary, or concluding).
5. Jot the main idea in the margin.

The first paragraph is done for you.

1. It's true. <u>Teachers learn more from a course than the students.</u> If you try to teach material to someone else, you are forced to grasp it in new ways, to express it in terms the other person can understand. This helps you remember. Tests at one university had a group of students study material using the SQ3R method. Another group also used the SQ3R method but was required to teach the material to other students. The student teachers did significantly better on tests than the control group. The catch in this technique is finding a "student" who is willing to learn biology or psychology or economics from you. But if you can talk someone into being your student, you may learn more than you ever have before.[10]

learn by teaching others

State the main idea: *You learn more when you teach.*

List any two supporting details: *Test proved*

Hard to find a student

Identify the type of paragraph: *Main idea*

[10] Patricia Westfall, "Teaching Others." Reprinted by permission from the 1978 issue of *Insider.*©1978, by Patricia Westfall.

2. If you're alert, what you learn from a midterm can help you through the rest of the term and the final. For instance, the midterm lets you know what kinds of questions—and answers—the instructor prefers. Armed with this information, you can more easily isolate what you should learn for the final. In addition, a midterm lets you doublecheck your own study habits and note-taking skills. If you missed important points or found your notes impossible to comprehend, you can fine-tune your study technique or note-taking for the rest of the course. Finally, the midterm can tell you a lot about your test-taking skills. Did you run out of time? Were you calm or frantic? Were you able to organize your thoughts? Analyze your strong and weak points and work to improve your test performance before the final.[11]

   1. Underline the topic sentence.

   2. State the main idea: _____

   3. List any two supporting details: _____

                             _____

   4. Identify the type of paragraph: _____

   5. Jot the main idea in the margin.

3. Are you a day person, ready to tackle studying as soon as you spring from bed? Or do you find the middle of the night the best time for intense learning? Keep a daily chart of your reaction to events for a week or so. Record when you wake up and how you feel (grumpy, full of pep?). During the day, write down the times when you feel tense and when you feel happy; when you are running at peak energy and when you start to slump. Soon you'll see a pattern developing. You can then plan your day around your ups and downs (known as biorhythms). For example, plan study times for when you are most alert and don't count on doing any heavy mental activity during your very low periods.[12]

   1. Underline the topic sentence.

   2. State the main idea: _____

   3. List any two supporting details: _____

                             _____

[11] Vicki Dennis, "Learn from Your Midterms." Reprinted by permission from the 1978 issue of *Insider*.© 1978, by Vicki Dennis.
[12] Vicki Dennis, "Determine Your Best Study Time." Reprinted by permission from the 1978 issue of *Insider*. © 1978, by Vicki Dennis.

    4. Identify the type of paragraph: _____

    5. Jot the main idea in the margin.

4.   Aztec social order was stratified into three main classes: nobles, commoners, and serfs. The nobles operated outside the lineage system on the basis
of land and serfs allotted them by the ruler from conquered peoples. The
commoners were divided into lineages, on which they were dependent for
land. Within each of these, individual status depended on the degree of
descent from the founder: those more closely related to the lineage founder
had higher status than those whose kinship was more distant. The third
class in Aztec society consisted of serfs bound to the land and porters
employed as carriers by merchants. Lowest of this class were the slaves.
Some had voluntarily sold themselves into boundage; others were captives
taken in war.[13]

    1. Underline the topic sentence.

    2. State the main idea: _____

    3. List any two supporting details: _____

                                         _____

    4. Identify the type of paragraph: _____

    5. Jot the main idea in the margin.

5.   Modern electronics has developed a wide range of easily hidden "bug-
ging" devices capable of eavesdropping on private telephone conversations in offices and homes. Police naturally find these devices very useful
in gathering information about the activities, associations, and plans of
suspected criminals, and the width of their electronic net was dramatized
by the revelation in the 1973 Watergate hearings that the private tele-
phones of many high officials in the Department of State had been tapped
on the orders of the President. Many citizens strongly object to the use of
these devices, arguing that they allow government to invade every area of
private life in the nightmare totalitarian fashion of George Orwell's *1984*.
Many law-enforcement officials argue with equal vehemence that depriv-
ing the police of this tool will benefit only criminals.[14]

---

[13] From *Anthropology,* 3rd edition, by William Haviland (New York: Holt, Rinehart and Winston, 1982), p. 381. Copyright © 1982 by CBS College Publishing. Reprinted by permission of CBS College Publishing.
[14] From *Governing: An Introduction to Political Science,* 3rd edition, by Austin Ranney (New York: Holt, Rinehart and Winston, 1982), p. 486. Copyright © 1982 by CBS College Publishing. Reprinted by permission of CBS College Publishing.

    1. Underline the topic sentence.

    2. State the main idea: _____

    3. List any two supporting details: _____

    4. Identify the type of paragraph: _____

    5. Jot the main idea in the margin.

6.   So far in this article the procedures for partitioning paragraphs have been pretty much intuitive; that is, I have not talked about formal markers of paragraph structure. I have generalized about the patterns my students and I find, and I have sketched out the basis for a taxonomy of expository paragraph patterns. Now I would like to describe the formal markers of paragraph tagmemes.[15]

    1. Underline the topic sentence.

    2. State the main idea: _____

    3. List any two supporting details: _____

                                        _____

    4. Identify the type of paragraph: _____

    5. Jot the main idea in the margin.

7.   This book will undertake a close examination of the management process. Before getting to that, however, it is important to understand the kinds of challenges management is going to be facing in the decades ahead. Conditions will continue to change, and the manager must be prepared to respond to these new developments. What will the future look like? This question is best answered by first examining the past, present, and future waves of change.[16]

    1. Underline the topic sentence.

    2. State the main idea: _____

    3. List any two supporting details: _____

                                         _____

[15] A.L. Becker, "A Tagmemic Approach to Paragraph Analysis," in Richard L. Graves, Ed., *Rhetoric and Composition* (Rochelle Park, N.J.: Hayden Book Company, 1976), p. 158.
[16] Richard M. Hodgetts, *Management: Theory, Process and Practice,* 3rd ed. (New York: Holt, Rinehart and Winston, 1982), p. 4.

4. Identify the type of paragraph: _____

5. Jot the main idea in the margin.

8. This chapter dealt with speech organization, a process that begins with the formulation of a thesis statement to express the central idea of a speech. The thesis is established in the introduction, developed in the body, and reviewed in the conclusion of a structured speech. The introduction will also gain the audience's attention, set the mood and tone of the speech, and demonstrate the importance of your topic to the audience.[17]

_____
_____
_____

1. Underline the topic sentence.

2. State the main idea: _____

3. List any two supporting details: _____

_____

4. Identify the type of paragraph: _____

5. Jot the main idea in the margin.

9. Genetic engineering is another example of technology that will affect business. Information on genetics is now doubling every two years, and major firms are currently using commercial applications of this "new biology." There is now talk of placing enzymes in automobiles; the enzymes would monitor exhausts and send data on pollution to microprocessors in the car, which would then adjust the engine. Other scientists are studying the possibility of using bacteria capable of converting sunlight into electro-chemical energy. Some scientists are also considering whether life forms can be bred to replace nuclear power plants.[18]

_____
_____
_____

1. Underline the topic sentence.

2. State the main idea: _____

3. List any two supporting details: _____

_____

4. Identify the type of paragraph: _____

5. Jot the main idea in the margin.

[17] From *Understanding Human Communication* by Ronald Adler and George Rodman (New York: Holt, Rinehart and Winston, 1982 p. 310. Copyright © 1982 by CBS College Publishing. Reprinted by permission of CBS College Publishing.
[18] Richard M. Hodgetts, *Management: Theory, Process and Practice,* 3rd ed. (New York: Holt, Rinehart and Winston, 1982), p. 7.

B. Read the following *section* of material. This is the complete text of the section on divorce that was sketched out and described for you on pages 160–161. Read and analyze this section to see how paragraphs 2 through 6 support and develop the main idea in paragraph 1. Jot a two-to three-word summary of each paragraph in the margin to help you concentrate. Then summarize the section and answer questions a through e at the end.

Divorce

1. As with marriage, divorce in non-Western societies is a matter of great concern to the families of the couple. Since marriage is primarily not a religious but an economic matter, divorce arrangements can be made for a variety of reasons and with varying degrees of difficulty.

2. Among the Gusii of Kenya, sterility or impotence were grounds for a divorce. Among the Chenchu of Hyderabad and the Caribou Indians of Canada, divorce was discouraged after children were born, and a couple was usually urged by their families to adjust their differences. A Zuni woman might divorce her husband by placing his belongings outside the door to indicate he was no longer welcome in the household. Divorce was fairly common among the Yahgan, who lived at the southernmost tip of South America, and was seen as justified if the husband was considered cruel or failed as a provider.

3. Divorce in these societies seems familiar and even sensible, considered in the light of our own entangled arrangements. In one way or another, the children are taken care of. An adult unmarried woman is almost unheard of in most non-Western societies; a divorced woman will soon remarry. In many societies, economic considerations are often the strongest motivation to marry. A man of New Guinea does not marry because of sexual needs, which he can readily satisfy out of wedlock, but because he needs a woman to make pots and cook his meals, to fabricate nets and weed his plantings. A man without a wife among the Australian aborigines is in an unsatisfactory position, since he has no one to supply him regularly with food or firewood. In all societies, the smallest economic unit is the family.

4. It is of interest to note that divorce rates in Western societies are low when compared to those in some societies, notably matrilineal societies such as that of the Zuni. Yet they are high enough to cause many North Americans to worry about the future of marriage and the family in the contemporary world. Undoubtedly, the causes of divorce in our society are many and varied. Among them are the trivial and transient characteristics that we have already discussed on which marriages may all too easily be based. Then, too, the stresses and strains inherent in the family organization typical of our society may result in the breakup of some marriages. We will discuss the nature of these at the end of this chapter.

5. Another contributing factor may relate to the demise of sex-role stereotypes. Although the sexual division of labor served humanity well in the

past, the demise of sex-role stereotypes is generally considered a good thing. In modern complex societies, they waste talents and abilities needed by society and greatly restrict a woman's chance for personal fulfillment. It is, of course, perfectly possible to do away with the stereotypes without at the same time doing away with the opportunity for individual men and women to cooperate in tasks that complement each other, so as to ensure relatively stable pair bonds. Unfortunately, in societies such as ours, which place high values on individual competitiveness, it is all too easy for couples to lose this, and with it one of the essential bases for family life.

6. As if these disruptive forces were not enough to contend with, a weakening of the taboo on all sexual activity out of wedlock further diminishes the need for a stable pair bond between individual men and women. With modern contraceptive devices, sexual activity need not lead to the birth of children, and even if it does, the child-rearing functions of the family are no longer as important as they once were. When all is said and done, we should perhaps not be dismayed that divorce is as common as it is in our society. The wonder of it is that divorce rates are not higher.[19]

    a. What is the main idea of this section? _____

_____

    b. How would you describe the focus? _____

_____

    c. List three subideas in this section:

_____

_____

_____

    d. List two bits of supporting material:

_____

_____

    e. What is the concluding idea? _____

_____

_____

[19] From *Anthropology*, 3rd edition, by William Haviland (New York: Holt, Rinehart and Winston, 1982), pp. 409-411. Copyright © 1982 by CBS College Publishing. Reprinted by permission of CBS College Publishing.

II. Application to Your Other Reading

A. Locate a paragraph in one of your textbooks, copy it, and mark and answer the same questions exactly as you did for the paragraphs in End-Chapter Exercise IA above. Remember to identify what *type of paragraph* it is.

B. Locate a section of material in one of your textbooks and summarize it paragraph-by-paragraph exactly as on pages 160-161. Write a final summary in phrases at the end. Finally, answer the same questions (a through e) about it as you did for the "Divorce" section in End-Chapter Exercise IB above.

III. Discussion and Class Activities

A. Describe how your expectations about reading paragraphs have changed since reading this chapter. What do you expect to find in paragraphs that you did not before?

B. Describe how your expectations about reading sections of material have changed since reading this chapter.

C. Read the final summary of the next chapter first, before you read the chapter itself. Then read the chapter, write your own outline summary, and compare it to the chapter summary. Does reading the summary first improve your comprehension and concentration? Try reading the summary first in some of your other textbooks.

D. Jot marginal paragraph summaries and section summaries for one week in your most difficult textbook. Describe how this practice affects your comprehension.

IV. Vocabulary Review
A. Specialized Terms

1. introductory paragraph _____

2. main idea paragraph _____

3. open-ended paragraph _____

4. subidea paragraph _____

5. transitional paragraph _____

6. summary paragraph _____

7. concluding paragraph _____

B. General Vocabulary

1. unit _____

2. function _____

3. unique _____

4. relative _____

5. visualize _____

6. cluster _____

CHAPTER 9
Reading Words and Sentences; Analyzing Style

In this chapter you will learn:

How to read the smallest parts of a text: the words and sentences.
How to analyze style.
How to identify the factors that influence style.

In the last chapter you learned to break a difficult text into paragraph and section units as an aid to understanding the whole. In this chapter you will learn to look at even smaller units in the text, the words and sentences. You will also learn to analyze how certain factors influence an author's style, and how insight into style can also help you understand difficult texts. Like the last chapter, this chapter will teach you to look at the parts of a difficult text so that you will later be able to reorganize them into a whole pattern of ideas that you can study, understand, and remember.

How Words Can Interfere with Comprehension

If you were to skim back through the preceding eight chapters, reviewing the text, the key reading strategies, and your summaries, you would find that you already have a great deal of information and skill to help you read most texts. There are times, however, when you bring your most powerful reading strategies to bear on a text, and you still find yourself staring at words rather than comprehending ideas. The problem is usually a simple one: You do not know the meanings of some of the words. Sometimes finding out the meaning of only one word will clear up an

Define:
obscure

otherwise obscure passage.

Look at the following group of words:

The iggle bombled and granded the blick.

You know from your past experience with syntax and punctuation that those words form a sentence in which *something* is doing *something* to *something* else. But you cannot get much farther than that in your comprehension because you do not understand the meaning of more than half of the words. The words in this sentence are, of course, not real words. Look now, however, at the following sentence from a biology textbook:

> After being removed and isolated from the bacterial cells, the plasmids are precisely cleaved by specific enzymes called restriction endonucleases.[1]

Unless you have studied biology and already know the meanings of all the words in that sentence, you will have difficulty understanding it until you get some definitions. Look at the sentence again to see which words interfere with your comprehension: *Something* having been removed from *something* has *something* done to it by *something*. Fill in specific meanings for those four words, and you will understand this sentence.

How To Read and Define Troublesome Words

There was information in Chapter 1 and the Preface to the Student on pages 4–5 and xi to heighten your awareness of unfamiliar words and to give you some strategies for dealing with them. The following list is an added attempt to heighten your awareness of difficult words. You will have to isolate these words and determine their meaning in order to read well.

Define:
syntax

1. *General vocabulary.* You have been defining general vocabulary throughout this book, so you know that it is not associated with a particular subject. There may not always be enough contextual information to help you define these words. Did you know, for instance, what syntax meant when you encountered it in the preceding section? You may have to consult the dictionary for the meaning of such words, write the meaning in the margin, and then re-read the passage again to make sense of it.

Define:
speaking vocabulary

2. *"Reading" vocabulary.* You possess both **speaking** and **reading vocabularies.** Your speaking vocabulary is composed of the words you know well enough to use when you speak or converse. It is smaller than your reading vocabulary, which is composed of many words you have seen in print many times but only half–know.

Define:
reading vocabulary

Here is an example: Suppose you have seen the word *incursion* several times in your reading. You have never looked it up, but you look at its parts and think about the clues they give to its meaning. *In,* you know, means in or into, and *cur* comes from the Latin word which means *to run.*[2] So the word should mean to run into or go into. That much meaning has been sufficient for most texts that you have read. But now you encounter this sentence:

> The principal made frequent *incursions* into the classroom and upset the teacher.

Suddenly you discover that the half–definition you have assigned this word in the past now seems to be inadequate. *Incursions* must mean more than going

---

[1] From *Biology: The Essential Principles* by Tom M. Graham (Philadelphia: Saunders College, 1982). p. 218. Copyright © 1982 by CBS College Publishing. Reprinted by permission of CBS College Publishing.

[2] See "The Vocabulary Builder" in the Appendix for the meanings of common word parts.

into a classroom because that in itself would not upset a teacher. So you consult a dictionary and learn that incursion means a hostile or sudden entrance into a place, or a raid. When you read the sentence again with that meaning in mind, the teacher's reaction makes sense. You jot the meaning of incursion in the margin to help you remember it. You may, in fact, by having paid this much attention to this word, feel confident enough now to transfer it from your reading vocabulary to your speaking vocabulary.

3. *Specialized vocabulary.* You have been defining specialized vocabulary throughout this book, so you know that it is the key vocabulary used to discuss a particular subject. You also know that the most troublesome specialized vocabulary can be the common words that are now used in a special and new way. The term *active reader,* for example, in Chapter 1 of this book has taken on meanings you may not have assigned to it in the past. If you were asked to define *active reader* on an exam testing knowledge of this book, you would be expected to give the meaning developed in Chapter 1 instead of your own definition. You will rely mainly on context to help you determine the meanings of many specialized vocabulary words.

Define:
technical vocabulary
_____
_____

4. *Technical vocabulary.* **Technical vocabulary** is specialized vocabulary associated with technical subjects such as mathematics, science, and engineering. Examples are **logarithmic statement** and **tangent function** from mathematics; **diploid** and **haploid** from biology; and **anion** and **oxyanion** from chemistry. You would not expect to see or use those words outside of the context of those subjects.

Define:
pervasive
_____
_____

Computer science has also developed its own technical vocabulary. Computers, however, are becoming such a pervasive force in our society that some of its technical terms are slipping into everyday speech to become general vocabulary words. You may hear people talking about giving *input* or *being programmed* or *interfacing* with someone else. Words formerly used only to describe computer communication, which are now being used to describe human communication, demonstrate the power of computers in our society. This is unusual, however. Most technical terms remain associated with their original subjects. You will have to look them up and learn their meanings to read technical subjects well.

5. *Allusions.* You have been identifying allusions throughout this book and know that they are references to people, places, events, and other literature and writings that the author assumes you know about. The essay "Of Reading Books" by John Livingston Lowes on pages 58–61 is full of allusions and, if you found it difficult, it was because of them. Allusions can be particularly troublesome when you read texts published in previous centuries. Authors of such texts often

Define:
contemporary
_____
_____

allude to their own contemporary events and people that we do not know about. Such texts either remain obscure for us, or we rely on information provided by scholars who have researched these allusions to make them clear to modern readers. Information about allusions of this type is often placed in

Define:
edition
_____
_____

footnotes in a modern edition of an old text. You should read such footnotes to understand the text. There are many such allusions with modern explanatory footnotes, for example, in Shakespeare's plays.

Define:
archaic
vocabulary

6. *Archaic vocabulary.* Words come and go in any language. You have just been given an example of new words entering the English language via computer science. Words also fall out of common usage and are labeled **arch.** for **archaic** in some modern dictionaries. You will encounter these words in material written in previous centuries, however, and you will have to find meanings for them to make complete sense of these texts. The modern word *tell,* for example, which means *to relate,* at one time meant *to count.* You may encounter a person in medieval literature who is telling, and you will be confused unless you discover the meaning of the word as it was used then. The best source we have for discovering what words meant when they were written is the *Oxford English Dictionary.* It is in more than 20 large volumes and is available in the Reference Room of most libraries. Use this dictionary when you want to know exactly what a word meant at a given time in history. All word definitions in this dictionary are labeled with dates. Thus, you can learn not only what a word meant at a particular time but also when it entered the language.

7. *Poetic diction.* Certain words, forms of words, and special spellings are found almost exclusively in poetry, and they can make comprehension difficult unless you pay them special attention. These words are used by poets mainly because of convention. It is conventional for scientists to write in scientific language. Poets, especially those who wrote before the twentieth century, write in poetic language. Here is an example of poetic diction from the poem *Paradise Lost.* Milton, the author, is describing Adam's and Eve's hair:

> His . . . hyacinthine locks
>
> Round from his parted forelock manly hung
>
> Clustering, but not beneath his shoulders broad:
>
> She, as a veil down to a slender waist,
>
> Her unadornèd golden tresses wore
>
> Dishevelled, but in wanton ringlets waved
>
> As the vine curls her tendrils.
>
> (Book IV, lines 301–308)

You can see that this description is more poetic than saying Adam had curly hair parted in the middle that came to his shoulders and Eve had long, blond hair that was curly and messy. Take another look at the poetic version. You will need to use a dictionary, your imagination, and your powers of association and visualization to read some of the words in this passage well. For example, by describing Adam's hair as "hyacinthine," Milton invites you to visualize the hyacinth and compare its tightly curled flowers with Adam's hair. Notice also that Eve's "tresses" fall in "ringlets," and curl like "tendrils," all poetic words not ordinarily used to describe hair in day-to-day conversation. You will need to visualize a vine with tendrils to understand this passage as you were meant to.

How To Use Context To Define Words

There were no context clues in the sentence about the iggle and the blick, quoted earlier. Read this next sentence, however, that also contains a nonsense word:

> The grugdub swam to the top of the aquarium and nibbled at the special grugdub food.

There are a number of clues in the context of that sentence to help you guess the meaning of the word grugdub. You know it swims, lives in an aquarium, and eats special food. Now read the following sentence.

> The *lebistes reticulatus* swam to the top of the aquarium and nibbled at the special *lebistes reticulatus* food.

This sentence may not be much easier for you to comprehend than the one about the grugdub. You have the same context clues in both sentences, however, and, if you guessed that these sentences were about a fish, you made a good guess. For complete comprehension, however, you would have to know that *lebistes reticulatus* is the scientific, Latin name for guppy.

In–Chapter Exercise 1

You may have contextual information as you did in the guppy sentence to help you guess the meaning of a word, or the author may go even further and spell out the meaning when a word or term is first introduced. Here are six examples from textbooks. Practice using contextual information to help you define the words being discussed.

1. From a Government Textbook

> One such device is the "run–off election": if no candidate receives an absolute majority in the first election, a second election is held between the two top candidates. and the one who wins a majority in the second election is declared the winner.[3]

Using context only, briefly define "run–off election": _____

_____

2. From a Speech Text

> One advantage of giving speeches to the same audience over and over is that you do not need to reassess it constantly. The audience in your class

---

[3] From *Governing: An Introduction to Political Science,* 3rd edition, by Austin Ranney (New York: Holt, Rinehart and Winston, 1982), p. 138. Copyright © 1982 by CBS College Publishing. Reprinted by permission of CBS College Publishing.

remains essentially the same through the term. A good class project may be to do a thorough demographic analysis of the class. Age, sexual balance, ethnic backgrounds, reasons for being in school, and vocational interests could be some of the factors to consider.[4]

What is the term defined in this passage? _____

Using context only, briefly define this term: _____

_____

3. From a Criminology Textbook.

The earliest example of the practice of ''psychiatry'' was during the Stone Ages, when cave men would use a crude stone to cut a hole in the skull of a person thought to be possessed of devils. The process, called trephining, was thought to permit the evil spirit to escape; there is evidence that some people survived the surgery and that in some cases the operation had beneficial results. But the usual treatment for evil spirits was exorcism.[5]

What is the term defined in this passage? _____

Using context only, briefly define this term: _____

_____

4. From a Political Science Textbook

On relatively rare occasions debate is a crucial step in the legislative process. The Senate allows unlimited debate, so in principle a few Senators can talk forever on a subject and thus kill a bill by preventing a vote. This is the so-called filibuster, which can be stopped only by invoking cloture, a vote by sixty Senators to end debate. Prior to 1975 cloture required two thirds of all Senators present and voting. Because two thirds was a difficult majority to achieve, and because many Senators supported the principle of unlimited debate, a cloture vote was difficult and occurred only rarely. Between 1917 and 1975, of 123 cloture votes taken only 34 succeeded (filibusters against civil rights bills were especially difficult to stop). Whether the new rule of sixty senators as opposed to two thirds of those present will make it easier to end debate remains to be seen.[6]

[4] Edwin Cohen, *Speaking the Speech* (New York: Holt, Rinehart and Winston, 1980), p. 36.

[5] Sue T. Reid, *Crime and Criminology*, 2nd ed. (New York: Holt, Rinehart and Winston, 1979), p. 162.

[6] From *Understanding American Government* by Robert Weissberg (New York: Holt, Rinehart and Winston, 1980), p. 302. Copyright © 1982 by Holt, Rinehart and Winston. Reprinted by permission of Holt, Rinehart and Winston, CBS College Publishing.

What is the term defined in this passage? _____

Using context only, briefly define this term: _____

_____

5. From an Algebra Book

Algebra is a mathematical system and, as such, similar to plane geometry; it has a logical structure. First, undefined terms are stated. For algebra, these consist of a set of numbers, relations, and operations. Definitions are then formed and assumptions, also called axioms, or postulates, are made about the undefined terms and definitions. A deductive reasoning process is used to obtain more statements about the subject matter. These statements, called theorems, are said to be proved statements. Most of the subject matter of a mathematical system consists of theorems.[7]

What is the term defined in this passage? _____

Using context only, briefly define this term: _____

_____

6. From a Biology Textbook

Water is cohesive and adhesive. Cohesion is the holding together of like substances; adhesion is the holding of one substance to a different one. You can fill a glass with water to above the level of the rim of the glass; a water strider can run across the surface of a pond. Both these facts are a result of the surface tension of water, which means that a water surface appears to be covered by a "skin." Surface tension results from the cohesion of water molecules to one another by their hydrogen bonds. Water is more cohesive than any other liquid except mercury. That it is both adhesive and cohesive accounts for its capillarity, the ability of water to move up a piece of porous paper or to creep through the fine pores in the soil or in a leaf. Because it is highly polar, water also adheres strongly to any surface that bears an electrical charge.[8]

What are the terms defined in this passage? _____

Using context only, briefly define these terms: _____

_____

_____

---

[7] Vivian Shaw Groza, *College Algebra* (Philadelphia: Saunders College, 1980), p. 1.

[8] From *Biology* by Karen Arms and Pamela S. Camp (New York: Holt, Rinehart and Winston, 1979), p. 21. Copyright © 1979 by Holt, Rinehart and Winston. Reprinted by permission of Holt, Rinehart and Winston, CBS College Publishing.

How To Read Difficult Sentences

The structure of some sentences can cause you to stare at words instead of comprehending ideas. Most authors write both long and short and simple and complex sentences. These add variety to their writing and enable them to express themselves adequately. Long and complex sentences can slow you down and interfere with comprehension, however, unless you know what to expect and how to read them.

It is some comfort to realize that basic English sentence structure has not changed since the earliest written records of the language. Texts published before this century may cause you difficulty because they contain longer sentences than you are used to. They will not be difficult because of unusual structures or word order, however. Additional difficulty with such texts may be caused by spelling and punctuation. Dictionaries (standardize) spelling and punctuation, and the first dictionary was not published until the beginning of the seventeenth century. Before that time, spelling was extremely (erratic,) differing from one text to another. Punctuation was not standardized until the nineteenth century, so material you read that was published before that time may break many of the rules you have learned in your English classes.

The basic convention that has governed word order in English sentences since the earliest times has been the subject–verb–object (s–v–o) or subject–linking–verb–predicate adjective (s–v–pa) or subject–verb–predicate noun (s–v–pn) order. Examples are: The boy hit the ball; the boy is hot; the boy is John. A sentence structured differently from this basic pattern, object–subject–verb (the ball the boy hit), for example, can be understood, but it is unusual.

Besides being able to expect a s–v–o order in most sentences you read, you can also usually expect that the subject and the verb will usually be next to each other or at least close together without much more than a clause or phrase separating them.

Define: standardize

——————

Define: erratic

——————

In–Chapter Exercise 2

Here are five sentences chosen at random from five different textbooks. Some of them are compound sentences (two sentences joined with an "and" or "but"). Or the object may be stated as a clause beginning with the word "that." Basically, however, they all follow the conventional s–v–o order of English sentences.

1. From a psychology textbook: "To put the matter another way, you are capable of exercising voluntary self–control, but machines aren't."[9]

---

[9] From *Understanding Human Behavior*, 3rd edition, by James V. McConnell (New York: Holt, Rinehart and Winston, 1980), p. 137. Copyright © 1974, 1977, 1980 by Holt, Rinehart and Winston. Reprinted by permission of Holt, Rinehart and Winston, CBS College Publishing.

2. From a physics textbook: "In 1650, Gassendi, an Italian physicist, revised the atomic theory, and Isaac Newton became a convert to the idea."[10]

Mark the subject, verb, and object in the next three sentences yourself:

3. From an algebra textbook: "A reason in a mathematical proof must be a definition, an axiom, or a previously proved theorem."[11]

4. From a chemistry text: "Experimental evidence shows that the reverse reaction does occur to a slight extent."[12]

5. From a political science textbook: "In analyzing and comparing political parties in modern democratic nations, political scientists often speak of "party systems."[13]

Define:
base clause

Whenever you have difficulty comprehending a sentence, make the task easier by locating the subject–verb–object core. This core is also called the **base clause.** It contains the main main idea of the sentence and is comparable to the topic sentence in a paragraph. The rest of the sentence, composed of phrases, clauses, and qualifying words, tells more about the elements in the base clause. These elements are comparable to subideas and supporting material in a paragraph. Once you locate the base clause, and analyze how the other parts of the sentence relate to it, you can then reread the sentence ard make better sense of it.

Locating the base clause can help you read sentences. So can an understanding of how sentences are built. Here is a s–v–o base clause:

The student played the harp.

Now, we add some more information:

He played like an angel.

The harp was large and golden.

---

[10] From *Physics in Your World,* 2nd edition, by Karl F. Kuhn and Jerry S. Faughn (Philadelphia: Saunders College, 1980), p. 121. Copyright © 1980 by Saunders College/Holt, Rinehart and Winston. Reprinted by permission of Holt, Rinehart and Winston, CBS College Publishing.

[11] Vivian Shaw Groza, *College Algebra* (Philadelphia: Saunders College, 1980), p. 12.

[12] Stanley M. Cherim and Leo E. Kallan, *Chemistry: An Introduction* (Philadelphia: Saunders College, 1980), p. 283.

[13] From *Governing: An Introduction to Political Science,* 3rd edition, by Austin Ranney (New York: Holt, Rinehart and Winston, 1982), p. 202. Copyright © 1982 by CBS College Publishing. Reprinted by permission of CBS College Publishing.

He played in the concert.

The concert was attended by more than 400 people.

The concert was last Sunday.

Most authors, unless they are writing primary reading texts, would avoid writing a string of sentences like those just listed. Instead they would combine the information into one sentence:

The student played the large, golden harp like an angel in a concert attended by more than 400 people last Sunday.

Note that the sentence is more complicated now, but it is still easy to read. Reread it and locate the subject, verb, and the object. You will find the usual s–v–o order. The other parts of the sentence tell more about the subject, the verb, and the object.

In–Chapter Exercise 3

Try combining the following lists of sentences into single sentences. There will be more than one correct way to write these. Compare your efforts with your classmates'. This activity will give you insight into the way authors compose complex sentences.

The book sat.

The book was ancient.

The book sat on the library shelf.

No one read it for years.

The book was lonely.

_____

_____

_____

The rock star stood on the stage.

He wore tight jeans and an open shirt.

His guitar was hung around his neck.

He sang his first note.

The crowd cheered.

_____

_____

_____

Go back now and label the subject and the verb in the two sentences you wrote.

Sometimes when authors are combining parts to form sentences, the parts end up in the wrong places and the sentences do not work. Here are some sentences written by actual accident victims in their accident reports to describe what happened at the scene. They were collected by an insurance company.

1. The indirect cause of this accident was a little guy in a small car with a big mouth.

2. I pulled away from the side of the road, glanced at my mother–in–law and headed over the embankment.

3. The pedestrian had no idea which direction to go, so I ran over him.

4. I saw the slow–moving, sad–faced old gentleman as he bounced off the hood of my car.[14]

Define:
Intact

You will probably agree that none of these sentences states exactly what their authors intended. Note, however, that the s–v–o word order is (intact) in all of them. Prove that to yourself by going back and labeling those parts in each sentence. The confusion in these sentences is caused by a faulty cause–effect relationship in the sentence. The glance at the mother–in–law in sentence 2, for instance, did not cause the driver to head over the embankment as the sentence implies.

Let us take sentence 1 apart and reduce it to a base clause and information about it in order to understand better what the author is trying to say:

$$\overset{s}{\text{The cause}} \text{ of this accident } \overset{v}{\underline{\text{was}}} \overset{pn}{\underline{\text{a little guy}}}.$$

The cause was indirect.

The little guy was in a small car.

The little guy had a big mouth.

Now let us recombine these parts into a more successful sentence:

The indirect cause of this accident was a little guy with a big mouth who was in a small car.

Here is a rewrite of sentence 2:

I pulled away from the side of the road, lost control of the car, and headed over the embankment. My mother–in–law was a passenger.

---

[14] These sentences come from actual insurance accident forms. They have been printed in newspapers including the *Toronto Sun,* July 27, 1977, and the *El Paso Times,* January 25, 1982.

In–Chapter Exercise 4

Try rewriting sentences 3 and 4 yourself so that they more nearly state what their authors must have intended:

3. _____

_____

_____

4. _____

_____

_____

These sentences have demonstrated the confusion that can occur in a sentence when its parts are either misplaced or the connections between the parts are not adequately stated. You can assume in reading most sentences, however, that the parts are well–placed and that once you discover the base clause, you can then determine how the other parts tell more about it.

The _periodic sentence_ is a special type of sentence that can present reading difficulties because of its unusual structure. They are common in literature written before this century when people studied Latin in school and followed Latin style in writing English sentences. Periodic sentences are not limited to early literature, however; they are also found in modern texts. Periodic Latin sentences are characteristically long with the verb at the end. English periodic sentences are also long and complex, they move in chunks, there are pauses at the ends of the chunks, and the base clause is at the end. You usually have to read such sentences slowly to understand them well. Here is a good example of a periodic sentence from a seventeenth-century source, Milton's _Paradise Lost_:

High on a throne of royal state, which far

Outshone the wealth of Ormus and of Ind,

Or where the gorgeous East with richest hand

Showers on her kings barbaric pearl and gold,

Satan exalted sat. (Book II, lines 1-5)

Mark the subject and verb, and note where they are located. To help you comprehend this sentence, here it is rewritten in a string of simple sentences, easy to understand:

Satan sat high on a throne.

Define:
exalted

Satan was (exalted.)

_____

_____

The throne was of royal state.

It outshone the wealth of Ormus and of Ind (allusions to islands in the Persian Gulf).

It outshone the gorgeous East where barbaric pearls and gold are showered on the kings.

Now, reread the sentence in its original form, and it should be easier to understand.

In–Chapter Exercise 5

Here is another periodic sentence from a modern text. It was written by a dean at the City College of New York during a time that was particularly discouraging professionally for the faculty of that institution:

What really gnawed away at our innards and left us hollow, what began to create a sad yet anxious look in our eyes and a dreadful listlessness in the way we moved through classes or sat at committee meetings, what dulled our lunch-room conversations and made us depend more on each other than on the students—who had always been the great reward for teaching at the City College—what coursed in our bodies like an incurable illness was our growing realization and fear that in middle age we no longer had a profession.[15]

Note how this sentence moves in chunks of descriptive material that lead up to the base clause at the end. Now that you have located the base clause of this sentence, state its main idea:

_____

_____

ANALYZING LEVELS OF STYLE

Having read the above information about words and sentences, you may be thinking now that authors could make it easier for readers if they wrote only with commonly used words and in simple, short sentences. There are at least three reasons why authors do not do this: (1) The manner in which an author writes reflects that author's thought. If the author thinks complexly, you can expect the text also to be complex. (2) It would be boring to readers if all texts were written at a simple level. (3) Uniform use of simple words and sentences would not satisfy the conventions of style. We expect, from habit, that certain types of material will be written in certain styles that are different from each other.

Define:
style

The word **style** needs to be defined as it is used here. When an author repeats

_____

[15] Theodore L. Gross, "How to Kill a College, the Private Papers of a Campus Dean," *Saturday Review*, February 4, 1978, p. 19.

Define:
idiosyn-
cratic

_____
_____

Define:
**personal
style**

_____
_____

Define:
**conven-
tional
style**

_____
_____

certain traits in a particular piece of writing, such as a special manner of expression, a particular level of word choice, certain types of supporting material, predictable types of sentence construction, and even varieties of punctuation, over and over again, the text can be said to have style. If the repeated traits are idiosyncratic to the author, the text is said to have a **personal style** typical of that particular author. You can read some texts, for example, and guess that Hemingway or Shakespeare wrote them because no one else thinks exactly like these authors or selects words or writes sentences exactly like they do over and over again. With reading experience, you can read some texts and usually guess quite accurately who wrote them if the author has a strong personal style and if you are familiar with it. One of the usual responsibilities of your English teachers in your literature classes is to help you learn to identify authors' personal styles.

If the repeated traits that we call style are idiosyncratic to a class or type of writing, such as the popular magazine article, the scholarly article, or the personal letter, the text is said to have **conventional style.** We associate, through habit, certain levels of word choice, types of sentence construction, types of supporting material, even types of punctuation with different types of writing. It will broaden your expectations of a text and help you read with better comprehension, concentration, and enjoyment if you are able to recognize the features of some conventional styles and then learn to associate them with certain types of writing.

In–Chapter Exercise 6

Here is a list of some types of writing that you can expect to have predictable styles dictated by habit and convention. Note that an attempt has been made to describe the style of the first five items on the list. See if you can describe the style you would associate with the other items on the list:

Type of Writing	Usual Style
1. Personal letter	short sentences, informal language, uncomplicated
2. Business memo	business language, sentences may be long and complex
3. Textbooks	specialized vocabulary, factual, complex
4. Popular magazine article	informal language, vivid supporting material, short sentences
5. Scholarly research article	specialized vocabulary, long, complex sentences
6. Advertisement in popular magazine	

7. Poem   _____

8. Newspaper editorial   _____

9. Children's book   _____

10. Philosophical essay   _____

The actual words that you selected to describe the usual style of these 10 examples of types of writing are not important. There are no correct descriptions. The purpose of this brief exercise, instead, was to point out to you that you already associate certain characteristics—what we call style—with certain types of writing.

An author's style is not only influenced by personal writing habits, the complexity of the ideas, and by habit and convention. It is also influenced by the degree of seriousness and complexity of the *subject;* the nature, education, and expectations of the *audience;* the author's *purpose* for writing; and the relative formality or informality of the *occasion.*

The following two passages demonstrate two distinctly different writing styles that might be described as basically *informal* and *formal.* These passages also demonstrate how the subject, audience, purposes, and occasion have influenced these authors' styles.

An Informal Letter

Dear Cheeselover,

Thank you so much for your order! I KNOW you can't wait to LEAP upon your delicious new cheeses and gobble them all up. *But would you please do me a favor first?* Set my mind at ease by following the few simple do's and don'ts below.

REMEMBER, your fine cheeses are a *living* food. And they have made a long journey to reach your home. So do let them rest a bit to regain their poise and composure. The few moments of care you give them now will repay you immeasurably in eating enjoyment later on.

**YOUR CHEESES ARE (PROBABLY) SOFT & PLIANT TO THE TOUCH*

This is understandable and natural, considering their journey. Simply place them in your refrigerator for an hour or two and they will be fine. If, however, it seems that an overexuberant parcel delivery boy has been "playing football" with your package, and that one or two cheeses have lost their shape, don't be afraid to mold them back into their original form with your hands before placing them in the refrigerator. Only their "vanity" has been hurt; their taste and texture will be as superb as ever. . . .

**ARE SOME OF YOUR CHEESES . . . "LEAKING"?*

This simply means (oh, stop worrying) that the air–tight wrapping or rind of your cheese has opened in transit and some of the natural oils have escaped. (Who can blame them? How would *you* like to be cooped up in a cheese all your life?) Yes, it may be messy. But no, it is not a problem—except perhaps an "aesthetic" one.[16]

---

[16] Gerard Paul, Cheeselovers International. Reprinted with permission.

A Formal Letter

Dear Degree Holder:

It is again time to report to you on the condition of graduate education at the University. The past year has seen continued progress toward the attainment of excellence in many of the programs in the Graduate School, continued use of funds for fellowships and for lectures and conferences to enhance the quality of intellectual life on campus, and continued struggle with the difficulties of inadequate and fragmented budgets.

In the past year, our ability to offer a limited number of large fellowships was extended, successful conferences and symposia were sponsored, several of our programs were reviewed, most of them quite favorably, and new housing was opened for graduate students. At the same time, the University's ability to provide adequate secretarial staffs, services, office budgets, student assistance, library collections and money for lectures, conferences, and travel remained inadequate, while facilities and equipment in some areas are seriously lacking. Further, we were compelled by the State Department of Higher Education to reduce our enrollments and this reduced our ability to maintain our extensive program of part–time and continuing education.

I am optimistic about the future of graduate education at the University. Our programs have gained national recognition. Our research activity has grown and our success at attracting external funding for research has grown even faster. The campus now faces the prospect of academic reorganization, which creates an opportunity to improve the way in which we conduct academic programs and therefore the effectiveness of those programs. The University administration continues to emphasize research and graduate education as the defining characteristics of the University and to search for means to help. These have included new money for recruitment of graduate students and a proposal to create additional tuition scholarships for graduate study.

Clearly, we need your help. In a time of great inflation and tight State budgets, we cannot realize the potential for each of our programs without additional money. . . .[17]

In order to gain insight into the reasons for the differences in style in these two letters, let's look first at what influenced these authors to write as they did:

Factors That Influence Style

	Informal letter	Formal Letter
Subject:	cheese	education
Audience:	anyone who likes cheese	a university graduate
Purpose:	tell how to care for cheese	persuade to give money
Occasion:	reader has just received cheese in mail	fund raising for university

[17] Kenneth G. Wolfson, Dean, Graduate School, Rutgers University. Reprinted with permission.

Now place yourself in the position of the authors of these two letters and look again at these two lists of influencing factors. Would you write differently in these two situations? Here is a list of some of the specific stylistic differences in the two letters that are caused by the differences in subject, audience, purpose, and occasion.

	Stylistic Differences in Two Letters	
	Cheeselover's Letter	Degree Holder's Letter
Word choice:	Slang: "gobble up; do's and don'ts". Conversational: "Oh, stop worrying; Yes; But, no"	Formal language: "continued progress, attainment of excellence"
Supporting material:	Informal images: delivery boy "playing football"; you cooped up in a cheese all your life. **Personification** of cheese: their "vanity"; let them regain their poise and composure.	Series of brief and general examples to show strengths and weaknesses of University. No anecdotes, visual imagery, or specific detailed examples.
Sentence structure:	Sentences short and almost all simple: There are 19 sentences in a passage of 262 words. Fifteen sentences are simple, two are compound, one is complex, and one is compound–complex. Average sentence length is 14 words.	Sentences long and either complex or contain series of items set off with commas. There are 13 sentences in a passage of 317 words. Only five of these are simple sentences. Average sentence length is 24 words.
Punctuation:	Informal punctuation including exclamation point, capital letters to emphasize words, parenthetical expressions in the middle of sentences, and words in quotes.	Formal punctuation, mainly commas and periods. No exclamation points, quotes, or words "shouted" in capital letters.
Effect on reader:	Humorous, fun, quick and easy reading; reader will care for cheese without worrying.	Reader takes problems seriously, considers them, and perhaps resolves to donate money.

Define:
personification

Here is a final example of Mark Twain having fun with conventional style. This sentence comes from *The Innocents Abroad,* an account of a group of nineteenth-century Americans traveling in Europe. The allusions in the passage tell you which country they are traveling in.

What is the
Parthenon?

Just as the earliest tinges of the dawn flushed the eastern sky and turned the pillared Parthenon to a broken harp hung in the pearly horizon, we closed our thirteenth mile of weary, round-about marching, and emerged upon the seashore abreast the ships, with our usual escort of fifteen hundred Pirean dogs howling at our heels.[18]

What is
Pirean?

Note that there are two types of style in this one sentence. The first part of the sentence is written in an exaggerated poetic style (tinges of dawn, turned the pillared Parthenon to a broken harp, pearly horizon). It suggests the ideal, the dream that tourists anticipate about their travel experiences in foreign countries. The second part of the sentence plunges the reader from the poetic dream into reality. Note particularly the stylistic changes in the language (the dawn flushing the eastern sky and the weary, round-about marching) and in the **imagery** (the pearly horizon and the fifteen hundred dogs howling at their heels). This quick and unexpected switch in style emphasizes the difference between the ideal and the reality, or the sublime and the ridiculous—the intended effect on the reader is to create humor.

Define:
Imagery

Chapter Summary

Improve your comprehension of a difficult text by looking at small units, the words and sentences, and at the text's special style. Clear up difficult passages by defining all words that you do not know, including general vocabulary, reading vocabulary, specialized vocabulary, technical vocabulary, allusions, archaic language, and poetic language. Whenever possible, rely on context to help you define words. Consult the dictionary for meaning not supplied by context. Analyzing the structure of long and difficult sentences can also help you comprehend difficult texts. The subject–verb–object order is standard in most English sentences. Learn to locate this part, which is called the *base clause,* first, and then analyze how the other parts of the sentence tell more about it. Style refers to certain characteristics and traits that are repeated over and over again in a text. When these traits are typical of the author, the text is said to have personal style. When the traits are characteristic of a particular type of writing, the text is said to have conventional style. We associate certain styles of writing with different types of texts. Style is influenced by the author's personality and by convention. It is also influenced by the subject, audience, purpose, and occasion. To analyze style, study the author's word choice, supporting material, sentence construction, and punctuation. Speculate about the intended effect of the text on the reader.

---

[18] Mark Twain, *The Innocents Abroad,* Vol. II (New York: Harper and Row, 1911), p.72.

Your Summary

Write a summary in outline form.

What is the subject of this chapter?

What did the author say about it?

END–CHAPTER EXERCISES

I. Practice
A. *Noticing and Defining Difficult Words*

1. The following two passages illustrate how textbook authors typically introduce specialized vocabulary and define it in the surrounding text. Read each passage, locate the specialized terms, and write them in the spaces provided below. Then, using context only, paraphrase (meaning rewrite in your own words) the meanings of the terms.
a. From a Marketing Textbook

What was the setting for the crucial change in management philosophy? Perhaps it can best be explained by the shift from a **seller's market**—one with a shortage of goods and services—to a **buyer's market**—one with an abundance of goods and services. When World War II ended, factories stopped manufacturing tanks and jeeps and started turning out consumer goods again—an activity that had for all practical purposes stopped in early 1942.[19]

[19] Louis E. Boone and David L. Kurtz, *Contemporary Marketing*, 3rd ed. (New York: Holt, Rinehart and Winston, 1982), p. 11.

Specialized terms: **Your paraphrased meanings:**

_____   _____

                             _____

_____   _____

                             _____

        b. From a Data-Processing Textbook

Two commonly encountered computer terms are hardware and software. Hardware refers to the physical components of the computer. This section of the book deals primarily with the hardware aspects of the modern *stored program digital computer*. (The meaning of the terms *program* and *digital* will become apparent as we progress.) Computer *software* refers to programs of instructions that make the hardware work for us. This topic is covered in Section 3.[20]

Specialized terms: **Your paraphrased meanings:**

_____   _____

                             _____

_____   _____

                             _____

      2. Read the following passage from a communication textbook. When you have finished, write, in your own words, what you think **semantics** means:

Semantic rules also govern our use of the language. But where syntax deals with structure, semantics governs meaning. Semantic rules reflect the ways in which speakers of a language respond to a particular symbol. Semantic rules are what make it possible for us to agree that "bikes" are for riding and "books" are for reading; they also help us to know who we will and won't encounter when we use rooms marked "men" or "women. Without semantic rules communication would be impossible, since each of us would use symbols in unique ways, unintelligible to one another.[21]

[20] From *Data Processing: The Fundamentals* by Wilson T. Price (New York: Holt, Rinehart and Winston, 1982), p.26. Copyright © 1982 by CBS College Publishing. Reprinted by permission of CBS College Publishing .

[21] From *Understanding Human Communication* by Ronald Adler and George Rodman (New York: Holt, Rinehart and Winston, 1982), p. 64. Copyright © 1982 by CBS College Publishing. Reprinted by permission of CBS College Publishing.

Your meaning for **semantics,** using context only:

_____

_____

Now look up **semantics** in the dictionary, and write the meaning that most closely describes the word as it is used in the above context.

The best dictionary meaning for **semantics** for this passage:

_____

_____

Now compare the two meanings. Did the context give you adequate information to define the word, or did you also need the dictionary for a satisfactory definition?

3. The following paragraph is taken from John Milton's _Areopagitica,_ an essay criticizing the practice of censoring books before they are published. This passage was written in the seventeenth century, and you may find it more difficult to read than a modern text. As you read it, underline all of the words and allusions that you do not understand. Then, answer the questions at the end.

Good and evil we know in the field of this world grow up together almost inseparably; and the knowledge of good is so involved and interwoven with the knowledge of evil, and in so many cunning resemblances hardly to be discerned, that those confused seeds which were imposed upon Psyche as an incessant labour to cull out, and sort asunder, were not more intermixed. It was from out the rind of one apple tasted, that the knowledge of good and evil, as two twins cleaving together, leaped forth into the world. And perhaps this is that doom which Adam fell into of knowing good and evil, that is to say of knowing good by evil. As therefore the state of man now is; what wisdom can there be to choose, what continence to forbear without the knowledge of evil? He that can apprehend and consider vice with all her baits and seeming pleasures, and yet abstain, and yet distinguish, and yet prefer that which is truly better, he is the true warfaring Christian.[22]

1. List general vocabulary words you do not know, look up their meanings in the dictionary, and write a _brief_ definition for each.

_____   _____

_____   _____

[22] John Milton, _Paradise Lost and Selected Poetry and Prose_ (New York: Rinehart & Co., Inc., 1951, p. 473.

_____   _____

_____   _____

_____   _____

What are the two key words that the whole passage is about?

_____   _____

Are there any old-fashioned words in this passage that seem dated to you? List these words, and write next to them synonyms that you might expect to find in modern prose:

_____   _____

_____   _____

_____   _____

List the two allusions in this passage and define them. Discuss why Milton refers to them in this text:

_____   _____

                              _____

_____   _____

                              _____

Now re-read the passage, and write, in your own words, a para-phrase of the main idea:

_____

_____

_____

B. *Reading and Analyzing Difficult Sentences*
    The following six exercises contain sentences from prose that was written in the sixteenth, seventeenth, eighteenth, nineteenth, and twentieth centuries. They are included here because in college you will be expected to read material written prior to the twentieth cen-tury. Since that is a difficult task for most students, you will need to practice some strategies for reading such material successfully.

1. *The Sixteenth Century.* From the second book of Sir Thomas More's *Utopia,* which is a description of an ideal society. Read the two sentences in this passage, and underline the subject–verb–

object base clauses. If there are difficult words that make it impossible for you to understand the meaning of the passage, look them up and jot their meanings to the side in the margin. You should not have to look up all the words. Use context, instead, to get clues to their meanings:

For in the circuit of the city, a little without the walls, they have four hospitals, so big and so wide, so ample, and so large, that they may seem four little towns, which were devised of that bigness partly to the intent the sick, be they never so many in number, should not lie too throng or strait, and therefore uneasily and incommodiously: and partly that they which were taken and holden with contagious diseases, such as be wont by infection to creep from one to another, might be laid apart far from the company of the residue. These hospitals be so well appointed, and with all things necessary to health so furnished, and moreover so diligent attendance through the continual presence of cunning physicians is given, that though no man be sent thither against his will, yet notwithstanding there is no sick person in all the city that had not rather lie there than at home in his own house.[23]

Now, re-read the passage and write a brief paraphrase in your own

words: _____

_____

_____

2. *The Seventeenth Century.* From Francis Bacon's *Of Studies,* an essay describing the value of reading and studying. You may have to look up some words in the dictionary and jot their meanings in the margin. Underline the subjects, verbs, and objects. (In the first sentence the subject *you* is understood.)

Read not to contradict and confute, nor to believe and take for granted, nor to find talk and discourse, but to weigh and consider. Some books are to be tasted, others to be swallowed, and some few to be chewed and digested; that is, some books are to be read only in parts; others to be read, but not curiously; and some few to be read wholly, and with diligence and attention.[24]

What is reading compared to in this passage? Speculate why:

_____

_____

---

[23] Alexander M. Witherspoon, Ed., *The College Survey of English Literature* (New York: Harcourt, Brace & Co., 1951), p. 187.
[24] Witherspoon, p. 321.

Write a brief paraphrase of this passage in your own words:

_____

_____

Define:
biography

_____

_____

Define:
lexico-
grapher:

_____

_____

3. *The Eighteenth Century.* From James Boswell's *Life of Samuel Johnson,* a well-known (biography) about a well-known poet and (lexicographer.) The two sentences in this passage describe Boswell's first meeting with Johnson. Underline the subject–verb–object base clause in each sentence, reread the passage, and write a brief paraphrase below:

At last, on Monday the 16th of May, when I was sitting in Mr. Davies's back-parlour, after having drunk tea with him and Mrs. Davies, Johnson unexpectedly came into the shop; and Mr. Davies having perceived him through the glass-door in the room in which we were sitting, advancing towards us,—he announced his aweful approach to me, somewhat in the manner of an actor in the part of Horatio, when he addresses Hamlet on the appearance of his father's ghost, "Look, my Lord, it comes." I found that I had a very perfect idea of Johnson's figure, from the portrait of him painted by Sir Joshua Reynolds soon after he had published his *Dictionary,* in the attitude of sitting in his easy chair in deep meditation, which was the first picture his friend did for him, which Sir Joshua very kindly presented to me, and from which an engraving has been made for this work.[25]

Your paraphrase: _____

_____

_____

Describe the effect of the allusion to Hamlet's father's ghost

in this passage: _____

_____

_____

4. *The Nineteenth Century.* From John Stuart Mill's essay *On Liberty,* where he describes his ideas about individual liberty. Underline the subject–verb–object base clause, and complete the exercises below:

[25] Witherspoon, p. 601.

If all mankind minus one, were of one opinion, and only one person were of the contrary opinion, mankind would be no more justified in silencing that one person, than he, if he had the power, would be justified in silencing mankind.[26]

Your paraphrase: _____

_____

_____

Make up a modern example to illustrate the generalization stated

in this sentence: _____

_____

_____

5. *The Twentieth Century.* From a government textbook. The author is describing the effect of adolescence on some people. Underline the subject–verb–object base clause, and then paraphrase the idea in the sentence.

The psychic maladjustments often produced by these personal crises sometimes find political outlets, particularly in strong commitments to utopian proposals both leftist *and* rightist, for sweeping away the corrupt institutions and hypocritical attitudes of the adult establishment and replacing them with a new society cleansed of war, greed, exploitation, racism, and all the other evils that adults perpetrate.[27]

Your paraphrase: _____

_____

_____

6. *The Twentieth Century.* The intent of both sentence 1 and sentence 2 listed below is to state cause–effect relationships. Read to determine which of them does so successfully and which does not. Answer the questions at the end of each of them.

[26] Witherspoon, p. 946.
[27] From *Governing; An Introduction to Political Science*, 3rd edition by Austin Ranney (New York: Holt, Rinehart and Winston, 1982), pp. 68-69. Copyright © 1982 by CBS College Publishing. Reprinted by permission of CBS College Publishing.

Sentence 1

When a metallic atom having a low ionization energy transfers one or more electrons (depending on the number of valence electrons) to a nonmetallic atom, strongly attracting ions result.[28]

Successful? yes _____ no _____

What is the cause? _____

What is the effect? _____

Sentence 2

I was on my way to the doctor with rear end trouble when my universal joint gave way causing me to have an accident?[29]

Successful? yes _____ no _____

What is the cause? _____

What is the effect? _____

If you marked one of the sentences above as unsuccessful, rewrite it in a more successful form below:

_____

_____

C. *Analyzing Style*

1. The following two passages are both on the same subject. They are descriptions of toads. The styles of the two passages are different, however. Read the two passages, and then speculate about the factors that influenced the different styles. Finally, describe the stylistic differences in the spaces provided below. Refer back to the analysis of the two letters on page 190 of this chapter for an example of how to proceed.

The Giant Flying Vampire Toad

The misnamed toad is actually a species of frog—a huge, wet, bile-green creature that can weigh up to ten kilograms. Translucent membranes of mucoid tissue are stretched between its fore and rear limbs like sails of bubbly slime, enabling it to glide for considerable distances from treetop perches, in the manner of a flying squirrel. . . .

[28] Stanley M. Cherim and Leo E. Kallan, *Chemistry: An Introduction*, 2nd ed. (Philadelphia: Saunders, 1980), p. 219.

[29] Another accident report from the same list quoted earlier in this chapter.

The toad, we now know, hangs upside down in the tops of trees, cunningly camouflaged in the rotting foliage. It hangs there motionless like a huge glob of goo until some as-yet-unelucidated heat sense detects the presence of a large, warm–blooded mammal.

The crafty creature waits until the mammal has passed well by its perch. Then it releases its grip, extends its "wings," and silently zooms in on its prey from directly behind in a long, low glide out of the wooded gloom. Fangs extended, it pierces the back of the neck like a double–headed arrow with the full momentum of its dive. An instant later it plasters its slimy, sticky body in the prey's hair, grabs on to the ears with its clawed forelimbs, fastens its powerful, rubberlike suction mouth around the point of entry, and hangs there upside down, throbbing, slobbering, and sucking blood through its long, hollow teeth. . . .[30]

General Appearance of the Giant Tree Toad

This is a large tree toad. The head is broad; the outline of the skull evident, as the skin is united to the skull; canthus rostralis and nostrils very prominent. The top of the head is smooth; the eyelids and back are roughened with large and fine tubercles. The most conspicuous characters are the very large disks on fingers and toes, those on the fingers being fully as large as the tympanum. The eyes are large and prominent, the iris with brilliant orange tints. The color, when the frog has been under cover, becomes a dull olive–green, but in the light becomes citrine, turtle green, or oil yellow, with indistinct dorsal spots of dull citrine or grayish olive. The legs are barred with the same. The rear of the femur is reticulated with the same. The throat is pale, buffy, and slightly granular; the rest of the venter is conspicuously and roughly granular and dull yellow in color, with the underside of the femur a deeper yellow, and the axilla bright yellow with a wash of the same color along the sides. The tubercles under the joints of feet and hands are prominent and pointed.[31]

Speculate on Factors that Influence Style

	Vampire Toad	**Giant Tree Toad**
Subject:	_____	_____
Audience:	_____	_____
Purpose:	_____	_____
Occasion:	_____	_____
	(consider the sources as named in footnotes.)	

---

[30] Norman Spinrad, "Save the Toad!" *Omni*, June 1980, p. 130.
[31] Albert Hazen Wright and Anna Allen Wright, *Handbook of Frogs and Toads*, 3rd ed. (Ithaca, N. Y.: Comstock Publishing Co., 1949), pp. 338–339.

Analyze the Stylistic Differences in the Two Descriptions

Vampire Toad	Giant Tree Toad

Word choice: _____   _____

Supporting
  material: _____   _____

Sentence structure: _____   _____

Punctuation: _____   _____

Effect on
  reader: _____   _____

2. The toad passages above are both from modern texts. The following are excerpts from a Meditation (short essay) written by John Donne in the seventeenth century. The author was ill, thinking about his own death, and listening to a tolling funeral bell. Read the passage and describe its stylistic features below:

Meditation 17
Now this bell, tolling softly for another, says to me,
"Thou must die."

Perchance he for whom this bell tolls may be so ill as that he knows not it tolls for him; and perchance I may think myself so much better than I am as that they who about me and see my state may have caused it to toll for me, and I know not that. . . . No man is an island entire of itself; every man is a piece of the continert, a part of the main. If a clod be washed away by the sea, Europe is the less, as well as if a promontory were, as well as if a manor of thy friend's or of thine own were. Any man's death diminishes me, because I am involved in mankind, and therefore never send to know for whom the bell tolls; it tolls for thee.[32]

Analysis of Stylistic Features

Word choice: _____

_____

Supporting material: _____

_____

[32] Witherspoon, pp. 340–341.

Sentence construction: _____

_____

Punctuation: _____

_____

Effect on reader: _____

_____

II. Application to Your Other Reading

A. Copy a brief passage (50 to 100 words) from one of your current reading assignments. Write your comments on the author's word choice, use of supporting material, sentence construction, and punctuation. Speculate about the effect of this passage on the reader.

III. Questions for Discussion and Class Activities

A. In doing the exercises above, you have read passages written during the sixteenth through the twentieth centuries. Discuss some of the ways English prose has changed during the last five centuries.

B. You may have found the passages in the exercises that were written prior to the twentieth century more difficult to read than modern prose. Why are the older passages more difficult for you to read? What can you do to read them more successfully?

IV. Vocabulary Review
A. Specialized Vocabulary

1. speaking vocabulary _____

2. reading vocabulary _____

3. technical vocabulary _____

4. archaic vocabulary _____

5. base clause _____

6. style _____

7. personal style _____

8. conventional style _____

9. personification _____

10. imagery _____

B. General Vocabulary

    1. obscure _____

    2. syntax _____

    3. pervasive _____

    4. contemporary _____

    5. edition _____

    6. standardize _____

    7. erratic _____

    8. intact _____

    9. exalted _____

    10. idiosyncratic _____

    11. biography _____

    12. lexicographer _____

C. Allusions

    1. Parthenon _____

    2. Pirean _____

CHAPTER 10
Remembering What You Read

In this chapter you will learn:

How to differentiate between short-term and long-term memory.
How to use special mental activities to help you remember.
How to use selected study methods to help you remember.

The last three chapters in improving close-reading skills have taught you to look at the whole or overall organization of the text first and then at increasingly smaller units, including the section, the paragraph, the sentence, and, finally, the words themselves. The purpose of this chapter is to teach you to look at the whole text again, and to think about it, and write about it in some specific ways in order to understand and remember it effectively.

In-Chapter Exercise 1

Before proceeding further, turn back and re-read pages 109–112 of the article entitled "Magical Memory Tour: The Unending Quest for a Study Formula That Works." Stop reading at the subhead about note taking. Now write a summary of what you have just read in phrases only and in your own words. Include in your summary general points about remembering and forgetting and ways to improve memory:

Your Summary of "Magical Memory Tour":

_____

_____

_____

_____

_____

_____

_____

Define:
encode

_____

In writing this summary, you have just accomplished three things: (1) You have once again practiced **encoding**, or rewriting material in your own words, as you have each time you have written marginal notations or summaries in this book. (2) You have reorganized the ideas in this essay slightly to form a pattern of ideas easier for you to remember. And (3) you have reviewed some important information on the nature of memory that will help you to read this chapter. Look back at your summary now, and make certain that, among other things, it includes the following items:

1. It is important to put what you learn in a pattern immediately in order to remember it.
2. Encoding immediately helps create memorable patterns.
3. You will forget at least half of what you learn within twenty-four hours of learning it if you do not take steps to remember.

The Nature of Memory

Define:
**rote
memoriz-
ing**

_____

Define:
integrate

_____

Memory, to many people, means the ability to parrot back memorized facts and then forget them. We do such **rote memorizing** occasionally but not often in our lives. More often we are expected to understand, think about, and finally learn and remember new material so that it will contribute to our education and stay with us for life. Rather than just memorizing, we integrate new knowledge with old and then use what we know to think, to solve problems, and to analyze and discuss ideas. In order to learn and remember new material, we use two parts of our memory system: the **short-term memory** and the **long-term memory**.

Define:
**short-term
memory**

_____

When material is first encountered, it enters the **short-term memory**, where it stays for only a brief time, and is then forgotten. Information, in fact, flits in and out of the short-term memory all day long. You cannot remember the faces of everyone you saw yesterday nor can you remember every telephone number you have called only once. Usually the short-term memory has a capacity for only seven items at one time. More than seven items causes an overload. You can, for example, usually remember a seven-digit telephone number long enough to dial it. If, however, you have to remember it along with an area code and the name of an unfamiliar person, you usually need to make some notes before you begin to call.

Define:
**long-term
memory**

_____

Some of the material that enters the short-term memory is transferred to the **long-term memory** where it becomes integrated with other material already there and then stays with you for life. Basically, four types of mental activity—encoding, associating, reorganizing, and reciting—can be used to transfer material from the short-term to the long-term memory.

Define:
distort

_____

1. **Encoding.** By encoding, you make meaning for yourself as you rephrase the author's language in easier, more familiar language. Be careful when you encode, however, not to alter or distort the author's original meaning.

Define:
associate

_____

2. **Associating.** You will remember new material better if you can associate it with something you already know. You can, for example, sometimes remember a new acquaintance by associating him or her with someone you already know or with a category of people such as athletes or doctors. Some psychologists think that we cannot remember experiences from the first year or two of our

lives because at that time we had nothing in our minds with which we could associate new material. At present, however, you have knowledge, experiences, and ideas already in your mind, and you use this information to interpret and understand new material. One purpose of education is to fill your memory with so much information that you will be able to learn through association throughout your life.

Define:
reorganize
———————
———————

3. **Reorganizing.** You will remember material more successfully if you not only encode and associate it, but also reorganize it so that it makes sense to you. Whenever you encode, or rewrite material in your own words, you reorganize and readjust it to some degree to help you understand and think about it. You can go even farther and reorganize the ideas in your mind or on paper according to the author's organizational pattern or one you devise. For example, if you use an organizational pattern, you might finish your reading by listing five topics, or three blocks of time, or one problem and three solutions. Or, you may want to finish your reading by making a **graphic post-organizer** that shows relationships among ideas in visual form. Two types of post-organizers, the outlined study sheet and the map, are described later in this chapter.

Define:
graphic post-organizer
———————
———————

Define:
Recite
———————
———————

4. **Reciting.** The last type of activity that can be used to help you transfer material from your short-term to your long-term memory is reciting. This involves writing or saying either aloud or to yourself, over and over again, the items of material to be learned until you know them. A few minutes spent on this activity can help make new material a part of your long-term memory.

Nine Activities to Help You Remember

You can see from the discussion so far that material does not automatically slip into your long-term memory and stay there. It takes an effort on your part to cause new material to be imprinted in your long-term memory. The following are nine thinking and study activities that will force you to encode, associate, reorganize, and recite material in order to remember it.

1. *First, consciously decide to remember.* It is almost impossible to work at remembering unless you are mentally set to do so, and that takes a conscious decision. The decision to remember the types of rocks described in a geology book, for example, activates the general category "rocks" in your mind, makes it easier to associate the new information with the old, and thereby improve your memory of the new types of rocks.

2. *Ask questions and answer them as you read.* Questioning also helps you associate new material with old because questions force you to remember what you already know about a topic. The questions presented at the beginning of each of the four parts of this book are designed to help you associate what you already know about reading with what you are about to learn. An even more effective memory aid is to create questions of your own. Some reading experts recommend that you ask a series of questions about each new title or subheading that you encounter. The heading above, "Nine Activities to Help You Remember," could, for example, be transformed into the following questions: What are some ac-

tivities? Do I do any of them now? Which will work best for me? When would I use them? Why do they work? Such questioning aids both comprehension and memory and also helps with concentration.

3. *Underline selectively, and write marginal notes and summaries.* You have been practicing this activity throughout your reading of this book, and you now know that it works because it forces you to encode and reorganize immediately. When the material is difficult for you to read, encode and write notes paragraph-by-paragraph. When the material is less difficult, encode and write summaries section-by-section or chapter-by-chapter. In general, write your notes in your words and phrases only, write only main ideas and important facts, and spend 80 to 90 percent of your time reading and only 10 to 20 percent writing.

4. *Identify the organizational pattern as you read.* As early as possible in your reading, identify the organizational pattern, and then read to locate its parts. If the pattern is topical, look for the number of topics and what they are. If it is chronological, look for the breaks in time. If it is problem–solution, locate the problem and the solutions, and so on. Then, when you think back through the material, use the organizational pattern to help you reorganize and remember the ideas. This will be easier if you have marked and numbered the chunks or sections of material within the overall pattern.

Define: visualize

5. *Mentally visualize descriptive passages.* This activity forces you to reorganize abstract ideas in concrete picture form. A mental picture is easier to remember than a verbal description. Create visual images and even draw pictures in the margins of books to aid your memory.

6. *Redraw or trace diagrams and graphs.* It is difficult to look at a completed diagram or graph and either understand or remember it adequately. Solve this problem by redrawing or tracing with a pencil or your finger each part of such a visual aid. In this way you will reorganize it in your own mind and thereby understand how its parts make up the whole. The whole will then be easier to remember.

   As you read, retrace, and thereby reorganize the information on graphs, be sure to do the following:

Define: horizontal axis

a. Determine what the graph is about in general by reading the title, caption, or surrounding discussion.

b. Discover what is being plotted on both the horizontal and vertical axes by reading the labels on each axis.

c. Note what the general trends are.

d. Notice the sizes of the numbers involved.

Define: vertical axis

e. Notice where the maximum and minimum numbers occur and see if you can give a plausible explanation for the reasons.[1]

When you have finished retracing the graph and noting the information just listed, encode by writing a brief summary of what you have learned from the graph.

---

[1] I am indebted to Dr. Barbara Prater for these suggestions on reading and interpreting graphs.

In-Chapter Exercise 2

Try using these steps to read and interpret the graph printed below.[2]

Anti-Vietnam War Protests. During the 1960s, in response to growing U.S. involvement in Vietnam, many people participated in peace marches, demonstrations, teach-ins, and other collective activity intended to influence government policy.

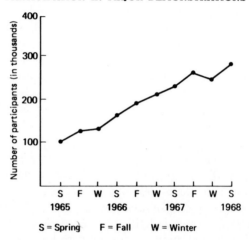

PARTICIPATION IN MAJOR DEMONSTRATIONS

S = Spring   F = Fall   W = Winter

Source. Jerome H. Skolnick, *The Politics of Protest.* A Staff Report to the National Commission on the Causes and Prevention of Violence (Washington, D.C.: Government Printing Office, 1969), p. 24.

1. What is this graph about? _____

_____

2. What is plotted on the vertical axis? _____

_____

3. What is plotted on the horizontal axis? _____

_____

[2] From *Understanding American Government* by Robert Weissberg (New York: Holt, Rinehart and Winston, 1980), p. 121. Copyright © by Holt, Rinehart and Winston. Reprinted by permission of Holt, Rinehart and Winston, CBS College Publishing.

4. What is the general trend? _____

_____

5. What are the sizes of the numbers involved? _____

_____

6. When is the minimum number? _____

_____

7. When is the maximum number? _____

_____

8. Can you explain why the maximum and minimum numbers occur where

they do? _____

_____

9. Write a brief summary of what you have learned from this graph: _____

_____

_____

_____

Treat complicated diagrams in a similar way. Discover what they are about in general, retrace until you understand each part that contributes to the whole, and then encode by summarizing.

Define:
**study
sheet**
_____
_____

7. *Make* **study sheets** *in outline form.* When you have finished reading, taking marginal notes, and writing summaries, you may find that you still have an imperfect grasp of the total text. You will be more effective in class discussions and examinations of the text if you reorganize the material in outline form on a brief study sheet that helps you see the main ideas. When making study sheets write the title at the top and underline it, place the main ideas next to the margin and number and underline them, and indent, list, and number the subideas. Add your own ideas in [square brackets,] draw simple diagrams, and include any other brief information that will help you understand and remember the material. Do not spend much time in making a study sheet for a chapter. Write fast and write big so that you can review the outline quickly before an exam or discussion. Figure 10.1 is an example of a study sheet on this chapter:

Figure 10.1 Example of study sheet for Chapter 10

Improving Memory

1. TWO *types memory*
   1. *short-term — seconds*
   2. *long-term — for life*
2. FOUR *mental activities for long-term memory*
   1. *encode — own words*
   2. *associate — new with old*
   3. *reorganize — ex: this study sheet.*
   4. *recite — say until know*
3. NINE *activities to help memory*
   1. *decide to remember*
   2. *questions — use titles*
   3. *marginal notes and summaries*
   4. *organizational pattern — look for [example: classification in this chapter]*
   5. *visualize — description*
   6. *retrace — diagrams and graphs*
   7. *study sheets — outline, brief*
   8. *maps — diagram of ideas*
   9. *go back over — recall, recite, reflect, review*

Define:
graphic

Your own study sheet of this chapter might have been even briefer than the one in Figure 10.1. Write only enough to jog your memory. Study sheets work because they force you to encode and associate as well as to reorganize the ideas in (graphic) form after you have finished reading. For this reason they are called graphic post-organizers.

Define:
map

8. *Make* **maps.** An excellent way to reorganize and then visualize the ideas in a chapter or article is to put them on a map, another type of graphic post-organizer. You may use your imagination in creating the form your map will take. Figure 10.2 is a map of the ideas in this chapter to demonstrate one possibility.[3]

Figure 10.2   Map 1 of ideas in Chapter 10.

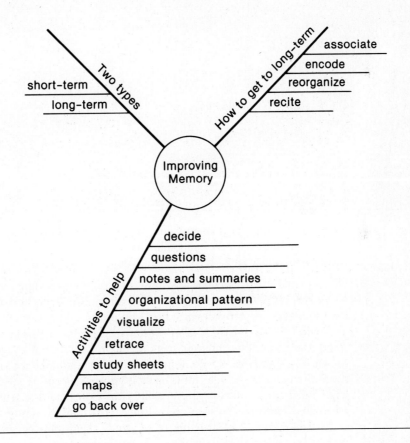

[3] For a more detailed explanation of mapping, see the essay by M. Buckley Hanf, "Mapping: A Technique for Translating Reading into Thinking," *Journal of Reading*, XIV, 4 (January 1971), pp. 225–230.

In-Chapter Exercise 3

Here is another form that a map might take. Complete this map of the ideas in Chapter 10 yourself.

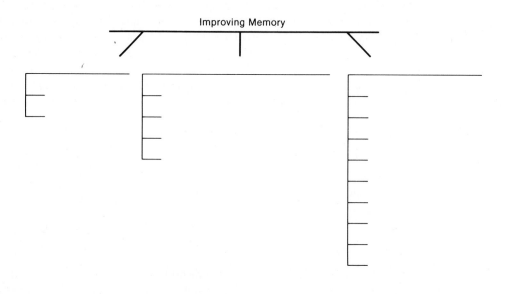

Define:
prominent
_____
_____

Notice that it is important to put the title of the map in a prominent place at the top or in the middle, and that the main ideas and subideas should also be easy to recognize quickly.

Define:
recall
_____
_____

9. *Go back and learn.* Spend a few minutes with your thoughts, notes, summaries, study sheets, or maps to imprint the material in your long-term memory. At least four types of activities will help you do this. They are **recall, recite, review,** and **reflect.** Note that all four of those words begin with the prefix *re* that means to *go back*. Recall by thinking back through the material you are trying to learn to see how much of it you remember without looking at your notes. If you cannot remember enough, look back at your notes and recite them a few times. Then look away and test your recall again. Continue this activity until you can recall all of the material accurately. Review material from time to time by quickly re-reading marginal notes, summaries, study sheets, and the maps that you have made over a period of time. This activity imprints the material more deeply in your long-term memory. Finally, reflect or think about what you have just learned. As you do, try to associate new information with old and answer the question introduced in Chapter 2: Why is this information useful or important to me?

Define:
reflect
_____
_____

Chapter Summary

Rote memorization is not so important as learning new material and integrating it with old so that you can use it to think, discuss, and solve problems. New material is first processed by the short-term memory, where it remains for only a brief time. Material can be transferred from the short-term to the long-term memory, where it stays for life, but only as a result of special mental effort. The activities of encoding or rephrasing the material, associating it with old material, reorganizing it in clear and familiar patterns, and reciting it until it is learned will help effect this transfer. Some specific thinking and study activities to help you remember are: (1) Make a decision to remember; (2) ask questions and then answer them as you read; (3) underline and write marginal notes and summaries; (4) identify the organizational pattern; and (5) mentally visualize descriptive passages; (6) redraw or retrace diagrams and graphs; (7) make study sheets in outline form; (8) make maps; and (9) go back over the material until you learn it.

Your Summary

You have already mapped the ideas in this chapter on page 212. Study your map briefly, and then try to write your summary of this chapter without looking back.

What is the subject of this chapter?

What did the author say about it?

END-CHAPTER EXERCISES

I. Practice
A. Below are two people's names with a list of 10 descriptive details each. Give yourself one second to look at each name and each detail, counting "1 and," "2 and," and so on until you reach 22. Then, immediately cover the lists with a sheet of paper and see how many items you can reproduce in the space below.

1st person: Harry	**2nd person: Bill**
1. bald	1. glasses
2. red-faced	2. short hair
3. fat	3. necktie
4. laughing	4. sad
5. short-sleeved shirt	5. suit
6. plaid shorts	6. wrist watch
7. little eyes	7. cuffs in pants
8. big ears	8. pipe in hand
9. sandals	9. shoes that tie
10. no socks	10. belt

1st person's name: _____   2nd person's name: _____

1.

2.

3.

4.

5.

6.

7.

8.

9.

10.

If you followed instructions exactly, you will have involved your short-term memory only in this exercise. Most people will be able to remember fewer than eight of the details and may not remember the names.

Now go back to the original lists and work through the following activities that are designed to engage your long-term memory:

1. Visualize and draw pictures of Harry and Bill. Label the 10 features in each picture.

Harry	Bill

2. Think of two specific people you have known or whose photos you have seen who remind you of Harry and of Bill. *Associate* Harry's and Bill's special features with the features of the people you have thought of.

3. Now *decide* that you will remember the original lists. Look away from the pictures you have drawn, and see if you can *recall* the 10 features of Harry and of Bill without looking. If you cannot, look back at the pictures and try again. Now cover up everything and reproduce the items in the orginial lists:

1st person's name: _____   **2nd person's name:** _____

1st person	2nd person
1.	1.
2.	2.
3.	3.
4.	4.
5.	5.
6.	6.
7.	7.
8.	8.
9.	9.
10.	10.

You should have a much better record this second time. Try tomorrow and a week from now to visualize Harry and Bill. You may not be able to recall all of their features exactly, but if you looked at the lists a few seconds, you could relearn them rapidly.

B. In Chapter 4, you were introduced to the memory technique of taking off the first letter or two of the key words you want to remember and making a nonsense word or phrase of them. See if you can still remember the nonsense words to remind you of the steps for:

Nonsense Word

Surveying a book   _____

Surveying a chapter   _____

If you cannot remember, look back at pages 76 and 78, and write the nonsense words in the blanks. Now look at these nonsense words and see if you can still write the steps they represent:

How to survey a book	**How to survey a chapter**
1. _____	1. _____
2. _____	2. _____
3. _____	3. _____
4. _____	4. _____
5. _____	5. _____
6. _____	6. _____

The nonsense word technique helps you *reorganize* material in a pattern that makes sense to you. Many students use this technique to remember difficult material for an exam. It is useful for retrieving information from your long-term memory quickly.

C. Read the following description of the room to which a depressed and morbid gentleman takes his young bride in Edgar Allen Poe's short story "Ligeia." Create a mental picture of everything in this room as you read. Then make a sketch of the room and answer the questions at the end:

The room lay in a high turret of the castellated abbey, was pentagonal in shape, and of capacious size. Occupying the whole southern face of the pentagon was the sole window—an immense sheet of unbroken glass from Venice—a single pane, and tinted of a leaden hue, so that the rays of either the sun or moon, passing through it, fell with a ghastly lustre on the objects within. Over the upper portion of this huge window, extended the trellice-work of an aged vine, which clambered up the massy walls of the turret. The ceiling, of gloomy-looking oak, was excessively lofty, vaulted, and elaborately fretted with the wildest and most grotesque specimens of a semi-Gothic, semi-Druidical device. From out of the most central recess of this melancholy vaulting, depended, by a single chain of gold with long links, a huge (censer) of the same metal, Saracenic in pattern, and with many perforations so contrived that there writhed in and out of them, as if endued with a serpent vitality, a continual succession of parti-colored fires.

Define:
censer
_____

_____

Some few ottomans and golden candelabra, of Eastern figure, were in various stations about—and there was the couch, too—the bridal couch—of an Indian model, and low, and sculptured of solid ebony, with a pall-like canopy above. In each of the angles of the chamber stood on end a gigantic (sarcophagus) of black granite, from the tombs of the kings over against Luxor, with their aged lids full of immemorial sculpture. But in the draping of the apartment lay, alas! the chief phantasy of all. The lofty walls, gigantic in height—even unproportionately so—were hung from summit to foot, in vast folds, with a heavy and massive-looking tapestry—tapestry of a material which was found alike as a carpet on the floor, as a covering for the ottomans and the ebony bed, as a canopy for the bed, and as the gorgeous volutes of the curtains which partially shaded the window. The material was the richest cloth of gold. It was spotted all over, at irregular intervals, with arabesque figures, about a foot in diameter, and wrought upon the cloth in patterns of the most jetty black. . . . The phantasmagoric effect was vastly heightened by the artificial introduction of a strong continual current of wind behind the draperies—giving a hideous and uneasy animation to the whole.[4]

Define:
sarcophagus
_____

Your sketch of the room:

[4] James A. Harrison, Ed., *The Complete Works of Edgar Allen Poe,* Vol. II (New York: Thomas Y. Crowell, 1902), pp. 259–261.

Questions about the room:

1. How many walls are there? _____

2. How many windows? _____ Describe and include the color: ___

_____

3. In what part of the building is the room located? _____

4. What is on the outside wall of the building? _____

5. Describe the ceiling: _____

6. What is hanging from the ceiling? _____

What color does it add to the scene? _____ Could it also add a

smell? _____ What? _____

7. Name some of the furnishings in the room: _____

_____

8. Describe the tapestry. Where is it used? _____

_____ What are

its colors and patterns? _____

9. What are the predominant colors in this room? _____

_____

10. Is there any movement in this room? _____

Describe it: _____

    Stop and reconstruct a complete mental picture of this room again in your mind. Now perhaps you can better understand the saying "a picture is worth a thousand words." A picture is certainly easier to remember than a thousand words.

D. The next three exercises (D1, D2, and D3) demonstrate the value of reorganizing by tracing and encoding by summarizing the information on graphs and diagrams in order to remember.

Define:
bar graph
_____
_____

    Look at the following bar graph. Actually retrace the parts of it with a pencil or your finger. Finally, answer the questions about it that appear below. Continue to retrace if necessary to find the answers.

AUDIENCE COMPOSITION BY SELECTED PROGRAM TYPE
REGULARLY SCHEDULED NETWORK PROGRAMS 6-11PM
(AVERAGE MINUTE AUDIENCES)

	GENERAL DRAMA (12)	SUSPENSE MYSTERY DRAMA (10)	SITUATION COMEDY (30)	FEATURE FILMS (7)	ALL REGULAR NETWORK PROGRAMS 7-11PM (71)	INFORMATIONAL 6-7PM ONE-A-WK. (5)	INFORMATIONAL 6-7PM MULTI-WK. (3)
TOTAL PERSONS 2+ (MILLIONS)	23.92	22.99	27.19	25.55	25.55	11.40	16.70
CHILDREN 2-5	.83	.72	1.43	.59	.96	.25	.36
CHILDREN 6-11	1.53	1.41	2.85	1.68	1.99	.42	.62
TEENS 12-17	1.39	1.79	2.51	2.22	1.94	.36	.61
MEN 18-34	2.65	3.03	3.44	4.08	3.51	1.26	1.67
MEN 35-54	2.25	2.83	2.45	3.24	2.84	1.28	1.89
MEN 55+	2.77	2.56	2.73	2.23	2.87	2.28	3.37
WOMEN 18-34	4.07	3.71	4.26	4.55	4.01	1.04	1.66
WOMEN 35-54	3.65	3.50	3.43	3.81	3.52	1.48	2.21
WOMEN 55+	4.78	3.44	4.09	3.15	3.91	3.03	4.31

( ) NUMBER OF PROGRAMS NOVEMBER 1981

From "1982 Nielsen Report on Television," A. C. Nielsen Company. Reprinted with permission.

1. What is the graph about in general? _____

_____

2. What is plotted on the vertical axis? _____

What is plotted on the horizontal axis? _____

3. What are the general trends? _____

_____

4. Make a statement about the sizes of the numbers involved: ____

_____

5. Where do the maximum and minimum numbers occur? _____

_____ Try to explain why: _____

_____

_____

Encode this graph by writing a brief summary, in phrases only, of what you have learned from it.

_____

_____

_____

Define:
line graph
_____

_____

2. Study the following (line graph,) retrace its parts, and answer the questions below:

Declining farm population in the United States.[6]

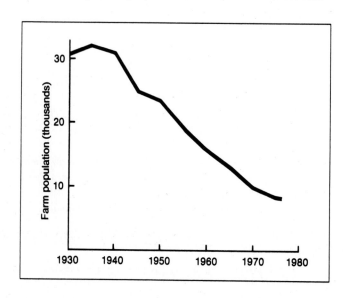

Source: U.S. Department of Commerce, Bureau of the Census, _Statistical Abstract of the United States_, 98th ed. (Washington, D.C.: Government Printing Office, 1977). Table 1132.

1. What is this graph about in general? _____

_____

2. What is plotted on the vertical axis? _____

_____ The horizontal axis? _____

_____

3. What is the general trend? _____

[6] From _Basic Economics_, 2nd edition, by Edwin G. Dolan (Hinsdale, Illinois: The Dryden Press, 1980), p. 442. Copyright © 1980 by The Dryden Press. Reprinted by permission of Holt, Rinehart and Winston, CBS College Publishing.

4. Note and comment on the numbers involved: _____

_____

5. Where do the maximum and minimum numbers occur? Why?

_____

6. Encode by writing a brief summary of the material presented:

_____

_____

3. Read the following description of a circuit breaker and then study the diagram that accompanies it. Now redraw the diagram yourself in the space provided to help you understand and remember it.

Circuit Breakers

In most new homes, a **circuit breaker** is used instead of a fuse. (See figure below.) In this device, current passes through a bimetallic strip, the top of which bends toward the left when excessive current heats it (see Chapter 8 for a discussion of bimetallic strips). If the bimetallic strip bends far enough to the left, it will settle into a groove in the spring-loaded metal strip. When this occurs, the metal strip drops downward sufficiently to open the circuit at the contact point and also flips the switch to indicate that the circuit breaker is now nonoperational. After the overload is removed, the switch can be flipped back on, and you're back in business.

A circuit breaker can be used instead of a fuse. It needn't be replaced when overloaded. (Arrows indicate path of current.)[7]

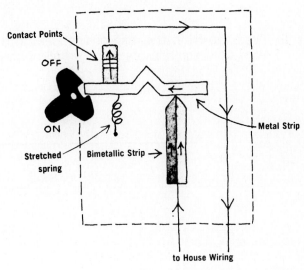

Contact Points

OFF

ON

Stretched spring

Bimetallic Strip →

Metal Strip

to House Wiring

[7] From *Physics in Your World,* 2nd edition, by Karl F. Kuhn and Jerry S. Faughn (Philadelphia: Saunders College, 1980), pp. 272–273. Copyright © 1980 by Saunders College/Holt, Rinehart and Winston. Reprinted by permission of Holt, Rinehart and Winston, CBS College Publishing.

Redraw the diagram:

Briefly summarize in your own words how a circuit breaker works:

E. Read and fill in the map of the ideas in the passage entitled "The Family," which appears on page 145 of this book.

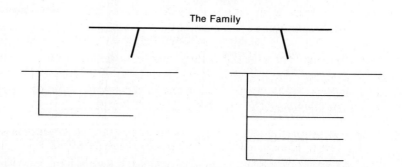

F. Read and fill in the map of the ideas in the passage entitled "Advantages of Active Listening" that appears on pages 146–147 of this book.

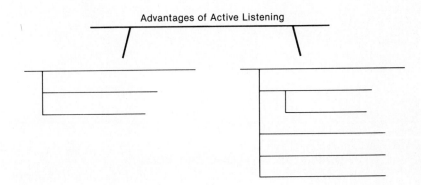

Advantages of Active Listening

G. Read the following passage from a biology textbook, and map the ideas in it. Since this is a difficult passage, you may want to map the title and the main ideas only on your first reading. Then re-read a second and even a third time to map the details.

Factors Affecting Enzymes

Three major factors influence the functioning of enzymes. First, there must be a sufficient amount, or *concentration,* of substrate molecules. If there are more enzyme molecules than substrate molecules, the reaction slows down. One way to speed up the reaction is to add more substrate. By so doing, more of the enzyme molecules become involved in the reaction. Once a sufficient substrate concentration is reached that involves all the enzyme molecules, the reaction will then proceed at its maximum rate. Beyond this point, however, adding more substrate will not further increase the rate of the reaction.

Second, the *temperature* of the cellular environment is crucial. At very low temperatures the rate of a chemical reaction is greatly slowed. If the temperature rises too high, the bonds holding the enzyme molecule intact are disrupted. As with other proteins, disruption of its bonds causes the enzyme molecule to unfold and lose its activity permanently. Enzymes affected in this manner are said to be *denatured.*

Third, every enzyme works most effectively at a certain *pH.* In your stomach, for example, some enzymes function at a pH well below 2; in your mouth, however, the enzyme in saliva is active at a pH of about 7. If either of these environments became too acidic or basic, the respective enzymes would cease to function.[8]

8. From *Biology: The Essential Principles* by Tom M. Graham (Philadelphia: Saunders College Publishing, 1982), p. 61. Copyright © 1982 by CBS College Publishing. Reprinted by permission of CBS College Publishing.

Your map:

II. Application to Your Other Reading

Map the ideas in one of your current reading assignments and submit it.

III. Discussion and Class Activities

A. Turn back to pages 59 to 60 and re-read what John Livingston Lowes says about "magnetic centres." How do his ideas about magnetic centres illustrate some of the theory about memory presented in this chapter?

B. Do some group mapping as a class activity. Four or five people may work together. Use large sheets of newsprint and ink pens. Make a large map of the ideas in Part III of this book (Chapters 7, 8, 9, and 10). Use masking tape to exhibit the various maps made in class and compare them.

C. Recite the information on one of the maps out loud as a group. Then look away and recall the information without looking. In three days try to recreate the map. Compare what you now remember from Part III of this textbook with what you remember from your other textbooks that you have not mapped and recited.

D. Think back through the activities to aid memory that you have read about in this chapter and practiced in these exercises. Which of them will be of the greatest value to you as you read and learn material for your other classes?

IV. Vocabulary Review

A. Specialized Terms

1. encode _____

2. rote memorizing _____

3. short-term memory _____

4. long-term memory _____

5. associate _____

6. reorganize _____

7. graphic post-organizer _____

8. recite _____

9. study sheet _____

10. map _____

11. recall _____

12. reflect _____

B. (General Vocabulary)

1. integrate _____

2. distort _____

3. visualize _____

4. horizontal axis _____

5. vertical axis _____

6. graphic _____

7. prominent _____

8. censer _____

9. sarcophagus _____

10. bar graph _____

11. line graph _____

Further Reading

The following works provide further information about some of the ideas discussed in Part III of this book.

Adler, Mortimer J. and Charles Van Doren. *How to Read a Book*. revised ed. New York: Simon and Schuster, 1972.

Corbett, Edward P. J. *The Little Rhetoric.* New York: John Wiley and Sons, 1977.

Graves, Richard L. *Rhetoric and Composition: A Sourcebook for Teachers.* Rochelle Park, N.J.: Hayden Book Company, Inc., 1976. Especially useful articles in this book are Francis Christensen's "A Generative Rhetoric of the Paragraph" and A. L. Becker's "A Tagmemic Approach to Paragraph Analysis."

Hairston, Maxine. *A Contemporary Rhetoric.* 3rd ed. New York: Harcourt, Brace & Jovanovich, 1982.

Hanf, M. Buckley. "Mapping: A Technique for Translating Reading into Thinking," *Journal of Reading* XIV, 4 (January 1971), pp. 225–230.

McConnell, James V. *Understanding Human Behavior.* 3rd ed. New York: Holt, Rinehart and Winston, 1980.

Puff, C. Richard, Ed. *Handbook of Research Methods in Human Memory and Cognition.* New York: Academic Press, 1982.

Smith, Frank. *Writing and the Writer.* New York: Holt, Rinehart and Winston, 1982.

Tulving, Endel and Wayne Donaldson, Eds. *Organization of Memory.* New York: Academic Press, 1972.

PART IV
The Critical, Evaluative Process

Part IV of this book will help you become a critical reader. The following ideas will be given special emphasis in the next three chapters:

1. All books are not of equal value or worth. Learn to discover which are the best books available on a topic and which are of value to you.
2. Authors have purposes or motives for writing. At times they write only to inform. More often they write to persuade. It is not always easy to discover which they are doing, but it is important to try to find out.
3. Some of the aims of critical reading are to discover authors' biases, to analyze authors' techniques of persuasion, and, finally, to make critical judgments of your own about particular topics.

Prepare for your reading by trying to answer the following questions:

1. Do you know how to find the best and most reliable books on a subject?
2. Do you know how to discover personal value in the material you read?
3. Do you know how to distinguish between factual and informative and opinionated and persuasive texts?
4. Do you know some ways to discover an author's real attitudes and beliefs about a subject?
5. Do you know how you should read when you disagree with the author?
6. Do you know some of the methods and techniques authors use when they deliberately set out to persuade?
7. Do you know how to recognize some of the signs of bias that the author may or may not be consciously aware of?
8. Do you know how to protect yourself when you do not want to be persuaded?

CHAPTER 11
Estimating the Comparative Worth of Reading Materials

In this chapter you will learn:

How to judge whether particular books and articles are useful to you.
How to locate the most competently written books and articles on a particular subject.

Define:
judgment

_____

Define:
dogmatic

_____

Define:
criteria

_____

Define:
evaluate

_____

_____

You make judgments about the people you meet all the time. Some are likable and some are irritating, some are intelligent and some are dull, and some seem fair and objective, while others seem biased and dogmatic. Books are the same, and you need to learn to make judgments about them also. This chapter and the two that follow will provide you with criteria to help you make critical judgments about what you read. Like people, books are all different, and you will enjoy and profit more from your reading if you regularly evaluate how the material you read is valuable to you personally, how it compares in quality to similar texts on similar topics, and how it influences your ideas and opinions.

Critical reading skills have been separated out from other skills in this book for instructional purposes. In actual practice you will integrate them with your other reading skills and use them every time you read.

The Value of Your Reading to You

Define:
liberal
education

_____

_____

Everything you read is conceivably of some potential use or value to you. Its use will be governed by your personal needs at the time you read, and these needs will help you form your reading purpose. Your calculus textbook, for example, will be useful to you while you are studying calculus; _People_ magazine may be useful when you have time to kill in a dentist's office; directions for assembling a stereo system will be useful to you if you are building one. The "classics" or "great books" will be useful if your goal is to get a broad, liberal education; and light, detective fiction may be useful for putting you to sleep at night. Even the back of the cereal box may be useful when it tells you how to save money on the next box of cereal.

This list is included here to remind you of the wide variety of purposes you can have for reading and the wide varieties of reading materials available to satisfy those purposes. Reading research shows that little children have to be taught reasons for reading—they do not automatically perceive reading as a valuable or useful activity. Many adults do not rely on printed material as much as they could to satisfy various needs in their lives. Some people, for instance, rely on television solely for the daily news and ignore the value of the combination of newspaper and television for more complete and accurate coverage. Other people try to follow complicated instructions given to them verbally when they would feel less frustrated and achieve better results if the instructions were written down.

Relying on the printed page to help satisfy many of your needs can result in a more satisfying and richer life. In order to accomplish that goal, however, you have to learn to make judgments regularly about what to read and how to use what you have read. Important and effective questions that will help you make these judgments include:

What are my immediate needs?
Will reading help me meet them?
What should I read to help me meet them?
How can I use what I have just read?

In answering those questions, you are not usually concerned with the comparative quality of the books and articles themselves. Badly written books can sometimes be entertaining, and poorly written memos can give information. If you need to read such material, you will perhaps only make a passing judgment about the quality of the text itself.

At other times, however, particularly when you are reading a number of sources about a particular topic, you will have to know how to make comparative judgments about the books and articles you read in order to find the best ones. The purpose of the rest of this chapter is to suggest ways to estimate the comparative worth of books and articles. Judging fiction—novels, poetry, short stories—will not be included here. Rather, the focus will be on ways to judge those texts that you rely on for information and informed opinion—material written to inform and/or to persuade you.

How To Find the Most (Competently) Written Material on A Subject

Define
competent
_____

_____

Define
contro-
versial
_____

_____

Suppose you have been assigned to do some reading on the history of the women's movement. You know that this is a (controversial) subject. Consequently, you can expect to find some material in favor of it, some against it, and some presenting both sides. You can also expect that some of the material will be written by authors who have done research, who will use mainly personal experience, or who are emotional and may not make much sense. You could form similar expectations about reading several sources on U. S.–China relations or day-care centers. In the next two chapters, you will be taught how to discover the author's stand on controversial issues and how to discover the ways in which authors work to persuade you. In this chapter, however, you will be concentrating on how to select books and articles best-suited to give you the most informed, detailed, up-to-date, reliable, and intelligent information available on your subject. Here are some suggestions to help you accomplish this:

1. *Analyze the author's qualifications.* Read through the introductory material to see if there is any information about the author's background and experience that suggests that he or she can write on the subject with authority.

In-Chapter Exercise 1

Here is an explanation of an author's qualifications in a book about U. S.–China relations. These "credentials" have been included at the beginning of the book to help establish the author's authority to write reliably on this subject:

John Bryan Starr is Executive Director of the Yale–China Association, an international education and cultural exchange organization based in New Haven. He also serves as Lecturer in the Department of Political Science at Yale University and as Director of East Asian Projects at the United Nations Association of the USA in New York. In this latter capacity, he directs the UNA-USA National Policy Panel to Study US–China Relations, from whose work this book is derived. He has written extensively on contemporary Chinese politics and political thought. His most recent book is *Continuing the Revolution: The Political Thought of Mao* (Princeton University Press, 1979).[1]

List three reasons why this author would seem qualified to write about U. S.–China relations:

1. _____

2. _____

3. _____

You might also consult one of the biographical dictionaries in the Reference Room of your library to get additional information about the author. Reading the book jacket, head notes if it is an article, or prefatory notes by another person can give you more information about the author's background and experience, and perhaps additional information on why the author wrote the book.

[1] John Bryan Starr, Ed., *The Future of U. S.–China Relations* (New York: New York University Press, 1981), p. ii.

In-Chapter Exercise 2

The following are prefatory notes written by another person about the author of a book on migrant farm workers. Notice how this material establishes the authority of both people.

The author of this thoughtful, clear–headed analysis of the political, economic, and inevitably, legal situation of an exceptional American working "population," our migrant farm workers, does well to make mention of the other books, all too many of them, that have preceded his own. I am one who wrote such a book, and in it I did likewise—referred with a sense of mixed gratitude, admiration, and despair to colleagues who had tried to tell others of a particularly grim and shameful story, as I hoped to do. I fear that I knew then, what I also now know, that my book would not be the last one written even as this one done by Ronald Goldfarb will not be because, unfortunately, there seems to be little prospect that this nation is yet prepared to do what is so urgently required: once and for all to bring justice to an extremely hard–working segment of our so–called "labor force." . . .

Here is a strongly worded, trenchant, discerning, fair-minded analysis of a major American social problem. Here, too, is a kind of exemplary witness—what it means to be a compassionate, high-minded lawyer and what it means, as a matter of fact, to remember in one's mind and heart, in one's working life as an attorney, as a citizen, those words engraved on the Supreme Court Building in Washington, D.C.: "Equal Justice under Law." One concludes the reading of this book wishing (hope against hope!) that it will be the very last one written and wishing, too, that those who practice the law could claim more colleagues such as Ronald Goldfarb—a moral example to a profession, to all of us.[2]

List one special qualification of the book's author, Ronald L. Goldfarb, to write a book about migrant farm workers:

1. _____

List one special qualification of the author of this preface to write about Goldfarb:

1. _____

Such author information can help you form an opinion about the author's qualifications to write on a topic. You will still have to examine the text, however, to see how well, in fact, the author accomplished the writing task.

[2] Robert Coles, "Foreword" to Ronald L. Goldfarb, *Migrant Farm Workers: A Caste of Despair* (Ames, Iowa: The Iowa State University Press, 1981). pp. vi–vii.

2. *Notice when the material was published.* Sometimes you will need the most recent material available, particularly if you are reading about a subject like solar energy in which change is taking place rapidly. The best books could turn out to be the most recent ones. On the other hand, if you are reading about a subject like Watergate, you may want material published at the time to give a sense of what happened then as well as recent commentary to provide an historical perspective.

3. *Check the publisher and the nationality of the book or article.* Book publishers and magazine and journal publishers acquire reputations just like people do. With experience, you will learn which have the best and most reliable reputations in particular fields. Until you have this experience, ask either experts in the field or librarians to help you judge magazines, journals, and publishing companies. Look also for the nationality of the book. Was it originally published in America or in another country? If it was written by an author from another country, read the title page to learn whether or not you are reading a translation. Try to discover whether the translator has competently and accurately presented the original text.

4. *Ask for expert opinion.* Professors can tell you about the reputation, quality, and general worth of specific books and articles in their own fields. Usually, when asked, they are pleased to offer the titles of the classic works that have long been admired and also to offer recent titles of books and articles that are influential and important. Librarians can also give expert opinion on the quality and reputation of many books and articles.

5. *Read book reviews.* You can find out still more about the book and its author by consulting some book review indexes that will lead you to book reviews. The information you get from the reviews will give you some idea about how the book was originally evaluated by other experts in the field.

    The Book Review Index, which is issued periodically itself like magazines and journals, lists the original sources where reviews of particular books may be read. *The Book Review Digest* is also issued periodically and not only tells you the specific magazines and journals in which your book is reviewed, but also quotes excerpts from these reviews. You may read through these excerpts to learn some of the content of the book as well as its strengths and weaknesses. *The Technical Book Review Index* is like the *Book Review Digest* in that it locates book reviews and lists excerpts from them. Its subject matter, however, is limited to the pure sciences, life sciences, technology, engineering, medicine, and related subjects. In judging the book reviews themselves, you will usually find that if most of the reviewers are favorable, the book is probably a reliable one.

    Get in the habit of reading journals and magazines that review books. This will help you learn to judge books yourself. Some of the best ones are *The New York Times Book Review, The New York Review of Books,* and *The Saturday Review of Books.* Read the book review sections also in your Sunday newspaper and in *Time* and *Newsweek* magazines.

6. *Compare passages.* You can, finally, read part or parts of a book to get an idea of how competently it has been written. Look first at the title and Table of

Contents to see if you already know something about any of the topics covered. If one is familiar, look it up in the index and then read in the text to see how it is handled. If, judging by what you know, you think the author seems to do a competent job of discussing this topic, you have another indication of the general worth of the book. Here is a simple example to show how this system might work: Suppose you consider yourself somewhat of an authority on solar energy. Perhaps you have just had a course in which this subject was studied. You are writing a paper on energy sources, and you need the best books the library has on the subject. You collect several books about energy, consult the Index in each of them for information on solar energy, and then read to see how each author handles this subject. If one or two of the books seem to be more accurate and more fully documented than the others, you would probably be safe in choosing those books as the best available.

Suppose, however, that you know nothing about energy, and you still must select one or two books on the subject. The best thing you can do in this case is arbitrarily to select a topic from the Index or Table of Contents and then compare the material on this topic in the several books. As you do so, consider the *relative amount* of specific material that the authors have used. Notice also the *quality* of the detail. Is it recent and significant? If there is almost no specific material, and the author relies instead on generalizations and opinions, it may be an indication that he or she is not well enough acquainted with the subject to know current information and facts and to write with authority. Notice whether or not such authors refer to other writers and researchers and then give the results of that research. (You will often, by the way, be led to other good sources if you notice those sources competent authors quote.)

Some authors do not use much supporting material. When this is the case, note whether or not they have the perspective, experience, knowledge, and reputation to speak with authority without relying on others. Immanuel Kant, the philosopher, used few examples. We may wish that he had used more to make it easier for us to read his work. We do not discredit his works, however, because they lack supporting material. Rather, we know from accounts of his knowledge and reputation that he is a competent author, and we read with greater care to understand him. If a book contains mainly generalizations and opinions, with little or no supporting material, you have to be the judge of whether or not the author has sufficient knowledge and background to write reliably.

7. *Make a final judgment about the author and the quality of the writing.* There are many poorly thought out and poorly written books. Learn to distinguish these from the best books. Search for books that appear to be written by authors with high general intelligence and that are clear, well organized, well thought out, and well researched. The Table of Contents of a book can indicate whether or not it is well organized. Read a page or two to see if it is clear and intelligently written. Notice whether the material is dense with new ideas, or whether the ideas are few and far between and overexplained. Notice whether the author seems to have the ability to form valid judgments or whether there are many hasty generalizations instead. Analyze the cause–effect reasoning and judge whether it is valid or oversimplified. Look for internal inconsistencies in the reasoning. Notice the breadth and variety of the allusions to other books and

fields of learning. Ask, in other words, whether or not there is a broad and general education apparent in a work.

If you are a freshman in college and you have not read very many books, you will have trouble answering all of these questions at first. That does not mean, however, that you should not ask them. The more you ask them and the more you try to answer them, the better you will become at evaluating what you read. The reason your professors ask you to read "several," or "five," or "seven" different sources when you do a research project is to force you to read several different writers on a subject. As you do so, you encounter different opinions, points of view—even different facts. Your professor expects you then to extract the best materials, both facts and opinion, from these sources and to combine them so as to present a more fair and complete picture than was presented by a single source. Your professor also hopes that your interweaving and combining materials from multiple sources will, perhaps, provide new insights into your subject that have, until now, been overlooked by everyone. That is the basic purpose of research. You need to learn to do it intelligently and critically. It is an activity that, once learned, can be of great use to you in many jobs after you leave college.

Chapter Summary

Books, like people, are all different, and you need to learn to evaluate their potential use to you and to judge how they compare to other works of their kind. Any written work can be useful if it satisfies a need. Children have to be taught, however, that reading is a useful activity. Likewise, many adults could lead richer and more successful lives if they relied more on printed material to gain information and to help them solve problems. Learn to locate texts that can be useful to you, and then take advantage of them. At times you will want to select the best texts available on a particular topic. To help you do so, analyze the author's qualifications, note when the material was published, check the publisher and the nationality of the book, ask for expert opinion, read book reviews, compare passages, and make a final judgment about the author and the quality of the writing.

Your Summary

Look back through this chapter and then jot phrases only as you write your summary.

What is this chapter about?

What did the author say about it?

_____

END–CHAPTER EXERCISES

I. Practice

A. Select three books in the library that are about the same subject. Evaluate how competently these books have been written using the criteria developed in this chapter. Then answer the following questions about them:

1. Which was the most reliable book on the subject? _____

_____ Why? _____

_____

_____

2. Which was the least reliable book on the subject? _____

_____ Why? _____

_____

_____

3. What is your final judgment about the quality of each of the three books?

a. _____

_____

b. _____

_____

c. _____

_____

II. Application to Your Other Reading

A. Make a list of five texts of any kind that you have read in the past year that have been useful to you. Write also why they were useful:

Texts	Why Useful
_____	_____
_____	_____
_____	_____
_____	_____
_____	_____

B. Which of your current textbooks is the most competently written? Why do you think so?

C. Which of your current textbooks is the most useful to you? Why?

III. Discussion and Class Activities

A. Make a list of books that the class judges to be competently written and generally excellent. They should have been read by members of the class. Discuss what qualities these books possess that make them excellent. From this discussion, form a list of qualities that the class associates with excellent books.

B. Each class member should interview a professor, and ask for the titles of three important and influential books in the professor's field. Ask, also, what special contributions to the field each of these books made. Compile a class bibliography of these books, and make it available to students who wish to do exploratory reading in various fields.

IV. Vocabulary Review

A. General Vocabulary

1. judgment _____

2. dogmatic _____

3. criteria _____

4. evaluate _____

5. liberal education _____

6. competent _____

7. controversial _____

CHAPTER 12
Discovering the Author's Motives and Detecting Bias

In this chapter you will learn:

> How to become aware of bias.
> How to compare your biased reactions with those of the author.
> How to avoid letting your own biases interfere with your comprehension.
> How to analyze the author's motives and detect the amount of bias present.
> How to distinguish fact from opinion.

Define:
almanac

Define:
bias

Any time you get information from any source, unless it is a list of facts from an almanac, you are likely to encounter bias and prejudice on the part of the author. When you read newspapers or magazines, when you do research for a paper, when you listen to a friend give opinions about education or politics, when you listen to your professors lecture, and even when you read your textbooks, you are exposed to varying degrees of bias and prejudice. You will need to become aware of this in everything you read. And you will need to learn to compare authors' views with your own and then to make final judgments about what you think.

How To Compare Your Biases with Those of the Author

Bias is not a bad thing. Life would be dull if people did not form opinions and state them. You are biased yourself on many subjects. Look at the following list of 20 topics. You probably have an opinion about most of them, and your opinions will differ from those held by some of your classmates and by many authors you will read.

In-Chapter Exercise 1

Register your own present biases on these issues by checking the appropriate boxes below.

		Your Biased Opinion		
Define: issue	(Issue)	Yes	No	No Opinion
——— ———	1. Should substances that cause cancer in animals, such as saccharin, be banned from human use?			
	2. Should the food-stamp program be abolished?			
Define: initiative	3. Will <u>increased</u> reliance on computers reduce human (initiative) and intelligence?			
——— ———	4. Does television have an (adverse) effect on morality?			
Define: adverse	5. Do movies contain too much sex and violence?			
——— ———	6. Are the rights of criminals protected at the expense of society?			
Define: reimburse	7. Should victims of violent crimes be (reimbursed) by society?			
——— ———	8. Should the U.S. sell arms to other countries?			
	9. Should the Federal Government control education?			
	10. Should cigarettes be banned by law because they are injurious to health?			
	11. Should drug addicts be permitted to purchase drugs legally?			
	12. Should marijuana be legalized for personal use?			
	13. Should illegal drugs be administered to terminal cancer patients?			
	14. Is abortion ever justified?			
	15. Is capital punishment ever justified?			
	16. Are you in favor of daily prayers in the public schools?			
	17. Should the draft be reinstated and become compulsory for all males?			
	18. Should females be subject to the draft?			
	19. Should men and women have equal rights and equal responsibilities?			
	20. Should the Federal Government, instead of private agencies, own and control all energy sources?			

The issues you have just examined are all controversial. There are no simple answers to any of them, and the arguments you would use to support your biases could seem as convincing to a third party as those given by someone who completely disagrees with you. The issues in this list are, furthermore, representative of controversial topics you might encounter if you read a daily newspaper, a weekly news magazine, or current popular books. You can also expect to find such topics discussed in your textbooks.

Reading biased and opinionated material on controversial topics can be difficult, especially if you have strong opinions of your own. Your own ideas and feelings can sometimes cause you to distort the author's meaning and may even cause you to miss the author's main point. This is most likely to occur when you are reading opinions that differ significantly from your own. Authors who hold opinions similar to or identical to your opinions may actually seem less biased to you than those who differ with you. In other words, the amount of bias or prejudice that you perceive in what you read is influenced by your own personal biases.

Here are three hypothetical situations that illustrate how you might react to reading biased material. They are meant to suggest how your own ideas and feelings can influence your perception of the ideas presented in the text. Suppose that you have just read biased articles on three of the issues from the above list that you just checked. These articles are about a female draft, computers and human initiative, and abortion. The diagrams in Figures 12.1, 12.2, and 12.3 compare the relative degrees of bias that you and the author might hold in these three situations:

Figure 12.1

Situation 1:   You have just read an article about drafting females into the armed services.

The Issue: Should females be subject to the draft the same as males?

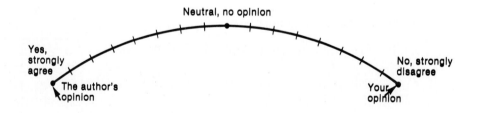

In Situation 1 (Figure 12.1), the author is biased in favor of a female draft and you are biased against it. Note that both of you are biased. You would be likely, in this case, to consider the author obviously biased because you disagree. You might also be in danger of letting your own ideas and feelings distort your understanding of this text.

Figure 12.2

Situation 2: You have just read an article about the effect of computers on society.

The issue: Will computers lower human initiative and cause people to be less creative and more dependent on computer technology?

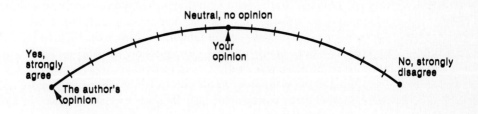

In Situation 2 (Figure 12.2), the author is biased against computer technology. Suppose that you know very little about how computers are used and have no opinion concerning their effect on human initiative. You are not biased. You probably would not complain about the author's biases either, since you have no strong opinions of your own. You would be able to read this article objectively without your own ideas and feelings interfering.

Figure 12.3

Situation 3: You have just read an article about abortion.

The Issue: Is abortion ever justified?

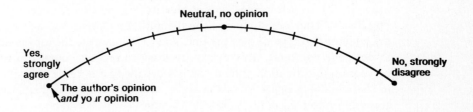

In Situation 3 (Figure 12.3), both you and the author are biased in the same way. Since you agree, you might not even consider this material to be biased. You would instead consider it to be accurate and true. In your eagerness to agree, however, you might impose some of your own ideas and values on the text and actually have difficulty comprehending those of the author.

How to Read Biased Material

Define:
perspec-
tive

_____

_____

Define:
dispassion-
ately

_____

These three diagrams provide you with a (perspective) to help you read opinionated and biased material. In the first situation, where you disagreed with the author on the female draft, you would be in danger of getting angry, hurling the book to the ground occasionally, writing rude remarks in the margin, and in your fury, perhaps missing much of what was said. In the second situation, where you had no strong feelings one way or another, you would read more (dispassionately) and probably more thoroughly. In the third situation, where you strongly agreed with the author, you would be writing "yes" in the margin, congratulating both the author and yourself for your shared good judgment, rushing next door to read passages aloud to a friend, and, again, in your glee, possibly missing or distorting in your own mind some of what was said.

What is the ideal attitude for you to foster whenever you are reading material that contains bias or prejudice? Usually such material is going to have some effect on your emotions. As a word of warning, you rarely will read critically and with good comprehension whenever you are eager to agree or disagree with everything the author says, even before you really understand it. On the other hand, it is impossible to deny your own biases and try to read as though you do not have them. The best you can do is to try to determine where you stand in relation to the author. Do you agree, disagree, or are you neutral? When you have answered this question, you can usually do a better job of temporarily setting aside your own strong opinions and feelings to hear the author out.

When you have read carefully and have analyzed how the material has been presented, you will then be in a position to make a final judgment about whether the author's position is good or bad and whether you agree or disagree with it. At this point you can ask such questions as, "Do I agree?" "What are the implications of this?" "Can I accept this?" "Can I live with the consequences of this?" or "Does my system of values permit this?" You can then use what you have read either to strengthen your existing opinions or to change your former opinions.

If your main job is not passionately to look for points with which to argue or agree while you are reading biased material, what should you be looking for instead? You have two objectives if you are to read biased material accurately and objectively. They are (1) to analyze the author's motives for writing and to detect the amount and type of bias present; and (2) to analyze the means the author uses to persuade you, and, if necessary, to learn to protect yourself against unwanted persuasion. Information to help you achieve the first of these objectives is presented in the remaining pages of this chapter, and information to help you achieve the second is presented in the following chapter.

Analyzing Motives and Detecting Bias

Define:
motive

_____

You may think (in fact, a lot of people do) that writers are either prejudiced and write biased material to get you to think as they do (Archie Bunker or Moral Majority-style), or that writers are not prejudiced and write objective material (newspaper style) to inform you. It is never this simple. Very seldom, in fact, do you meet an author who is genuinely objective and who writes completely factual

Define:
**overt
persuasion**

Define:
**covert
persuasion**

Define:
**objective
reporting**

Define:
**deliberate
persuasion**

Define:
guise

Define:
**hidden
persuasion**

Define:
**uncon-
scious
persuasion**

Define:
predisposi-
tion

material intended only to inform. Opinion creeps in, either deliberately or not, in all types of writing including textbooks and news stories. As soon as possible, you should determine each author's (motive) for writing. It may be to inform you, to persuade you, or to do both. Furthermore, if the purpose is persuasive, the author may openly admit it in a style of **overt persuasion**, or may attempt to disguise it in a style of **covert persuasion**. It will help you to analyze each author's motives for writing and to detect the degree of bias present in the work if you know the four different ways in which degrees of bias or objectivity may appear in what you read or hear.

1. **Objective reporting.** *Some expository material is genuinely objective.* Such material contains no lies, no distortions, and no opinions. It is made up of facts and data that you can verify by going to other sources. Newspaper reporters try for such objective reporting. They don't always succeed, however. Material that fits this first category is, in fact, comparatively rare.

2. **Deliberate, or Overt Persuasion.** *At the other extreme, some writiers are openly biased and deliberately, clearly, and admittedly trying to persuade you.* When this is the case, the title of the work itself often alerts you to the author's persuasive intent. You can usually then get a clear and accurate idea of the issues and the author's stand on them by reading the Preface or the Introduction and, perhaps, the first part of the first chapter.

3. **Hidden, or Covert Persuasion.** *Sometimes authors may deliberately try to persuade you under the* (guise) *of reporting.* Such persuasion is sometimes called **hidden persuasion**. It is usually accomplished by presenting facts, but *selected* facts that are carefully stacked to tell you only half of the story. The result is a one-sided and inaccurate "report." An author, for example, in writing about strip mining for coal in a wilderness area, might spend considerable space describing the beauty of the area before the mining began, and then print pictures that would show the landscape had been altered and made ugly by the mines. All of the information would appear to be factual and objective. All of the material in such a report would, in fact, be true. The strip mining would emerge as objectionable, however, to *any* reader who values undisturbed wilderness areas. Both description and pictures would be carefully pre-selected to persuade readers that strip mining in such areas is undesireable.

4. **Unconscious, Covert Persuasion.** Finally, authors may be influenced by their own prejudices while they think they are writing objective and accurate reports. Imagine a Catholic reporter for a Catholic newsletter assigned to write an objective report about worldwide efforts to control population. Even though this author tried to be objective and to give an accurate and unbiased account, it would be difficult. The author's Catholic values and strong (predisposition) to believe that population control is wrong could interfere with objective reporting. It would be the most natural thing in the world for this author to see and report more adverse than good effects of population control around the world. The reader would finish reading the "report" with a strong question about the morality and advisability of population control. Yet the author would not have intended such persuasion and probably would not even know that the article had been slanted in this way.

Define:
proliferation

_____

_____

Think also of articles about the use of torture in Latin America, the (proliferation) of nuclear armaments, or child abuse. It is extremely difficult for any reporter to be completely objective when writing about such subjects even though a sincere effort may be made to do so.

Define:
elicit

_____

_____

Define:
ostensibly

_____

_____

It would be a mistake to associate these last two ways in which bias may appear with evil causes. Many authors with good causes use hidden persuasion to deliberately persuade you even though they may seem to be reporting. Accounts of natural disasters, such as earthquakes and tornadoes, persuade people to send food and clothing to desperate people. The descriptions and pictures of their distress are calculated to (elicit) such response, even though the story (ostensibly) presents only the facts. Hitler, on the other hand, made no secret that he was deliberately and openly persuading people. Whenever persuasion is hidden, it is not necessarily bad.

Distinguishing Facts from Opinions

Define:
**popularly
held
opinions**

_____

_____

One way to detect bias and to determine whether an author does or does not have a persuasive motive is to learn to distinguish facts from opinions in the material you read. Remember that you can always verify or prove facts by checking them in other sources. Opinions, on the other hand, represent the author's personal ideas, values, or conclusions about the subject. You may find authors' opinions stated elsewhere by other authors because they are **popularly held opinions.** These opinions may seem true either because so many people hold them or because there seems to be convincing evidence to support them. Still, all opinions differ from facts because they cannot absolutely be proven to be true.

In-Chapter Exercise 2

The following are statements about Sigmund Freud that are adapted from a psychology textbook.[1] Place a checkmark in one of the columns to the right to identify each of them as a fact or as an opinion. Remember the test: Facts can be proved.

	Fact	Opinion
1. Freud was a genius.		
2. His theory of psychoanalysis was, in its own way, as bold and creative a step forward as was Darwin's theory of evolution.		
3. Freud developed his theory the way that you or I would.		
4. Most of the data that Freud reported were quite accurate.		

[1] From *Understanding Human Behavior,* 3rd edition, by James V. McConnell (New York: Holt, Rinehart and Winston, 1980), pp. 546, 562, and 563. Copyright © 1974, 1977, 1980 by Holt, Rinehart and Winston. Reprinted by permission of Holt, Rinehart and Winston, CBS College Publishing.

5. Freudian theory seems to fall down in two major areas.

6. Sigmund Freud had a problem. Or rather, he had several of them.

7. Freud was born in 1856 in what is now Czechoslovakia.

8. He lived for almost 80 years in Vienna.

9. Freud could not make up his mind what road to success he should follow.

10. Around 1885, Freud spent several months in Paris, studying hypnosis with Charcot.

You were correct if you identified all of the statements, with the exceptions of numbers 7, 8, and 10, as opinions. This author is persuading you to think about Freud in certain ways. Write a brief description of the man that emerges from these statements.

_____

_____

Do you think that all modern psychologists would present an identical portrait of Freud? Consult the Index and read about Freud in another psychology textbook to learn the answer to this question.

Analyzing the relative amount of factual and opinionated material in a text is only one way of detecting bias. In the next chapter, where you are taught to analyze persuasive texts, you will learn about several other signs in the text itself that demonstrate an author's persuasive intent.

Chapter Summary

Bias can be present in anything you read or hear. You need to learn to recognize it and also to compare your biases on particular issues with those of the author. Once you have established the author's biases and have compared them with your own, it is then easier to read objectively and to make a fair, final judgment. It is important to determine whether an author's motives are mainly to inform or to persuade you. To help you determine this, you need to analyze the amount and type of bias present in the text. Genuinely objective material that contains only facts is relatively rare. Instead, you can expect bias to appear in some form in nearly everything you read. Authors may be overtly persuasive and admit their intent, or they may be covertly persuasive and either deliberately hide or be unconscious of their intent. One way to recognize the degree of bias present in an author's work is to study the relative amount of fact and opinion present. Heavily opinionated material is meant to be persuasive and to influence your ideas about the subject.

Your Summary

Write a brief summary, in phrases only, of the main ideas in this chapter.

What is the subject of this chapter?

What did the author say about it?

END-CHAPTER EXERCISES

I. Practice
A. Compare your biases with those of the author.
Read the following passages and then notice that the central issue in each is identified at the end. Check the appropriate blanks that follow to compare your bias with the author's apparent bias on each issue.
1. From *The Origins of the Equal Rights Amendment: American Feminism between the Wars*

   Actually, equality with men is essential to feminism, but it does not necessarily mean adopting male defined values without reflection or reevaluation. At its best, feminism is a humanistic outlook which involves rights and responsibilities, free from sex stereotyping, for both men and women. However, in the short term, obtaining women's rights must come first for feminists.[2]

   Issue: <u>Women must be equal to men.</u>

   Your bias: Agree _____ No opinion _____ Disagree _____

   Author's bias: Agree _____ No opinion _____ Disagree _____

[2] By Susan D. Becker (Westport, Conn.: Greenwood Press, 1981), pp. 274–275.

2. From *The Conduct of Just and Limited War*

It is my position that the most original fresh reappraisal of war will, if it deals with reality, conclude that recourse to armed coercion is a perennial feature of the human condition. The use of armed force takes place, of necessity, at all levels of society from the local level of domestic police to the national level of revolutionary war to the international level of interstate conflict. If this is true, a fresh reappraisal that would simply wish away war is irrelevant to the problem and irresponsible.[3]

Issue: War is inevitable so we should accept it.

Your bias: Agree _____ No opinion _____ Disagree _____

Author's bias: Agree _____ No Opinion _____ Disagree _____

3. From the introduction to a collection of essays entitled *Day Care: Scientific and Social Policy Issues*

The quality versus cost debate is highlighted in the chapters by Senators Hatch and Kennedy. Both senators underline the importance of *quality* child care. Kennedy begins with the premise that child care is a right, not a privilege. He adds that the federal government has a responsibility to help parents pay the cost of quality care. Senator Hatch, however, not only opposes "a massive, federally funded network of child care facilities" but also does not voice support for other, more indirect subsidies such as child care tax credits. The ultimate responsibility for ensuring that children get quality care—and for paying for the care—should, he says, rest with parents.

Senators Kennedy and Hatch may represent two extremes of the political spectrum on day care. But they also help illustrate two peculiarly American traditions which have long complicated the provision of day care for children of working parents in this country. First, while European nations routinely accept the notion that society shares in the responsibility for child care, Americans have usually wanted to restrict this responsibility to parents. Thus, day care is bound to be controversial because it challenges this deeply entrenched tradition of family autonomy in the area of child care. Second, support for day care in the United States is complicated by the fact that the nation seems to vacillate between universal concern for the welfare of its citizens and the tradition of individual responsibility for one's own welfare.[4]

---

[3] By William V. O'Brien (New York: Praeger Publishers, 1981), p. 2.

[4] Reprinted by permission of the publisher, from Edward F. Zigler and Edmund W. Gordon (Eds.), *Day Care: Scientific and Social Policy Issues* (Boston: Auburn House Publishing Company, 1982), pp. vii–viii.

Issue: <u>The Federal Government should pay for child care.</u>

Senator Kennedy's bias: Agree _____ No opinion _____

    Disagree _____

Senator Hatch's bias: Agree _____ No opinion _____

    Disagree _____

Your bias: Agree _____ No opinion _____ Disagree _____

Author's apparent bias: Agree: _____ No opinion _____

    Disagree _____

B. Analyze the author's motives and the relative amount of fact and opinion in each of the passages below. Underline facts once and opinions twice as you read. The first one is started for you.

1. From *Knowing Right from Wrong: The Insanity Defense of Daniel McNaughtan*

The <u>most important</u> case in the history of the plea of insanity took place in London during the reign of Queen Victoria. A young Scotsman, Daniel McNaughtan, on a raw January afternoon in 1843, shot Edward Drummond, private secretary to Sir Robert Peel, believing him to be the prime minister. Five days later Drummond died of complications from his gunshot wound. The assassin was charged with murder in the first degree and tried in the Central Criminal Court of London, Old Bailey.

Daniel McNaughtan's defense rested upon the state of his mind at the time he committed the act, not upon the denial of the act itself. His learned counsel, Alexander Cockburn, argued that McNaughtan had been "the victim of a fierce and fearful delusion" which caused him to imagine that the Tories were his enemies. The solicitor general, Sir William Follett, acknowledged that McNaughtan suffered delusions that could not exist in a wholly sane person, yet he maintained that under English law McNaughtan could not be relieved of criminal responsibility unless he was totally incapable of knowing right from wrong. Nine medical experts appeared for the defense. When the solicitor general decided not to combat this testimony, Chief Justice Nichlas Tindal stopped the trial and practically directed the jury to return a verdict of "not guilty on the grounds of insanity."[5]

[5] By Richard Moran (New York: The Free Press, 1981), p. 1.

List some facts in this passage:

_____

_____

_____

_____

_____

_____

_____

List some opinions:

_____

_____

_____

How would you categorize this passage?

_____ Objective reporting (all facts)

_____ Deliberate persuasion (with persuasive intent stated openly)

_____ Hidden persuasion (author knows what he thinks and wants to cause you to agree although he does not say so)

_____ Unconscious persuasion (author influenced by unconscious prejudice)

Why?_____

_____

2. From *Long Memory: The Black Experience in America*
    This book tells the story of a people wrenched from their African homeland and scattered along the inhospitable shores of the

Americas. The black American was hewn from the massive rock of African civilization and sculpted into new shapes by the forces unleashed in the attempt to forge the first new nation on the continent of North America. From the black perspective, America has, throughout its history, been a country living in permanent contradiction between its ideals and its practices. Still, the oppression and exploitation the blacks endured made them the quintessential Americans. The reason for this development, Jean-Paul Sartre wrote, was that "the exploited man doesn't separate his destiny from that of others. His individual misfortune is, in fact, a collective misfortune; it is due to the economic, political, and social structures of the society in which he lives." The history of the Afro-American, as the great novelist Richard Wright observed in 1941, is the history of other citizens of the United States: "We black folk, our history, and our present being, are a mirror of all the manifold experiences in America. What we want, what we represent, what we endure, is what America *is*."[6]

List some facts in this passage:

_____

_____

_____

List some opinions:

_____

_____

_____

How would you categorize this passage?

_____ Objective reporting

_____ Deliberate persuasion

_____ Hidden persuasion

_____ Unconscious persuasion

Why? _____

_____

[6] By Mary Frances Berry and John W. Blassingame (New York: Oxford University Press, 1982), Preface.

II. Application to Your Other Reading

A. Select a passage from one of your textbooks, write a brief paraphrase of it, and then write answers to the following questions. Submit both the paraphrase and your answers.

1. Is there a controversial issue in this passage? What is it?

2. What is your opinion on the issue?

3. Can you tell what opinion the author seems to hold? What is it?

4. List one fact and one opinion from the passage.

5. Is this passage primarily an example of objective reporting, overt persuasion, covert persuasion, or a combination of these? Why do you think so?

III. Discussion and Class Activities

A. In the next lecture you attend, listen for both fact and opinion. Underline facts once and opinions twice in your lecture notes, and bring them to class to discuss.

B. Find a newspaper article that contains both fact and opinion. Underline the facts once and opinions twice, and bring it to class to discuss.

C. Look back at the list of issues on page 239 of this chapter. Notice that these issues in their present form are opinions. Select one of the issues, and make a list of facts about it to support your point of view. Now make a list of facts to support the opposite point of view. Use your list to write two paragraphs, one with factual material stacked in favor of your point of view, and the other with factual material stacked to support the opposite point of view.

D. Go back to the three passages in End-Chapter Exercise I of this chapter, and notice whether you agreed or disagreed with the authors or the senators mentioned. How do your biases influence the way in which you regard these authors and these senators?

IV. Vocabulary Review
A. Specialized Vocabulary

1. overt persuasion _____

2. covert persuasion _____

3. objective reporting _____

4. deliberate persuasion _____

5. hidden persuasion _____

6. unconscious persuasion _____

7. popularly held opinions _____

B. (General Vocabulary)

    1. bias _____

    2. issue _____

    3. initiative _____

    4. adverse _____

    5. reimburse _____

    6. perspective _____ _____

    7. dispassionately _____

    8. motive _____

    9. guise _____

    10. predisposition _____

    11. proliferation _____

    12. elicit _____

    13. ostensibly _____

C. Allusions

    1. almanac _____

CHAPTER 13
Analyzing Persuasive Texts

In this chapter you will learn:

> How to recognize persuasive appeals.
> How to recognize signs of bias.
> How to protect yourself against unwanted persuasion.
> How to make inferences.

In the last chapter you learned that one way in which authors work to persuade you to change your beliefs and values is to bombard you with their own opinions. This chapter explains some of the other persuasive techniques that authors use when they are trying to change your ideas or actions. These techniques can be used for both overt and covert persuasion.

The Persuasive Appeals

Define:
persuasive appeal

The persuasive techniques used by authors with overt persuasive intents are known as **persuasive appeals**. By recognizing and analyzing these appeals, you will understand how you are being persuaded and, if necessary, learn to protect yourself against unwanted persuasion.

Define:
rhetoric

Some of the best advice about how to be effectively persuasive can be found in the (rhetoric) books written during the Greek and Roman classical period. Classical rhetoric is useful to modern readers who need a systematic explanation of how authors manipulate us to change our thoughts and actions.

Classical writers recognized that there are three ways in which authors can appeal to you and thereby change your views. These are (1) **ethical appeals**, (2) **emotional appeals**, and (3) **logical appeals**.

Define:
ethical appeal

1. **Ethical appeal.** Authors often gain your attention and persuade you to accept their views by causing you to admire them, to trust their judgment, and to believe what they say. Either directly or indirectly persuasive authors work to make you believe that they possess intelligence, knowledge, integrity, good judgment, and good will towards you the reader. You are more likely to be persuaded by authors when you are convinced that they have such admirable qualities.

Define:
emotional appeal

2. **Emotional appeal.** One of the quickest ways an author can gain your attention and influence your thought is by appealing to your emotions. Most authors know this intuitively even though they may know nothing of classical rhetoric. Tear-jerking stories, vividly descriptive passages, and allusions to people and causes that you are likely to feel strongly about all engage your emotions.

Define:
**logical
appeal**
3. **Logical appeal.** Finally, authors influence and persuade you by using logical arguments that appeal to your sense of what is reasonable, acceptable, and true. These arguments may be presented inductively or deductively. Recall that inductive arguments begin with a list of examples, anecdotes, or other supporting material that lead up to the final, main point of the argument. In deductive argument, the main point is stated at the beginning, and arguments and supporting material are then used to prove it. Your textbook authors make use of logical appeal when they state generalizations, and then prove them with a line of logical argument or with diagrams, statistics, or references to research and studies.

In-Chapter Exercise 1

Ethical and emotional appeals are used by the author of the following passage from a book about migrant farm workers. As you read, write one line in the margin next to material that engages your *emotions* and two lines next to material that gives you a *favorable impression of the author.*

In 1975 a federal court in Washington, D.C., appointed me to monitor how well the Department of Labor provided government services to migrant and seasonal farm workers. One afternoon when I was traveling in the home base of what is known as the East Coast "migrant stream," I stopped unannounced at a union hiring hall in Avon Park, Fla. With a small group of state and federal labor officials, I was traveling throughout farming areas of Florida to learn about the lot of farm workers there. This world was strange to an urban man with only the vaguest notions about how crops were planted and harvested and found their way to my table.

Avon Park is a poor, scruffy, agricultural town; paradoxically, it is not far from the luxury of Miami and Palm Beach. The union building was spare but well used. The young woman in charge of the office there seemed wary of us; she was plainly skeptical about our interest in her union's affairs. We persuaded her to accompany us to a modest luncheonette on a nearby back street and to sit and talk with us awhile.

On first impression she seemed to be a contentious if not a surly person—one not to be taken seriously. She wore a tight Mickey Mouse T-shirt and dungarees. Her body was thickset, and her language was coarse. But as she spoke, it was clear that, however rough-hewn, she was a bright and engaging person, full of insights, convictions, opinions, and commitment. She was a forceful, challenging, and compelling advocate with a one-track mind that governed a one-track life. She was a child of farm worker parents who had committed herself completely to the union movement. Her whole life was devoted to getting farm workers the justice they deserved. Without stint, single-mindedly, she pounded at strangers about the needs and problems with which her impoverished but dedicated union was engaged.

First impressions of a brazen dame faded fast; they were replaced by the reality of a savvy, sensitive, probing, and extraordinarily dedicated working woman. We spent several hours debating life and labor over a simple lunch of collards, crackers, and tea; then we returned to the union hall where we watched the operation work. When my party had to leave, the tough, cynical woman we had met upon arrival embraced us, imploring us not to forget the farm workers' needs. The memory of the magnetism and energy of this committed woman remained long after we left Avon Park and Florida.[1]

1. *Author's motive.* Is this author's primary purpose to inform or to persuade you? Why do you think so? _____

_____

2. *Emotional appeal.* How does the author engage your emotions about the subject of migrant farm workers? Name at least two instances of material

that seem to be included for their emotional appeal: _____

_____

3. *Ethical appeal.* What information does the author include about himself to cause you to consider him an authority as well as a trustworthy spokes-

man on the topic of migrant farm workers?_____

_____

_____

Define:
ethos

_____

_____

4. *Ethical appeal.* How else does the author establish his (ethos) by causing you to think that he is flexible, reasonable, and has good judgment? Consider especially the judgments he makes about the young woman de-

scribed in this passage:_____

_____

_____

5. *Author's bias.* Do you think this author will be in favor of continued or increased government aid or in favor of discontinuing aid to migrant farm

workers? Why do you think so?_____

_____

_____

[1] Ronald L. Goldfarb, *Migrant Farm Workers: A Caste of Despair* (Ames, Iowa: The Iowa State University Press, 1981), pp. viii–ix.

6. *Your bias.* What is your position on government aid to migrant farm

   workers? _____

   _____

7. *Effectiveness of persuasion.* Were your ideas influenced by any of the

   persuasive appeals used in this passage? _____

   _____

_____

The Signs of Bias

Define:
**signs
of bias**

_____

You can train yourself to become aware of various signs that an author is biased
or prejudiced by doing a close analysis of the author's use of the three persuasive
appeals. This is especially useful when the author's motives and purpose are not
stated or immediately clear. When you can spot **signs of bias** and thereby understand
the author's motives, it is both easier to comprehend the text and to protect yourself
against it, if that seems important.

Analyze the author's outside influences along with the source of the published
material to gain greater insight into the author's *ethical appeal*. Analyze the author's
use of emotionally loaded material to gain insight into the author's use of *emotional
appeals*. Finally, analyze the author's use of all materials that appear to be logical
and reasonable. Some will be, but some may actually be incomplete or represent
faulty reasoning. Biased authors sometimes misuse *logical appeals* in order to cloud
your reason and encourage you to accept biased views. Some of the signs of bias
along with some suggestions for analyzing and resisting their persuasive force follow.

The Author and the Source

Define:
affiliation

_____

1. *The author's* (*affiliations.*) Look for information in introductions, in book reviews, or in biographical indexes to see if authors have interests, background
   experiences, or affiliations that can also often tell you whether or not authors
   are biased on particular subjects.

2. *The author's assumptions.* Another sign of bias, which may be consciously or
   unconsciously used by an author, derives from those values, opinions, and assumptions that an author personally holds to be true. Such assumptions are
   usually not directly stated in the work, but they influence the way in which the
   author presents the ideas. Authors are not always aware of their own basic
   assumptions. You can make yourself aware of them, however, if you regularly
   ask the question, "What general basic belief caused this author to make this
   statement?"

In-Chapter Exercise 2

Try to identify the underlying values and assumptions that influence the authors of the following statements:

Statement 1

For those guided by just-war and limited-war doctrines, the problem is to set morally acceptable goals for and limits on war....[2]

1. What beliefs does the author hold about the nature of war that cause

   him to make this statement?_____

   _____

Statement 2

Assassinations generally occur during periods of social and political upheaval—when there are major disturbances in the social structure.[3]

1. Would this author be likely to attribute the cause of assassinations to the

   personality disorders of the assassin? yes _____ no _____
2. What assumption does the author make about the main cause of assas-

   sinations? _____

   _____

By asking yourself what authors assume to be true, it is then easier to understand why they say some of the things they do. This, in turn, helps you understand them, their positions, and their degree of bias towards their subjects. In the foreword to Carlos B. Embry's book *America's Concentration Camps: The Facts about Our Indian Reservations Today*, the author writes:

> In this book I have tried not to act as a judge or a moralist, but only as an objective observer. My purpose is not to proselyte but to state the facts as I found them, so that the reader may draw his own conclusions.[4]

In spite of this promise of objectivity, in the first sentence of the same foreword, the author states: "The Indian is the worst fed, the worst clad, and the worst housed of any racial group in the United States" (p. ix). The author

[2] William V. O'Brien, *The Conduct of Just and Limited War* (New York: Praeger Publishers, 1981), p. 3.
[3] Richard Moran, *Knowing Right from Wrong: The Insanity Defense of Daniel McNaughtan* (New York: The Free Press, 1981), p. 5.
[4] (New York: David McKay Company, 1956), p. xiii.

here is not stating facts, as he has said he would do, but is stating opinions. Furthermore, these opinions clearly illustrate his own assumptions about the Indian condition. It would not be difficult to predict his stand if he were to debate the "Indian problem." From this first sentence on, you should realize that this is a biased author and read to see how his assumptions influence the way in which he "states the facts as he found them" and then generalizes from these "facts."

3. *The author's organizational pattern.* You learned in Chapter 7 that in most patterns used to inform you, such as the topical and chronological, the intent or purpose is stated right away in the introductory remarks. When the author does not immediately state the intent but, rather, reserves it until the end, you can usually anticipate a persuasive purpose. Watch a few television commercials to test this out. You know they are meant to be persuasive. Notice how often the point of the commercial—what you are supposed to do or believe—is reserved until the end.

4. *The source of the published material.* If you are trying to judge the degree of bias in a magazine or newspaper article, find out if the publication itself is noted for printing material that is slanted and biased in a particular direction. Determine, particularly, if you can expect an identifiable political or religious slant from a particular magazine or newspaper.

In-Chapter Exercise 3

The following excerpt comes from a newsletter that is affiliated with a political party. Read it through, and write in the blank provided which party was responsible for printing it.

More Party Lines

We hate to keep doing this to you every month, but we can't seem to restrain ourselves. Yes, this is yet another tale of mirth and/or woe about those folks on the other side of the fence, THE REPUBLICANS.

As you know, the GOP has at its disposal a batallion of computers to aid them in their fund-raising activities. During one such money-making effort, President Reagan signed a computerized letter that was addressed to the Church of God in Comack, N.J. It began like this:

"Dear Mr. God: As Your President, I am calling upon you to make a most unusual sacrifice." He then asked Mr. God to contribute $120 to help GOP senatorial candidates and further added, "I'm not asking everyone to contribute . . . only proud, flagwaving Americans like you who I know are willing to sacrifice to keep our nation strong."

To date, the White House has received no reply from its Heavenly Correspondent.[5]

Which political party do you think printed this? _____

[5] From the *Texas Democratic Party Lines*, Vol. III, No. 4, May 1982.

You can expect publications of this type to contain bias and prejudice, and it is more fun to read them when you are able to spot it. Expecting it can also make you more resistant to it.

Deliberate Emotional Appeals

1. *The use of emotionally loaded language.* Notice the language used by the author. You have learned that the quickest and easiest way to change your attitudes or to persuade you is to use language that will create a strong emotional reaction. When authors regularly use language that arouses you emotionally, instead of neutral, objective language, it is often a sign of bias and a sign that they are either consiously or unconsciously trying to persuade you to accept their views.

In-Chapter Exercise 4

Read the following paragraph from an article entitled "The Worldwide Epidemic of Drug and Alcohol Abuse," and underline all words that could cause an emotional response in a reader.

Each year millions slide down the slippery slope of alcohol and drug abuse into addiction, illness, crime and death.

In the United States alone, 10 to 12 million men and women—and their loved ones and families—are crippled by the ravages of alcoholism. Additional millions abuse alcohol at immense cost in health and in lost productivity.

In Canada, it is said, "Alcohol increases business—for hospitals, ambulance drivers, doctors, nurses, undertakers and grave diggers" (E. C. McKenzie).

Alcohol abuse, heroin and other dangerous drugs have swept through Europe like a brushfire. Soviet culture, too, is paying enormous social and economic costs.

Developing nations are plagued with drug problems—both ancient and modern. In this part of the world hundreds of millions crave addicting agents to ease their miseries and problems in life.

These methods of coping are unhealthy solutions! It is time we understood why—and found the way out of today's greatest social plague besetting this supposedly enlightened 20th century.[6]

Define:
denotative meaning

Define:
connotative meaning

Did you underline the word "alcohol" in In-chapter Exercise 4? Notice how it is used. You could consult the dictionary for the **denotative** or dictionary meaning of this word and find that it means "the intoxicating principle of fermented liquors, produced by fermentation of certain carbohydrates." The writer of this passage did not, however, have only that meaning in mind when he refers to alcohol. The word, *as he uses it*, is accompanied by strong negative feelings about the effects of alcohol abuse that give the word "extra" meanings beyond the dictionary definition. The "extra" meanings are called **connotative** meanings.

[6] By Donald D. Schroeder in *Plain Truth*, May 1982, p. 5.

Define:
**meaning-
less
words**

_____

Define:
semanti-
cist

_____

If you were to ask several people to define such words as "good," "bad," or "progress," each person would probably give you a slightly different definition, and none of the definitions would correspond exactly with the dictionary definition. Words with strong connotative meanings that evoke different emotional responses from different individuals are called **meaningless words** by some general (semanticists) because there is no specific meaning held in common by all people. Such words are also sometimes called **emotionally loaded words**.

Define:
**emotional-
ly loaded
word**

_____

Notice some other examples of such language in the passage just quoted. Did you underline "slide down the slippery slope of alcohol and drug abuse," "loved ones and families . . . are crippled by the ravages of alcoholism," "alcohol increases business—for . . . grave diggers," "dangerous drugs," "millions crave addicting agents," and "today's greatest social plague?" If one of your family members is an alcoholic, such language will evoke especially strong emotional responses in you. On the other hand, if you have never seen anyone drunk or high, you will still adopt a negative attitude toward alcohol and drug abuse if you allow the language in this paragraph to affect your emotions.

Define:
**vivid
emotional
description**

_____

2. _The use of **vivid emotional description.**_ Vivid emotional description can create a mental picture that works on your emotions and persuades you to change your views and even your actions. An author writing about child abuse, for instance, can create a mental picture of an abused child that might persuade you to contribute time or money to prevent such abuse.

3. _The use of **figurative analogies.**_ The figurative analogy compares two items from radically different categories. When it is used to support, it is actually little more than an embellishment. It is impressive to say that the present government policy toward inflation is "a double-edged sword," or that Communist governments are "like hungry wolves devouring innocent sheep." These statements prove nothing, however. Governments are not literally like swords or wolves. Figurative analogies, like emotionally loaded language, usually appeal to your feelings rather than to your reason. They are usually also evidence of an author's strong feelings and own personal bias.

Define:
**figurative
analogy**

_____

Define:
**emotional-
ly
loaded
example**

_____

_____

4. _The use of a single **emotionally loaded example.**_ The single, emotionally loaded example is also usually a sign of bias. Suppose, for instance, that an author were arguing that the drinking age should be raised to age 21. Rather than quoting available statistics about how damaging alcohol is to most teenagers, you read instead about an 18-year-old boy who got drunk, wrecked the car, killed his friend, and injured himself for life. This is an impressive example, but by itself it cannot be used to prove that the drinking age should be raised. A more effective proof might be statistics showing the effects of alcohol on a large group of teenagers. The 18-year-old boy, interesting and memorable as he is, appeals to your emotions. Used alone as "proof," he is also a sign of the author's own bias against teenage drinking.

Define:
tone

_____

_____

5. _The manipulation of **tone.**_[7] The tone of an author's writing will often give you an idea of the author's true feelings and attitudes toward the subject and, con-

_____

[7] Turn back to page 27 and reread I. A. Richards's observations about tone for a more complete understanding of how it influences meaning.

sequently, can also indicate bias. You know that the tone of voice you use in speaking tells your listener a great deal about how you feel and think about your subject. You can say, for example, that "that professor is really something else" in a complimentary or in an insulting tone of voice. Tone is present on the written page just as it is in speech. It is somewhat more difficult to detect there because there is no vocal inflection to indicate attitude. Instead, the reader has to look at the writer's choice of language to discover the tone and attitude toward the subject.

In-Chapter Exercise 5

Here are two sentences that say the same thing, basically. Notice, however, how the choice of words indicates two very different attitudes:

Sentence 1

The prisoner was executed according to schedule.

Sentence 2

The prisoner was dragged from his cell, strapped to the electric chair, and murdered right on schedule.

1. If these sentences were read aloud, which would probably be read with a calm, unemotional tone of voice?

   _____

2. Which sentence would you guess was written by an author strongly biased against capital punishment?

   _____

Define:
irony

_____

_____

Define:
satire

_____

_____

Define:
deride

_____

_____

Notice, as you read anything, whether the author's "tone of voice" is formal, informal, angry, serious, solemn and inspiring, insulting, or funny as another means for discovering strong feelings and bias.

It is particularly important that you be sensitive to tone when an author is being ironic. **Irony,** or an ironic tone, is used by satirists to deride and ridicule, usually with the hope that a bad situation will be improved or changed. The technique of irony is to say exactly the opposite of what is actually meant. The author counts on the reader, however, to be clever enough to see what is actually meant. The author also hopes to persuade the reader to believe the opposite of what is actually said.

In-Chapter Exercise 6

Here are some excerpts from Art Buchwald's newspaper column of May 23, 1972, in which he speaks ironically about the ownership of handguns. He entitles his piece "Make Handgun Ownership Mandatory for Everyone," and says that Congress should require by law that everyone in the United States own a gun. He adds:

No country in the world offers its citizens a greater choice of guns than the United States. There are snubnosed guns that can fit in a woman's handbag . . . For those who are on relief and unemployed the government could supply surplus weapons from the armed forces at the same time they give out food stamps and unemployment checks.

1. What does this author, on the surface, seem to be saying about handgun

   ownership? _____

   _____

2. What is he actually saying? _____

   _____

3. What effect does he expect this text to have on the reader?_____

   _____

In-Chapter Exercise 7

Handgun ownership is still a controversial issue. Here is Ann Landers, writing 10 years after Buchwald, on July 19, 1982, and expressing exactly the same opinion. She does not use irony, however, but states her opinion directly:

No one goes hunting with a Saturday-night special, nor have I ever seen one decorating a wall. Palm-sized guns are made for one reason only—to kill people. I agree there should be a stiff penalty for anyone who commits a crime with a weapon but there should also be a law that requires the registration of all guns, and it should be strictly enforced, which it is not.

1. What does the author say about handgun ownership? _____

   _____

2. What effect does she expect this text to have on the reader?

   _____

3. In your opinion, which was the more persuasive, the Buchwald or the Landers text? _____ Why? _____

_____

_____

Both direct statement and irony can be effective ways of persuading readers to accept certain beliefs. An author who uses irony, however, adds a compliment to the reader. Irony always suggests that the reader is intelligent enough to read a passage and recognize that the author is biased and actually means exactly the opposite of what the words seem to say.

Irony is an old technique. You will find it employed not only in modern but also in ancient writings. Whenever you overlook it, however, you virtually miss the main idea of the text.

Incomplete or Faulty Reasoning

1. *The use of incomplete supporting material.* In Chapter 12 it was pointed out that authors sometimes select and stack their supporting material to favor a particular stand or point of view. Such stacking is misleading and can cause you to make faulty judgments because you do not have complete information.

In-Chapter Exercise 8

The following excerpt is from a criminal justice textbook. Note how the author has selected a particularly forceful example to support his position on prisoner abuse.

A final kind of prison violence is regulatory violence carried out under the auspices of the prison organization and administration. . . . One drug, Anectine, is used systematically as part of a program to modify the behavior of uncooperative prisoners, and while it may not be effective, its proponents talk about it in a way that provides adequate evidence that it is a form of violence.

According to Dr. Arthur Nugent, chief psychiatrist at Vacaville and an enthusiast for the drug, it induces "sensations of suffocation and drowning." The subject experiences feelings of deep horror and terror, "as though he were on the brink of death." While he is in this condition a therapist scolds him for his misdeeds and tells him to shape up or expect more of the same. Candidates for Anectine treatment were selected for a range of offenses: "frequent fights, verbal threatening, deviant sexual behavior, stealing, unresponsiveness to the group therapy programs." Dr. Nugent told the *San Francisco Chronicle*, "Even the toughest inmates have come to fear and hate the drug. I don't blame them, I wouldn't have one treatment myself for the world." Declaring he was anxious to continue the experiment, he added, "I'm at a loss as to why everybody's upset over this" (Mitford, 1971:142).

Because the violence is carried out under the auspices of "treatment" does not make it any less real.[8]

1. What is the example in this passage?

   _____

2. What main idea is this example used to illustrate?

   _____

3. How does this selected example stack the argument against prisoner abuse?

   _____

4. How does the author feel about this type of prisoner violence?

   _____

5. How does Dr. Nugent, the psychiatrist in the passage, feel about it?

   _____

6. How do you feel about it?

   _____

Besides noticing how authors select their supporting material, there are other specific questions you can ask about authors' use of supporting material, which may also reveal their biases. These questions include: (1) *How much supporting material is used?* Do authors get specific, and support what they have to say, or do they stay on an abstract, general level throughout, stating mainly opinions rather than facts? Remember the old statement, "Don't confuse me with the facts." Whenever authors are free from facts, it is easier for them to wander from the truth. If an author says, in effect, that this is true because I say it is true, look carefully to see if there is any evidence for you to believe that it is. (2) Ask also *whether or not the facts authors use are verifiable.* Could you, for instance, go to another source and find the same facts stated there? Or are they, perhaps, modified or even invented by the author? (3) Note particularly *how authors use statistics.* They also can be carefully selected and stacked to defend a particular point of view.

Define:
historical analogy

_____

_____

2. *The use of the **historical analogy**.* The historical analogy, which is a comparison of a present condition with a past condition, usually carries with it the implication that if something worked or was desirable in the past, it will likewise work or be desirable now. Authors who argue that the United States will lose

---

[8] Howard C. Daudistel, William B. Sanders, and David F. Luckenbill, Eds., *Criminal Justice: Situation and Decisions* (New York: Holt, Rinehart and Winston, 1979), p. 324.

power because Rome and England did, or that depression always follows inflation because it did in the 1930s, always lay themselves open to the following question: Are the two time periods being compared so similar in every respect that the end result of one will necessarily be the end result of the other? When the answer is "no," this form of support loses its persuasive power.

Define:
**literal
analogy**

3. *The use of **literal analogies**.* The same question as to comparability can be asked when a literal analogy (a comparison of two items from the same general category, like a government or school system) is used to prove a statement. If an author argues that the honor system will work in high school because it works in college, the test, again, is to ask if high school and college are so similar that what works in one place will work in the other. An answer of no demonstrates faulty reasoning.

Define:
**Irrelevant
data**

4. *The use of **irrelevant data**.* Another sign of bias is the use of irrelevant data that may be impressive or persuasive in itself, but which really has nothing to do with the main argument. The use of statistics sometimes falls in this category.

One of the purposes of the book *Alcatraz Is Not an Island* is to show why American Indians should be given free and clear title to Alcatraz Island. In the book the island is personified as a woman: "her joy knew no bounds . . . Soon her elder children came to purify her desecrated body and to relieve and release the tortured ghosts that suffered there."[9] You might find this passage persuasive and impressive, but it is irrelevant to the argument and does not prove that anyone should do anything. Other types of irrelevant argument that are used to mislead your thoughts and feelings rather than to logically prove or disapprove an argument are (1) to attack the source of the argument rather than the argument itself ("How can you believe men who argue against legalized abortion when you know that they don't have to have the babies?") and (2) to suggest guilt and consequent incompetence because of past or present casual associations ("How can we trust a politician who runs around with chorus girls?").

Making Inferences

Define:
imply

Define:
inference

Authors do not always state all of their meaning in clear, straightforward language. You have learned, in this chapter, in fact, that authors sometimes use irony to state the exact opposite of what they mean. You also learned earlier in this chapter that authors' unstated values and assumptions sometimes cause them to hold a particular position and to present their ideas in a biased way. At other times, authors may deliberately state only part of what they have to say and imply the rest, expecting the reader to fill in what is left out. As the reader, you will have to make inferences about what is unstated in such texts if you are to comprehend them accurately. As in the use of irony, the author pays you a compliment at such times by assuming that you are intelligent enough to read what is there and infer the rest. The rest can be either part of the argument or even the conclusion.

[9] Peter Blue Cloud, Ed. (Berkeley: Wingbow Press, 1972), p. 15.

You will understand the idea of supplying part of the meaning better if you think about nonverbal communication that might take place between two people who are conversing. Gestures, body movements, facial expressions, and the tone of voice all tell more than the mere words themselves. In a conversation we listen to the words but add what we learn from the nonverbal cues to gain total comprehension. The Doonesbury strip in Figure 13.1 provides an example of Duke (with the gun) making an inference about why Thadius keeps running. Duke's inference demonstrates his own unstated values and assumptions, a frequent source of humor in the *Doonesbury* strip. Duke's inference is, of course, incorrect and the other character in this strip has to spell out for him what actually can be inferred from Thadius's actions: the fact that he did not hear the command to stop.

Figure 13.1 An incorrect inference.

DOONESBURY   **by Garry Trudeau**

Incorrect inferences can distort your reading of a text just as Duke's interpretation of this situation distorts his perception of what is actually happening. When this occurs, the cause is usually the same as that demonstrated in this Doonesbury strip. You, too, can allow your own assumptions, values, and opinions to interfere with your comprehension of the text. For this reason it is important to try to put aside your own ideas and feelings until you have accurately understood the author.

Authors often imply rather than directly state as a means of persuasion. Authors know that you are more likely to be persuaded if you have to supply some of the connections among ideas or even an unstated conclusion on your own. When you find yourself making a lot of inferences, analyze the text to see if it is primarily factual and informative or opinionated and persuasive. If it is persuasive, as it is likely to be, the inferences you will be drawing will probably help to advance the author's argument.

In-Chapter Exercise 9

In the following example, the author asks a question and makes some observations, but leaves you to infer the answer:

"Moon Shot" Public Policy Making

Can we conquer drug abuse the same way we conquered the moon? America's tradition of "good old Yankee know-how" has led citizens and governments to believe there are "quick-fix" solutions to age-old people problems like crime and addiction, misbehavior, mental illness, overanxiety, underanxiety, unhappiness, nervousness, sadness and rage. Policymakers, their advisers and constituents presumably believe that if some terrible social problem exists, government need only pass the necessary laws, erect the agencies to implement them, pour in the money and manpower, and somehow out will pop the magic solution.[10]

Which of the following conclusions are you expected to infer?

_____ Government programs solve social problems.

_____ There are no simple, quick answers to social problems.

If you checked the second answer, you were correct. The author has led you to accept this conclusion. Go back through the passage and underline the words and phrases that urge you to think that there are no quick answers to social problems. Notice, also, that you may find it easier to accept this conclusion since you derived it yourself from the material stated. If it had been directly stated at the beginning of the paragraph in topic sentence form, the passage might have been less convincing.

Chapter Summary

In order to analyze persuasive texts you need to be able to detect the ways in which authors work to change your beliefs and actions. In overtly persuasive texts, where the author's motives are clearly to persuade, you can expect to find appeals to your judgment of the author's character, to your emotions, and to your reason. When the author's motive is not clear, but you think that it leans towards persuasion, you should analyze the persuasive appeals further and look for additional signs of bias in the text. Detecting signs of bias will not only help you determine the author's motive—it will also help you protect yourself against unwanted persuasion. The signs of bias associated with the author and the text may include the author's affiliations, the author's underlying assumptions, the organizational pattern, and the source of the published text. The signs of deliberate emotional appeal are the use of emotionally loaded language, vivid description, figurative analogies, single, emotionally loaded examples, and the manipulation of tone, including the use of irony. Signs of incomplete or faulty reasoning include carefully selected and stacked supporting material to represent only one side of an issue, sketchy or nonverifiable supporting material, the use of historical and literal analogies and of irrelevant data. Some authors with a persuasive intent deliberately leave some of their meaning

[10] David J. Bellis, *Heroin and Politicians: The Failure of Public Policy to Control Addiction in America* (Westport, Conn.: Greenwood Press, 1981), p. xiv.

and sometimes even their conclusions unstated. When this is the case the reader must make inferences. The reader should read objectively in order to make accurate inferences and not distort the author's meaning.

Your Summary

Jot a summary of the main points in this chapter in brief outline form.

What is the subject of this chapter?

What did the author say about it?

END-CHAPTER EXERCISES

I. Practice in Detecting Bias

   A. *Emotionally Loaded Language.* Read the brief passages below, under-line the emotionally loaded language, and answer the questions:

1. Psychologists are still debating whether Eichmann possessed a grossly de-mented personality or whether he was a cowering bureaucrat deferring to the demented Nazis above him.[11]

   a. How does the loaded language in this passage influence your

   attitude toward Eichmann and the Nazis? _____

   b. Is it convincing proof? yes ____ no ____ Why or why not?

---

[11] Reprinted by permission of G. P. Putnam's Sons from *The Survival Factor: Israeli Intelligence from World War I to the Present* by Stanley A. Blumberg and Gwinn Owens, p. 19. Copyright © 1981 by Stanley A. Blumberg and Gwinn Owens.

2. Mention natural gas regulation and you will probably produce a shudder in the average congressman or presidential aide, as he or she recalls the monumental battles that have been fought since the 1940's over federal control of the industry. The combatants tend to view their opponents in exaggerated terms: they are either the minions of the devilish oil lobby or northern socialists bent on pillaging southwestern colonies of their natural resources. The regulation of natural gas is, in the words of a House committee staffer, ''a theological issue.''[12]

    a. Identify the two factions in the regulation of the natural

    gas issue: _____

    _____

    b. What is the effect of describing them both in loaded language?

    _____

    _____

B. *Predicting Bias from Titles*
    1. Read through the following list of actual book titles and place a checkmark next to the ones that are probably controversial and probably contain bias:

    a. *Long Memory: The Black Experience in America* _____

    b. *Migrant Farm Workers: A Caste of Despair* _____

    c. *The Future of U.S.–China Relations* _____

    d. *Heroin and Politicians* _____

    e. *Knowing Right from Wrong* _____

    f. *The Regulation of Natural Gas* _____

    g. *The Conduct of Just and Limited War* _____

    h. *The Survival Factor* _____

    i. *The Origins of the Equal Rights Amendment* _____

    j. *Class and Culture in Cold War America* _____

    k. *Day Care* _____

[12] M. Elizabeth Sanders, *The Regulation of Natural Gas: Policy and Politics, 1938–1978* (Philadelphia: Temple University Press, 1981), p. xiii.

What types of clues caused you to check the titles you did? _____

_____

_____

    C. *Emotionally Loaded Examples.* Read the following passage, and number the emotionally loaded examples. Then make some observations about the quality and quantity of these examples by answering the questions below.

A few days before Christmas, 1943, gangs of workers armed with scissors and matches roamed through one of Detroit's largest aircraft factories, cutting neckties off supervisors and management personnel and placing lighted matches in the shoes of fellow workers.*

    St. Louis bus drivers staged a surprise strike on Memorial Day, 1944, congregating jovially around the bus barns by day, but disrupting a government-sponsored back-to-work meeting at night as they drank, played cards, and heckled anti-strike speakers.**

    Three hundred welders employed by Cadillac in Detroit walked off the job in December, 1944, to protest restrictions against smoking at work.***

    These bizarre and seemingly trivial outbursts, along with thousands of other disruptions, demonstrations, and strikes like them, expressed rebellion against work, authority, and hierarchy, and they constituted an important manifestation of the working class for independence that emerged during and after World War II.[13]

    a. What does the author want you to believe as a result of reading these examples?

_____

_____

    b. Is this a fair sample of examples or do they seem to be selected and stacked to favor a particular point of view?

_____

_____

* *Business Week*, March 18, 1944, p. 88. *Detroit Free Press*, December 25, 1943, p. 1.; December 27, 1943, p. 1.

** *St. Louis Post-Dispatch*, June 2, 1944, p. 31.; June 3, 1944, p. 1.

*** *Detroit Times*, December 17, 1944, p. 3.

[13] George Lipsitz, *Class and Culture in Cold War America: "A Rainbow at Midnight"* (New York: Praeger Publications, 1981), p. 1.

    c. Note that the author gives sources for the examples listed in the starred footnotes on page 270. Are citing these sources a convincing form of proof?

_____

Why or why not? _____

_____

  D. _Figurative Analogy_

    1. Read the following sentence and answer the questions that follow it.

Cracking down on worldwide narcotics trafficking is like emptying the ocean with a teacup.[14]

    a. What two objects are being compared? _____

    b. What is the main idea of this sentence? _____

    c. Does this figurative analogy provide convincing proof of the

main idea? yes _____ no _____ Why or why not? _____

_____

  E. _Irrelevant Information._ Underline the material in the following passage that is mainly irrelevant and ornamental and that is included to influence your thoughts and feelings about Israel.

Zionism was fathered by a vision, mothered by necessity, and nurtured by political and military intelligence. The vision is almost as old as Judaism, the necessity was made acute by Adolf Hitler, and the intelligence explains to a great degree why the State of Israel exists today.[15]

    a. Is this material convincing proof? yes _____ no _____ Why or

why not? _____

  F. _Statistics._ Underline statistical information in the following passage that might influence your thinking about the effectiveness of government programs in controlling heroin addiction:

1. Since 1969 the federal government has spent several _billion_ dollars treating heroin addicts. While in 1971 there were only three hundred federally

---

[14] Jeff Zhorne, "The Drug Smugglers' Challenge," _The Plain Truth,_ May 1982, p. 34.

[15] Reprinted by permission of G. P. Putnam's Sons from _The Survival Factor: Israeli Intelligence from World War I to the Present_ by Stanley A. Blumberg and Gwinn Owens, p. 17. Copyright © 1981 by Stanley A. Blumberg and Gwinn Owens.

funded programs treating 16,000 addicts, by 1973 over 1,000 such centers were providing drug-free and methadone maintenance treatment to about 75,000 addict-clients. In 1977 100,000 addicts were enrolled in federally funded treatment projects, and an additional 170,000 nonfederally funded treatment "slots" were available nationwide. Between 1969 and 1974. . . . federal addiction treatment and rehabilitation budgets jumped from $28 million to over $300 million a year. What has this outlay accomplished?[16]

    a. What is the issue in this passage? _____

    _____

    b. What conclusion are you to infer about the effectiveness of

    these programs? _____

    _____

    c. Are the statistics in the passage convincing proof of the con-

    clusion? yes _____ no _____ Why or why not? _____

    _____

Underline statistical information in the following paragraph that might influence your thinking about the importance of providing day-care centers for children:

2. Today over 50 percent of mothers in the United States work outside the home, and this figure is expected to rise to 75 percent by 1990. Still more striking, the fastest-growing segment of working mothers is among those with children under two. Whether one sees this trend as good or bad, potentially reversible or here to stay, it is a demographic reality of tremendous import. For the question is not only who will care for these children while their parents work, but also who will pay for the care, and will it help or harm children?[17]

    a. What is the issue in this passage? _____

    _____

    b. What main idea are the statistics used to prove? _____

    _____

[16] David J. Bellis, *Heroin and Politicians: The Failure of Public Policy to Control Addiction in America* (Westport, Conn.: Greenwood Press, 1981), pp. xii–xiv.
[17] Reprinted by permission of the publisher, from Edward F. Zigler and Edmund W. Gordon (Eds.), *Day Care: Scientific and Social Policy Issues* (Boston: Auburn House Publishing Co., 1982), p. v.

    c. Do the statistics convincingly prove this idea? yes _____

no _____ Why or why not? _____

_____

    G. *Tone.* Read the following passage, underline the words and phrases that express the author's attitude toward the subject, and answer the questions about tone that appear below:

Fifteen years after the end of World War II a pitiable figure lay blindfolded on a bed in a suburban house near Buenos Aires. He was a prisoner in a hideout, the captive of the State of Israel. An efficient and dedicated corps of secret intelligence agents had ended one of the great manhunts of all time by tracking him down, ending his routine, middle-class existence in Argentina, ten thousand miles from Germany.

The helpless prisoner accepted his fate. His concern was for his family. ''How will my wife and sons live?''

His guard was not without compassion. ''No harm will come to them. They'll manage all right without you. But tell me, please, you who worry so much about *your* children, how could you and your colleagues murder little children in the tens and hundreds of thousands?''

The prisoner was willing to respond. ''Today I don't understand how we could have done such things. I was always on the side of the Jews. I was striving to find a satisfactory solution to their problem. I did what everybody else was doing—I wanted to get on in life.''

Thus did Eichmann explain away 6 million murders.[18]

    a. What attitude toward Eichmann does the author seem to hold

in the first part of this passage? _____

_____

    b. What does the last sentence indicate about the author's actual

attitude? _____

_____

    c. This author has used a technique in the first part of this passage to state the opposite of what he actually thinks about

Eichmann. What is this technique called? _____

_____

[18] Reprinted by permission of G. P. Putnam's Sons from *The Survival Factor: Israeli Intelligence from World War I to the Present* by Stanley A. Blumberg and Gwinn Owens, p. 18. Copyright © 1981 by Stanley A. Blumberg and Gwinn Owens.

H. *Making Inferences.* Read the following passage about the importance of studying the future need for day-care centers, and answer the questions:

We do not know what we need to know about day care because, as a society, we have so far failed to commit ourselves to the kind of longitudinal studies required. Soon it may be too late. Perhaps the most relevant parallel is to research on the effects of television. How could we have allowed such a major influence as television to develop without better research on its effects on children? We certainly would not allow a new drug to be introduced without more adequate inquiry into its likely effects.[19]

a. What three items are being compared in this passage that, according to the author, should be carefully monitored and studied?

(1) _____

(2) _____

(3) _____

b. What type of analogy is being used here where a current prob-

lem is compared with a problem in the past? _____

_____

c. Is this type of analogy an effective type of proof? yes _____

no _____ Why or why not? _____

d. As a result of these comparisons, what can you infer that the author believes about the importance of studying the future

need for day-care centers? _____

_____

I. The following excerpt comes from an article written by the columnist George F. Will right after the historic Supreme Court vote of 9–0 in favor of legalized abortion. The author uses a number of persuasive techniques in this passage. Get ready to read by setting aside your own present ideas about abortion. Then read the passage and answer the questions:

[19] Reprinted by permission of the publisher, from Edward F. Zigler and Edmund W. Gordon (Eds.), *Day Care: Scientific and Social Policy Issues* (Boston: Auburn House Publishing Co., 1982) p. vi.

Discretionary Killing

But for now the issue is abortion, and it is being trivialized by cant about "a woman's right to control her body." Dr. Kass notes that "the fetus simply is not a mere part of a woman's body. One need only consider whether a woman can ethically take thalidomide while pregnant to see that this is so." Dr. Kass is especially impatient with the argument that a fetus with a heartbeat and brain activity "is indistinguishable from a tumor in the uterus, a wart on the nose, or a hamburger in the stomach." But that argument is necessary to justify discretionary killing of fetuses on the current scale, and some of the experiments that some scientists want to perform on live fetuses.

Abortion advocates have speech quirks that may betray qualms. Homeowners kill crabgrass. Abortionists kill fetuses. Homeowners do not speak of "terminating" crabgrass. But Planned Parenthood of New York City, which evidently regards abortion as just another form of birth control, has published an abortion guide that uses the word "kill" only twice, once to say what some women did to themselves before legalized abortion, and once to describe what some contraceptives do to sperm. But when referring to the killing of fetuses, the book, like abortion advocates generally, uses only euphemisms, like "termination of potential life."

Abortion advocates become interestingly indignant when opponents display photographs of the well-formed feet and hands of a nine-week-old fetus. People avoid correct words and object to accurate photographs because they are uneasy about saying and seeing what abortion is. It is not the "termination" of a hamburger in the stomach.[20]

a. Is the author biased in favor of or against abortion?_____

b. What are your biases on this issue?_____

Were your beliefs influenced or changed by reading this?

yes _____ no _____

c. Look up "discretionary" if necessary. What is "discretionary killing?"

_____

Does this title give a clue to the author's motives and whether

or not you can expect bias to be present? yes _____ no _____

d. Is the language primarily objective or emotional? Give some

examples:_____

_____

[20] *Newsweek*, September 20, 1976, p. 96.

e. What types of supporting materials are used to advance this author's argument? Are they primarily factual and verifiable or are they slanted and emotional? Give some examples:

_____

_____

_____

f. What is the author's object in commenting on the opposition's use of ``terminate'' instead of ``kill?''

_____

_____

g. Are there any vivid emotional descriptions in this passage?

Give examples:_____

_____

h. What basic assumptions do you think this author holds about human life that cause him to take this particular stand on abortion?

_____

_____

i. The author refers to sources that are both for and against abortion. Which is his anti-abortion source?

_____

Which is his pro-abortion source?_____

Which of these sources seems to be more reliable in this passage?

_____

Give reasons for your answer._____

_____

_____

_____

j. How would you describe the tone of the last sentence in the passage?

_____

What does it tell you about the author's attitude toward abortion?

_____

II. Application to Your Other Reading

A. Look through the Tables of Contents of your textbooks, and list one chapter title on a controversial issue and define the issue. Read selectively in this chapter to determine the author's position on this issue. List at least two signs of bias that helped you determine the author's position. Your completed assignment should look like this:

---

1. Textbook: _Management: Theory, Process and Practice_ [21]
   Controversial chapter title: "Modern Schools of Management Thought"
   Issue: Which is the best school?
   Author's position: A synthesis of the three schools would be best
   Signs of Bias:
   1. States position directly—overt persuasion
   2. Uses loaded language to describe individual schools: "gives lip service," "fails to see the complete picture."

B. Go to the browsing section of your library ard copy down five book titles that indicate probable controversial topics and biased authors.

III. Discussion and Class Activities

A. Bring one magazine to class, and describe whether or not it seems to be biased in favor of or against a particular political or religious ideology.

B. Read the letters to the editor in your newspaper, and find one that contains examples of some signs of bias. Identify and analyze the persuasive effectiveness of these signs. Discuss them in class.

C. Listen to a political speech on television, and make a list of emotional, ethical, and logical appeals used by the speaker. Discuss them in class.

IV. Vocabulary Review
A. Specialized Vocabulary

1. persuasive appeal _____

2. emotional appeal _____

[21] By Richard M. Hodgetts, 3rd ed. (Hinsdale, Ill.: The Dryden Press, 1982).

3. ethical appeal _____

4. logical appeal _____

5. signs of bias _____

6. denotative meaning _____

7. connotative meaning _____

8. meaningless words _____

B. (General Vocabulary)

1. rhetoric _____

2. ethos _____

3. affiliation _____

4. semanticist _____

5. satire _____

6. deride _____

7. imply _____

8. inference _____

C. Match the following signs of bias with their descriptions. Locate the best description and write the number next to the sign of bias.

_____ **1.** author's affiliations

_____ **2.** author's assumptions

_____ **3.** persuasive pattern of organization

_____ **4.** source of the published material

_____ **5.** emotionally loaded words

_____ **6.** vivid, emotional description

_____ **7.** figurative analogy

_____ **8.** emotionally loaded example

_____ **9.** tone

_____ **10.** irony

_____ **11.** selected and stacked supporting material

_____ **12.** historical analogy

_____ **13.** literal analogy

_____ **14.** irrelevant data

1. states the exact opposite of what the author really means.
2. indicates the author's attitude toward the subject.
3. main point reserved until the end.
4. words with strong connotative meanings that engage one's emotions.
5. impressive or persuasive material that has nothing to do with the main argument.
6. material carefully selected to favor a particular point of view.
7. creates a mental picture that causes an emotional response.
8. indicate author's background, interests, experience that might lead to bias.
9. one example that engages your emotions.
10. comparison of two items in same general category with implication that both will turn out the same.
11. the magazine or newspaper itself may be biased or slanted.
12. comparison of something in present with something in past with implication that both will turn out the same.
13. compares two items from radically different categories.
14. values and opinions an author assumes to be true.

D. Group the signs of bias listed in End-chapter Exercise C in categories to help you remember them. Use the maps below to help you.

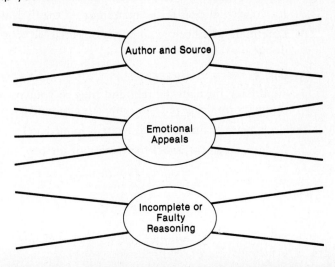

FURTHER READING

The following works provide further information about some of the ideas discussed in Part IV of this book.

Aristotle. *The Rhetoric.* Trans. Lane Cooper. New York: Appleton-Century-Crofts, 1932.

Corbett, Edward P. J. *Classical Rhetoric for the Modern Student.* New York: Oxford University Press, 1965.

Goodman, Kenneth S. and Olive S. Niles. *Reading: Process and Program.* Champaign, Ill.: National Council of Teachers of English, 1970.

Hayakawa, S. I. *Language in Thought and Action.* New York: Harcourt Brace, 1949.

Richards, I. A. *Practical Criticism.* New York: Harcourt Brace, 1929.

Develop a System for Close, Critical Reading

Because of its complexity, reading is difficult to systematize in a step-by-step process. It can be organized somewhat, however. Study the following three-stage system for doing close, critical reading. Then, adapt it to your own reading purposes.

STAGE 1   Before You Read

1. Survey and mark the major chunks of material. Number the chunks.

2. Ask questions about the author, the author's purpose, the subject, the occasion, and the intended audience. Classify the text. Anticipate what the author might say.

3. Think about your purpose for reading the text and the reading methods and strategies you will use.

STAGE 2   As You Read

1. Read actively, looking for the subject, focus, and main ideas.

2. Underline selectively, take marginal notes, and/or write brief summaries of sections of material.

3. Circle or underline words that interest you or that you must learn to understand the subject. Jot word meanings in the margin.

4. Jot your own ideas in the margin or on the fly leaves of the book.

5. Determine whether the author is objective or biased and whether you agree or disagree.

STAGE 3   After You Read

1. Skim back through the text and then in your own words write a summary in outline form using phrases only. An alternative is to map the chapter.

2. To remember the material, recite it immediately and review it periodically.

3. Make a judgment about the quality of the text and its final value to you.

APPENDIX
A Vocabulary Builder

There is a high correlation between vocabulary and success. Studies of the vocabularies of business executives show that top executives have more extensive vocabularies than the people they supervise. Other studies have made it clear that the best students also have the best vocabularies. For this reason almost 50 percent of the Scholastic Aptitude Test consists of a vocabulary test. College administrators know that a good vocabulary is the mark of a good student and so, in order to locate good students, they administer vocabulary tests to find them.

If you are worried that you do not have a good vocabulary at present and, therefore, may not ever be a good student, stop worrying. At some colleges, students have been given courses in vocabulary building and their grades have improved. You can do the same thing yourself. One reason studies improve when vocabularies improve is because we think with words. Consequently, the more words we know, the better we are able to think. Another reason students improve when their vocabularies improve is because larger vocabularies permit them to read and listen to more complicated material and to express themselves more effectively. Academic communication, which is the heart of education, relies on the student knowing and being able to learn and retain many new words.

If this book accomplishes its purpose and turns you into an habitual reader, your vocabulary will automatically begin to improve. You can speed up this process of improving your personal vocabulary with some systematic vocabulary improvement work. You will be most effective in acquiring an improved vocabulary if you select words to learn that you half-know already, that interest you, and that you know will be useful to you. You are most likely to encounter such words in the books you read and in the college lectures you attend. Search for new words in these sources, and then use the suggestions below to help you learn them.

Use Context

Throughout your reading of this book you have been encouraged to study context to help you determine the meanings of many words. In this book both general and specialized vocabulary was identified for you, and you were asked to jot definitions of them in the margins. Continue to develop this habit in the other books you read. Circle or underline words you do not know and want to learn, read through to the end of the chapter, and then go back and write brief meanings in the margin. Rely on context as much as possible to help you determine word meanings. Go to the dictionary or the glossary if the context does not yield enough meaning.

This practice of underlining and defining words will help you with test preparation as well as reading. Transfer the specialized terms and their meanings to vocabulary lists like those found at the end of each of the chapters in this book, and then memorize these lists before the test. This practice will help you read exam questions as well as answer them effectively.

Analyze Latin and Greek Elements

Besides context, another way of gaining clues to the meanings of words is to break a word down into its prefix, root, and suffix elements, then to determine the meaning of each of these elements and, finally, to use these meanings to help you to form guesses about word meaning. This method of analyzing a word's meaning through its elements is possible because roughly 75 percent of the words in the English language contain elements from the classical Latin and Greek languages. Consequently, if you learn the meanings of some of the most common classical elements that are found over and over again in English words, you will have clues to the meanings of thousands of English words.

You will not be able to use this type of word analysis for all English words. There are three categories of words in your English vocabulary, and word analysis will only work for the third category. The categories are (1) *simple*, (2) *compound*, and (3) *derivative* words. **Simple words,** such as *know, faith, hope, father, learn, under,* are English-root words that do not contain prefixes, suffixes, or roots from classical languages. **Compound words** are made by joining two or more English-root words to give one meaning. Examples are *stepfather, earthquake,* or *son-in-law.* Notice that earth and quake can stand alone as English words. **Derivative words,** however, are made up of one or more classical elements, and their meanings can be analyzed by studying the meaning of their parts. There are thousands of derivative words in the English language, and they are often also the most difficult and most uncommon words. Most derivative words contain two or more syllables. They are formed by adding a prefix, a suffix, or both to a root word. Here is an example:

un	*happi*	*ly*
prefix, meaning not	root	suffix, meaning how done; *ly* is a sign of the adverb

Notice that, unlike the parts of compound words, the prefix and suffix elements in *"unhappily"* cannot stand alone. Nonetheless, by knowing the meanings of the prefix and suffix of this word, you can figure out that it means *not done in a happy manner.* Here is another word that is put together in the same way but that has a less familiar root:

un	*abated*	*ly*
prefix, meaning not	root, meaning to reduce in force or to hold back	suffix, meaning how done; sign of the adverb

An analysis of its parts tells you that *"unabatedly"* means *not held back,* or done with "full steam ahead."

Look at the following list of common elements from Latin and Greek and their meanings. Then use the meanings of these elements to help you take the vocabulary test that follows. Do not use the dictionary. Use only the list of elements and their meanings to help you answer the questions.

Some Latin and Greek Elements and Their Meanings

Latin Prefixes	Meaning
ad-	to
ben-, bon-	good
circum-	around
con-, com-	with, together
de-	away from
e-, ex-	out
in-	not, against
inter-	between
mal-	bad
mis-	wrong
poly-	many
post-	after
pre-	before
pro-	for
re-	back, again
sub-	under
trans-	across

Greek and Latin Roots	Meaning
anthrop-	man
appell-	name
aut-	self
can-, cant-	sing
cid-, cis-	cut, kill
corp-	body
cur-	run

Greek and Latin Roots	Meaning
dic-, dict-	say
duc-, duct-	lead
fac-, fact-	do
grand-	great
gyn-	woman
loc-	speak
man-	hand
medi-	middle
mon-	warn
nasc-, nat-	to be born
nomen-	name
port-	carry
pseud-	false
rect-	right, straight
sanguin-	blood
semi-	half
ten-	have, hold
termin-	boundary, end
ver-	true

Vocabulary Test

1. Circumnavigating a lake is accomplished by sailing (a) rapidly (b) across (c) over (d) around it.
2. When something is transported across the plains, it is carried (a) slowly (b) across (c) rapidly (d) around them.
3. When a week intervenes, it comes (a) between (b) before (c) after (d) during.
4. An automaton is capable of operating (a) skillfully (b) by itself (c) many things (d) one thing at a time.
5. When an employee's position is terminated, it is (a) continued (b) redefined (c) ended (d) begun.
6. A maladjusted mechanism runs (a) well (b) often (c) badly (d) quietly.
7. A polyglot can speak (a) no language (b) one language (c) two languages (d) many languages.
8. A subterranean passage is (a) above ground (b) on the ground (c) in the air (d) under the ground.
9. A premonition is a warning that comes (a) too late (b) before (c) from an authority (d) from superstitious people.
10. Elocution lessons are lessons in (a) speech (b) driving (c) grammar (d) manners.

Match the following words with their meanings. Write the numbers of the definitions in the blanks.

_____ 1. anthropoid   1. bloody

_____ 2. appellation   2. make truthful

_____ 3. autonomous   3. draw forth

_____ 4. cantata   4. a person who does evil

_____ 5. concurrent   5. happening at the same time

_____ 6. educe   6. false name

_____ 7. grandiose   7. not material; without a body

_____ 8. incisive   8. self-governing

_____ 9. incorporeal   9. curse

_____ 10. indict   10. manlike

_____ 11. malediction   11. cutting, sharp

_____ 12. manipulate   12. one who hates mankind

_____ 13. misanthrope   13. story set to music

_____ 14. nativity   14. bring charges against

_____ 15. mediocre   15. name, title

_____ 16. pseudonym   16. birth

_____ 17. rectify   17. impressive, imposing

_____ 18. malefactor   18. operate with the hands

_____ 19. verify   19. to make right, to correct

_____ 20. sanguinary   20. commonplace

More Latin and Greek Elements

The following are additional lists of some of the most common classical prefixes, roots, and suffixes. Memorize them and their meanings. A combination of analyzing the meanings of a word's parts and using context clues to meaning can help you determine the meaning of many difficult words without ever having to look them up in the dictionary. When you have studied the elements and their meanings, try thinking of English words that contain these elements and write them in the blanks provided. Use the dictionary if you need to.

Prefixes	Meaning	English Example
Negative prefixes		
anti-, contra-, contro-, counter-	against	_____
a-, un-, non-, in-, im-, il, ir-	not	_____
Time prefixes		
fore-, pre-, ante-	before	_____
post-, after-	after	_____
Place prefixes		
over-, super-	over	_____
under-, sub-	under	_____
Value prefixes		
pro-	for	_____
ben-	good	_____
Number or size prefixes		
micro-	small	_____
macro-	large	_____
mono-, uni-	one	_____
bi-, di-	two	_____
tri-	three	_____
quad-, tetr-	four	_____
pent-, quint-	five	_____

Prefixes	Meaning	English Example
hex-, sex-	six	_____
hept-, sept-	seven	_____
oct-	eight	_____
nona-	nine	_____
dica-, deci-	ten	_____
centi-	hundred	_____
mil-, kilo-	thousand	_____
prim-, pro-	first	_____
semi-, hemi-	half	_____
multi-, poly-	many	_____
omni-, pan-	all	_____

Latin Roots	Meaning	English Example
agr-	farm	_____
alter-, altra-	other, change	_____
am-, amic-	love, friend	_____
anim-	mind, soul, spirit	_____
aqu-	water	_____
aud-, audit-	hear	_____
cap-, capt-, cept-, cip-	take, seize	_____
carn-	flesh	_____
cogn-	know, be acquainted	_____
cred-	belief, trust	_____

Latin Roots	Meaning	English Example
ego-	I, self	_____
equ-	equal	_____
err-	wander	_____
ferre-	to bring	_____
fin-	end, limit	_____
frag-, fract-	break	_____
grad-, gress-	step, go	_____
homo-	man, human being	_____
junct-	join	_____
jus-, juris-, leg-	law	_____
lev-	light, rise	_____
magn-	large	_____
mar-	sea	_____
mini-	small	_____
mit-, miss-	send	_____
mor-, mort-	die, death	_____
ped-	foot	_____
plic-, pli-	fold	_____
rupt-	break	_____
simil-	like	_____
spec-	see	_____
stat-	stand	_____

Latin Roots	Meaning	English Example
tempor-	time	_____
terr-, ter-	land	_____
turb-	agitate	_____
und-	wave	_____
verb-	word	_____
viv-	live, lively	_____

Greek Roots	Meaning	English Example
arch-	chief, rule	_____
astron-	star	_____
biblio-	book	_____
bio-	life	_____
chrome-	color	_____
chron-	time	_____
cosmo-	world	_____
dent-, dont-	tooth	_____
eu-	well, happy	_____
ge-	earth	_____
gen-	origin, people	_____
graph-	write	_____
gyn-	woman	_____
homo-	same	_____
hydr-	water	

Greek Roots	Meaning	English Example
meter-	measure	_____
pathos-	feeling	_____
philo-	love	_____
phobia-	fear	_____
phone-	sound	_____
psych-	soul (mind)	_____
scope-	see	_____
soph-	wisdom	_____
tele-	far off	_____
theo-	god	_____
thermo-	heat	_____

Latin Suffixes	Meaning	English Example
-able	capable of being	_____
-acity	character, quality	_____
-ferous	bearing, producing	_____
-fy	to make	_____
-ity	state of	_____
-lent	full of	_____
-ment	act of, state of	_____
-mony	state	_____
-ule	small	_____

Greek Suffixes	Meaning	English Example
-geneous, -genous	capable of producing	_____
-graph, -graphy	write	_____
-ite	one of, a follower of	_____
-logy	a way of speaking, the study of	_____
-meter	a measure	_____
-pathy	state of feeling	_____
-scope, -scopy	seeing	_____

Use Spanish If You Know It

Spanish has become the second most commonly used language in the United States. If you know or have studied Spanish, you can often use it to help you determine the meanings of many Latin elements in English words. This works because Spanish is closer to the original Latin language than English is. In some cases, you can use your knowledge of Spanish as a frame of reference to help you remember Latin word parts. For example, you can associate the Latin prefix *ab* meaning *away from* with the Spanish word *abcensia* meaning *absence*. This association will help you remember the meaning of *ab*. Then, when you encounter the word *abstemious,* you will know that it has something to do with keeping away from or being absent from something (in this case, food or drink).

At other times you can use your knowledge of Spanish directly to help you analyze the meaning of an English word. This is most effective when the Latin and the Spanish are almost the same. The Latin prefix *ante*, meaning *before*, for example, is so close to the meaning of the Spanish *antes*, that you do not have to learn the Latin word. Your knowledge of Spanish alone is sufficient to help you discover the meaning of *ante-dated.* Other examples are Spanish *tierra* and Latin *terra,* both meaning *land,* or Spanish *cuerpo* and Latin *corpus,* both meaning *body.* If you know some Spanish, look back at the lists of Latin roots and prefixes, and think of some additional Spanish words that are so close to the Latin that you can use Spanish instead of Latin to help you analyze English words.

Create Word Families

As you study classical roots, in particular, you will begin to notice that several English words are often derived from one root word. It will help you learn whole families of them if you group them on maps, in brief outlines, or in some other form[1] so that you can see the relationships among them and thereby learn them more quickly. Figure A.1 shows a map of words derived from the Latin root *corp-,* meaning *body:*

Figure A.1   A map of words derived from the Latin *corp.*

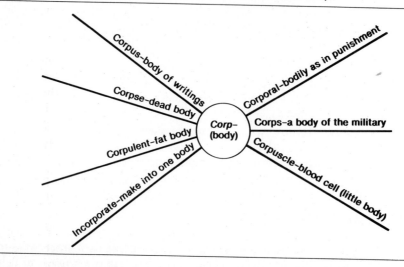

Try making similar maps of *auto* words (meaning *self*) or *phobia* words (meaning *fear of*) or words that derive from *man-/manus-* (meaning *hand*). You can also make entire lists of words that begin with the negative prefixes or with the number and quantity prefixes.

If you are taking biology or some other science, go back through the Latin and Greek elements and think of scientific words that have been created from these elements. You may be able to think of whole families, using such elements as *logy* (meaning *study of*) or *tele* (meaning *far off*).

Use the Dictionary

Every college student needs a good dictionary. Any one of those listed in the bibliography at the end of this appendix will serve you well. Once you acquire a good dictionary you only need to learn to use it. To begin, survey your dictionary just as you would a textbook. See pages 70-75 to remind you how to do this. Notice that besides the words and their definitions your dictionary contains several pages of information at the beginning, including advice on how to use the dictionary;

---

[1] Lou E. Burmeister recommends making word-family "trees" with the root word written on the trunk and the derivative words written on the branches. See her article "Vocabulary Development in the Content Areas through the Use of Morphemes," *Journal of Reading,* March 1976, pp. 481–487.

information on the history of the language; and information on abbreviations, pronunciation, and other matters. At the back of your dictionary will be such information as a directory of colleges and universities, tables with meanings of various symbols, and information that will help you prepare college papers. Check the insides of the front and back covers as well for other useful information.

The words themselves are listed in alphabetical order and set in boldface type. These words are known as **main entries.** The following information will help you read a main entry.

1. Main entries can be both simple and compound words as well as prefixes, suffixes, roots, proper nouns, phrases, foreign phrases, and abbreviations. All are arranged in alphabetical order and defined. Use the guide words at the top of the pages to help you locate the entry you are looking for.

2. Spelling and syllable division are given for all main entries. The preferred spelling is given first. The syllables are separated with dots. Hyphens indicate the word should be hyphenated when you write it.

3. The pronunciation of each main entry is indicated in parentheses following the word. If you do not know how to interpret the pronunciation symbols, refer to the section of your dictionary that explains these.

4. The part of speech for each word is also provided. You will notice that some words may be listed as more than one part of speech. The word *fathom,* for example, can be both a noun and a verb depending on its use in a sentence.

5. The *etymology,* or information about a word's origin, is also included. A great many of the words in English come from Latin, Greek, Old English, and Middle English, which are abbreviated L., Gk., OE., and ME. We have also borrowed words from many other languages, however. Catsup, for instance, comes from Chinese. Look at the etymology key in your dictionary for a list of languages from which English words have been derived, and then notice where words come from when you look them up. The more information you have about a word, the easier it is to remember it.

6. The actual meanings of the word are numbered with the most common meaning or the oldest meaning listed first. Check your dictionary to find out what rationale has been followed to order and list the meanings. You will also have to sort through the meanings for a word to find the definition most suitable to the context.

7. Sometimes the definitions are more difficult to understand than the word itself. When this is the case, look at the *synonyms* (words that are similar in meaning) at the end of the entry to see if they help. Look, for instance, at the following meanings for the word *fatuous* in *The Random House College Dictionary:* "1. complacently foolish or inane; silly. 2. unreal; illusory." Those meanings may help a bit, but the *synonyms* (abbreviated *syn.*) that are listed at the end of the entry may help more. They are: 1. *dense* and *dim-witted. Antonyms* (words that mean the opposite) are also given for some words and can help you arrive at a definition you can understand.

The following[2] is an example of the main entry that illustrates the various types of information that the dictionary can provide:

ec·cen·tric (ik sen′trik, ek-). *adj.* **1.** deviating from the recognized or customary character, practice, etc.; irregular; erratic; peculiar; odd. **2.** *Geom.* not having the same center; not concentric: used esp. of two circles or spheres at least one of which contains the centers of both. **3.** (of an axis, axle, etc.) not situated in the center. **4.** (of a wheel, cam, etc.) having the axis or support away from the center. **5.** *Astron.* deviating from a circular form, as an elliptic orbit. —*n.* **6.** a person who has an unusual or odd personality, set of beliefs, or behavior pattern. **7.** something that is unusual, peculiar, or odd. **8.** *Mach.* a device for converting circular motion into reciprocating rectilinear motion, consisting of a disk fixed somewhat out of center to a revolving shaft, and working freely in a surrounding collar (**eccen′tric strap′**), to which a rod (**eccen′tric rod′**) is attached. [< ML *eccentric(us)* < Gk *ékkentr(os)* out of center (see EC-, CENTER) + L *-icus -IC*] —**ec·cen′tri·cal**, *adj.* —**ec·cen′tri·cal·ly**, *adv.* —**Ant. 1.** normal, ordinary.

Eccentric circles A, Center of small circle; B, Center of large circle

When you have finished reading the entry, answer the following questions about it:

1. If you were typing this word in a paper and had to break it at the end of a line, where could you place the hyphen?

   _____

2. Notice that this word can be pronounced two ways. Which is the most usual

   pronunciation?_____

   How do you pronounce it?_____

3. What is the general meaning of this word when it is used as an adjective?

   _____

4. What is its specialized meaning for geometry?_____

   _____

   For astronomy?_____

5. What is the general meaning of this word when it is used as a noun?

   _____

6. What is its specialized meaning when it is used as part of a machine?

   _____

7. What languages does this word derive from?_____

[2] *The Random House College Dictionary*, Rev. ed. (New York: Random House, 1980), p. 417.

8. What is the meaning of the main, original source word?_____

   _____

9. What are its two antonyms?_____

   _____

10. Which of the meanings of the word does the diagram illustrate?

    _____

In using the dictionary to define difficult words, read the entire entry carefully, as you have just done for the word *eccentric*. Then, select the meaning that best fits the word as you have encountered it, and jot down a simplified meaning in a familiar word or two that will help you remember it. Never copy long dictionary definitions that mean nothing to you—a waste of time that will not help you learn anything.

Other Methods for Vocabulary Development

Besides the recommendations already made, the following ideas can also help you speed up the process of vocabulary development:

1. *Work through the exercises in vocabulary-improvement books.* You can find them in any bookstand. Those that help students prepare for standardized tests such as the Scholastic Aptitude Test (SAT) or the Graduate Record Exam (GRE) can be particularly useful.

2. *Make vocabulary sheets for each class you are taking.* Fold a piece of paper lenghwise twice so that you create four columns. Write the word you want to learn in the first column, the context in which you found it in the second column, the meaning in the third column, and an association to aid your memory in the fourth column.[3] Study these sheets until you know the words.

3. *Make vocabulary cards.* Write the word on the front of the card and the meaning on the back. Or write lists of several words with their meanings on one card. Look at the words and then look away and say the meanings until you have memorized them. You will memorize more quickly if you write the word, say it out loud, and then associate it with something familiar or with a bit of context to help you remember it.

Finally, use the new words you have learned. Don't show off, of course, and use fancy words when it is inappropriate to do so. But begin to notice how other people use the words you have learned and use them yourself in both your writing and your speaking whenever you can.

---

[3] This method is described in more detail in Nancy V. Wood, *College Reading and Study Skills,* 2d ed. (New York: Holt, Rinehart and Winston, 1982), pp. 51–52.

BIBLIOGRAPHY
For Vocabulary Building

Dictionaries

The American Heritage Dictionary, 2nd college ed. New York: Houghton Mifflin, 1982.
The Random House College Dictionary, revised ed. New York: Random House, 1980.
Webster's New Collegiate Dictionary. Springfield, Mass.: G. & C. Merriam, 1981.

Workbooks, Pamphlets, and Texts

Donald M. Ayers. *English Words from Latin and Greek Elements*. Tucson, Ariz.: The University of Arizona Press, 1980.

Edgar Dale, Joseph O'Rourke, and Henry A. Bamman. *Techniques of Teaching Vocabulary*. Palo Alto, Calif.: Field Educational Publications, 1971.

George W. Feinstein. *Programed College Vocabulary 3600*. Englewood Cliffs, N.J.: Prentice-Hall, 1969.

An Outline for Dictionary Study. Springfield, Mass.: G. & C. Merriam, 1954.

GLOSSARY

All specialized vocabulary in this Glossary is printed in bold-face type; general vocabulary is printed in regular type; and allusions are identified with a wavy line. See pages 4–5 for additional explanation about these three types of vocabulary.

active reader   a reader who interacts with the text in order to concentrate and comprehend

active reading strategy   an activity to help you concentrate, think about, and understand a text

advance organizer   a naming of the topics that will be developed later; also called a preoutline

adverse   unfavorable

affiliation   association, connection

allusion   a brief mention or reference to a person, place, or event

almanac   a publication containing facts and statistical data

ambiguity   suggesting more than one possible meaning and, consequently, unclear

analogy   a similarity, either exact or partial

anticipate   to look ahead and expect

archaic vocabulary   wording outdated and no longer in use

Aristotle   a Greek philosopher of the fourth century B.C. who wrote, among other things, the *Rhetoric*

associate   to make mental connections and see relationships

assume   expect to be true; to take for granted

assumption   the taking of something for granted; the supposition that it is true

back matter   the material in a book that comes after the last chapter

bar graph   a graph that employs vertical bars to plot the data

base clause   the subject–verb–object core, or main idea, of a sentence

bias   a strong opinion about something

biography   an account of another person's life

blunt   obvious, easy to recognize

category   a class or a group of similar, related items

cause–effect pattern   material arranged to explain the effects of certain ideas or events

censer   a container in which incense is burned

chronological   refers to events arranged as they occurred in a sequence in time

chronological pattern   material arranged as it occurred in time

classification pattern   a main topic divided into subtopics, types, or parts

classify   to place in a general category with other similar items

cluster   to group closely together

collaborate   to work together with one or more persons to accomplish something

comparison   a process showing how two ideas, events, or objects are alike

comparison and contrast pattern   material organized to show similarities and differences

competent   capable and qualified

component   one element or part of something larger

compulsive   refers to a strong desire to repeat an act even though one's conscious mind says not to

concede   to acknowledge or to admit

concluding paragraph   a final paragraph that emphasizes an important point

conclusion   the important, final idea emphasized at the end of a book or chapter conform   to fit; to be in harmony with

conjunction   the state of being combined or joined with

connotative meaning   the feeling that we associate with a certain word that is not part of its dictionary definition

contemporary   living or happening at the same time

context   the words that precede or follow a particular word that influence and give clues to its meaning

contrast   a process showing how two ideas, events, or objects are different

controversial   debatable, having two sides

convention   a cultural habit that causes certain behavior

conventional   the usual or accepted standard or way of doing something

conventional forms   common formats for writing certain types of material such as letters or news articles

conventional style   certain traits that we associate with a particular type of writing

Copland, Aaron   a twentieth-century American composer

covert persuasion   disguised or hidden efforts to change another person's ideas and opinions; same as hidden persuasion

criteria   standards of judgment to help one form opinions

deceased   dead

deductive pattern   a form of logic in which a general statement is supported by details; same as general to specific pattern

definition pattern   material organized to define an idea or concept

delete   omit; strike out

deliberate persuasion   openly, obviously, and admittedly trying to change another person's opinions; same as overt persuasion

denotative meaning   the dictionary meaning of a word

deride   make fun of

Dickens, Charles   a nineteenth-century English novelist who wrote *David Copperfield, A Tale of Two Cities,* and other novels

dispassionately   calmly, without strong feelings

distort   to change the meaning; to misrepresent

dogmatic   opinionated and arrogant

dominant   main, chief, or controlling

edition   an individual printing of a text, sometimes with changes of the original text

elicit   to call forth

Emerson, Ralph Waldo   nineteenth-century American essayist and poet

emotional appeal   technique to change people's minds by creating strong feelings

emotionally loaded example   an example that creates a strong emotional response

emotionally loaded word   a word that evokes an emotional response

empathy   imagining and sharing the feelings and attitudes of another person

encode   to rewrite material in your own words without changing the meaning in order to understand it better

erratic   differing from what is usually considered normal

estimate   a judgment or initial opinion

ethical appeal   a technique to change people's minds by causing them to admire, trust, and believe the author

ethos   moral character

evaluate   to determine how valuable something is

exalted   ennobled, elevated, honored

exhaustive   thorough, complete

eye fixations the points at which the eyes stop and see during reading, usually several fixations or stops per line

eye movements the pattern one's eyes make during reading

fiction text material containing imaginative, made-up material

figurative analogy a comparison of two items from radically different categories

flexibility ability to adapt to the demands of different situations

focus the central or main point that the author makes about the subject

front matter the material in a book that precedes the first chapter

function role or purpose

funnel to channel or pour into

general the overall aspects of a subject; the main ideas

general to specific pattern a form of logic in which a general statement is supported by details; same as deductive pattern

generate bring into existence, create

Gettysburg Address speech made by Abraham Lincoln in 1863 at the dedication of a civil war cemetery

graphic easy to visualize or imagine in picture form

graphic post-organizer a map or diagram that visually organizes ideas so that one can easily see all parts and how they interrelate

guise the external appearance

hidden persuasion disguised or hidden efforts to change another person's ideas and opinions; same as covert persuasion

historical analogy comparison of a past condition with a present condition

horizontal axis the line at the bottom of a graph that extends from left to right across the page and intersects with the vertical axis

hypothesis an explanation for a group of phenomena that can be proven or disproven through experimentation

idiosyncratic peculiar to or characteristic of

imagery mental images

imply to indicate or suggest without stating directly

inductive pattern a form of logic in which details are arranged to lead up to a general statement; same as specific to general pattern

inference a guess or conclusion drawn from what is directly stated and indirectly suggested

initiative the taking of responsibility for deciding and acting without being told and prodded

intact whole or complete

integrate to combine parts to make a whole

interactive referring to the taking of meaning from a text and contributing meaning from one's own background

internal summary a restatement of the main ideas in a section of material within the body of a text; to be distinguished from a final summary at the end

introduction the beginning of a book or chapter in which the author describes the subject and focus and gives other information to help one read the main body

introductory paragraph the paragraph at or near the beginning in which the author usually states the subject and often tells how it will be developed

irony the technique of appearing to say one thing while actually meaning the direct opposite

irrelevant data material used to further an argument that may be impressive but has nothing to do with the main point

issue a controversial topic that might cause people to disagree and argue

jargon language associated with a particular subject that has been so overused that it is almost meaningless

jot to make brief, quick notes

judgment   opinion

lexicographer   a dictionary writer or compiler

liberal education   a broad education that includes instruction in arts, sciences, social sciences, and humanities

limitation   restriction or boundary

line graph   a graph that employs a line to connect and thereby depict relationships among the data

literal analogy   a comparison of two items in the same general category

literary   having to do with excellent and permanent works that are designated as literature

logical appeal   technique to change people's minds with logical arguments

long-term memory   the part of the memory system where learned material is stored permanently for life

macabre   horrible and having to do with death

main body   the part of a book or chapter that follows the introduction where the main ideas are explained in detail

main idea   an idea that helps set forth the author's major line of thought; written at Roman-numeral level in the outline

main idea paragraph   a paragraph that presents a major idea and then develops it

manipulate   to change or adapt to suit one's own purpose

map   a visual representation of ideas

master example pattern   a single example used throughout to illustrate all of the main ideas

meaningless words   words that have strong feelings associated with them and that may, consequently, not mean the same thing to everyone

metaphor   suggests close similarities between two unlike objects in order to invite comparison

misrepresent   to give an incorrect or false impression

mnemonic   an aid to help one remember a body of material; may be a nonsense word or picture

motivated sequence pattern   ideas arranged to motivate readers to find a solution and take action

motive   something that prompts one to act

nonfiction text   material containing facts and theory instead of made-up stories

objective reporting   material that is totally factual with no opinion or distortion

obscure   unclear, difficult to understand

open-ended paragraph   a paragraph that is not summarized at the end and leads into additional details in the next paragraph

opposition   a group that represents a different or an opposite point of view

oral reading rate   the rate at which one reads aloud, usually around 150 words per minute

ostensibly   apparently

outline   a brief sketch of main ideas, subideas, and supporting material that shows the relationships among these parts

overt persuasion   open, obvious, and admitted efforts to change another person's ideas and opinions; same as deliberate persuasion

paraphrase   to rewrite a passage in your own words

Parthenon   an ancient temple in Athens, Greece

patterns of organization   established ways to think about, develop, and order ideas

peripheral vision   the capacity to see the material on either side of a fixation point that may not be in sharp focus but is still visible

personal style   certain writing traits that particular authors repeat regularly and which help us identify their work

personification   the assigning of human qualities to an inanimate object

perspective   a mental view of how facts and ideas interrelate that can help one understand other things

persuade   to change another person's mind to agree with your own

persuasive appeal   a technique in which special means are used to change another person's mind

pervasive   spread throughout every part

Pirean   adjective form of Piraeus, a seaport in Greece

pompous   inflated; showing off

popularly held opinions   opinions that seem to be true because so many people hold them

predict   to know or guess what will happen beforehand

predisposition   a tendency or inclination

predominant pattern of organization   the main pattern that organizes the entire body of a piece of writing or a speech

preoutline   a transition that names at the outset the main ideas that will be introduced; also called advance organizer

pretentious diction   words that are unnecessarily formal, complicated, fancy, or showy

preview   the looking through and reading of only parts of a text so that it will be easier to read closely later

private product   the final result of a process that belongs to the person who completed it rather than to the general public

problem–solution pattern   material arranged to present one or more problems and one or more solutions

process   a procedure for completing a task

process pattern   material arranged in a step-by-step sequence to describe how to accomplish a goal

proliferation   a rapid growth or spread

prominent   conspicuous, easy to see

purpose sentence   sentence usually located in the introduction, stating author's subject, focus, and purpose; also called thesis sentence

reading communication process   the procedure whereby meaning is transmitted from an author to a reader via a text

reading vocabulary   words that one understands or at least partially understands while reading but would be unlikely to use in writing or speaking

recall   to see how much one can remember without looking at notes

recapitulate   to restate or briefly summarize

recite   to repeat or write material over and over again until it is learned

reflect   to think about newly learned material and associate it with what one already knows

regression   the act of going back to reread a passage that was just read

reimburse   to pay back

relative   comparative

reorganize   to arrange ideas in a new order that makes better sense and is easier to remember

restrict   to limit or confine

review   to go back to reread and relearn previously learned material to refresh it in one's mind

rhetoric   the study of the effective use of language; in classical times, the study of the effective means of persuasion

Rhetoric   a book by Aristotle that describes how to persuade others

rote memorizing   the process of memorizing and parroting back without thinking

sarcophagus   a stone coffin

satire   the use of ridicule to improve or correct a wrong

scanning   the process of using special eye movements to locate bits of information on a page as quickly as possible

selective reading   the process of locating passages that contain needed information and then slowing down to read them closely

semanticist   a person who studies the meanings of words

short-term memory   the part of the memory system that remembers only a few items at a time for a brief period and then forgets them

signal word   a transitional word that alerts one to a new idea, a new relationship, or a new section of material

signs of bias   techniques that authors use to manipulate a reader's thoughts, feelings, and actions

silent reading rate   the rate at which the eyes can see and the mind comprehend without involving the speech mechanism; the usual range is 250 to 800 words per minute

simile   a comparison stating directly how two unlike objects are alike; usually with "like" or "as"

skimming   a rapid reading technique that enables you to get the subject, focus, and some of the ideas and details very quickly

sophisticated   worldly-wise because of education and experience

spatial pattern   a form of organization in which material is arranged according to its location in an area or space

speaking vocabulary   the vocabulary one relies on while speaking or conversing

specific   details that tell more about a general subject; the subideas and supporting material

specific to general pattern   a form of logic in which details are arranged to lead up to a general statement; same as inductive pattern

speed-reading   a rapid-reading skill that involves seeing most of the words as opposed to skipping over large chunks of material

standardize   to set a model or pattern of excellence

strategy   a special activity or skill that you can use, for example, to improve your reading

structure   something composed of organized and interrelated parts

study sheet   a brief outline of material on a specific topic to aid in exam preparation

style   certain traits repeated over and over in a piece of writing that give it a distinctive character

subidea   supporting material that gives more information about main idea; written at level of A., B., etc. in the outline

subidea paragraph   a paragraph that gives additional details about a main idea introduced in a previous paragraph

subject   the most important main idea or topic in a text

subpattern of organization   a minor pattern that organizes a small segment of material in a piece of writing or a speech

summarize   to restate briefly and, often, in one's own words the subject and main points of a reading passage

summary   a restatement at the end of a book or chapter of the most important ideas made by the author

summary paragraph   a paragraph that restates the main ideas made previously

supplementary   added or extra

supporting material   bits of material that can be imagined, visualized, or sensed that make main ideas clear, interesting, and memorable, such as an example

surveying   the process of locating and reading only specific parts of a text in order to preview or review it

syntax   word order or pattern of words in a sentence

synthesize   to combine parts into a whole

technical vocabulary   specialized vocabulary associated with technical subjects such as math, science, and engineering

thesis sentence   a sentence usually located in the introduction, stating author's subject, focus, and purpose; also called purpose sentence

tone   the quality reflected by a particular choice or combination of words that shows the author's attitude towards the subject

topic sentence   the sentence usually located at the beginning of a paragraph, stating the main idea; may also be at the end or in the middle of a paragraph

topical pattern   a form of organization in which material is grouped in categories by subject

topoi   Greek for topics, which are ways to think about and develop a subject

transition   words, phrases, or longer blocks of material used to change the subject, to emphasize ideas, and sometimes to state relationships among ideas; transitional words are sometimes called signal words

transitional paragraph   a paragraph that changes the subject from one main idea to another

unconscious persuasion   a technique to change another person's ideas or opinions even though the author or speaker may not be aware of this intent

unique   special; nothing else like it

unit   something that forms a united whole

validate   make or prove to be true

vertical axis   the line along the side of a graph that extends from top to bottom and intersects with the horizontal axis

visualize   to form mental pictures

vivid emotional description   a description that creates a strong mental picture and emotional response

Vladivostok   a Russian seaport

vocalization   word-by-word reading in which the reader may whisper each word or think about each word while reading

voracious   having an appetite characterized as always hungry for huge quantities of food

ANSWER KEYS

CHAPTER 1   In-Chapter Exercises

---

1. Interactive strategies: 4, 6, 8, 9, 11, 12, 13, 15
   Sample outline summary of chapter:
   What is the subject? ways to become an active reader
   What did the author say about it?

   1. Blind student active—concentrating, comprehending
   2. Reader passive—no meaning

   Learn Vocabulary
   3 types
   1. specialized—associated with subject—boldface
   2. general—used for any subject—circled
   3. allusions—place, people, events—wavy line

      Select interesting words
      Define briefly in margin
      Use context and dictionary

   The Active Reading Process
   Use a process that includes activities before, during, and after reading.
   Use active strategies that include reading, writing, and thinking.

   Mark the Text
   Mark and define vocabulary in margin.
   Underline important ideas and jot in margins.
   Write summaries.
   Jot down own ideas.

   Summarize
   Ask, what is subject? What does author say about it?
   Summarize briefly at end of sections, chapters, and book.

   Become Active
   Use strategies.
   Collaborate with other readers.

End-Chapter Exercises

I. C.   Sample outline summary of "Safety Problems with Nuclear Power Plants"
   What is the subject? Safety problems with nuclear reactors
   What does the author say about it?
      5 Dangers
       1. May explode
          —water used to avoid
       2. Water flow may be interrupted
          —everything overheats, melts, including ground
          —a nonnuclear explosion from overheating would spread radioactivity

  3. Small radioactive leaks
     –into water
     –into air
  4. Waste difficult to dispose of
     –now sealed and buried
     –could be sabotaged or stolen
  5. Stream water for cooling is hotter when returned to stream and kills
     fish.

CHAPTER 2   In-Chapter Exercises

1. 1. Sydney Piddington
    2. Educated—reads; a professional man
    3. Australian
    4. In army and POW when young, business, reading to relax and solve
       problems
    5. living
    6. _____
    7. Educated businessperson, reflective
    8. Believes slow reading can help solve problems
    9. Yes—comment on *The Importance of Living*
   10. Yes—passing on advice that helps him
   11. Personal experience
2. 1. Inform about slow reading
    2. Persuade reader to try it.
       Entertain reader with personal experiences.
       Express values about reading.
3. 1. Women speakers
    2. ?
    3. Try the advice, whether male or female
4. 1. Author writing article about effective speaking
5. 1. Listen for method of organization when taking notes
    2. Research—Dr. Lyman Steil
    3. 4 ways to organize: points, cause–effect, chronology, pictorial
    4. Yes—4 points
    5. Quotes from source that include examples to clarify
    6. Yes—says "some of the most common techniques"; then underlines 4 main
          points to make them stand out
    7. Relatively informal—contractions and conversational words

Sample outline summary of chapter:
What is the subject? Types of questions readers should ask to help them read
    actively
What does the author say about it?

   Reading as Communication
   1. Author ⎫
   2. Text   ⎬   Ask questions about all
   3. Subject ⎪
   4. Reader ⎭

Questions to Improve Comprehension
  Who wrote it? (author)
  Why wrote it? (author's purpose)
  Who wrote it for? (author's idea of reader)
  What caused it? (author's occasion)
  What is it about? (subject)
  What type of text? (classify)
  How written? (difficulty of text)
  How benefit me? (reader)

  Ask questions before, during, and after reading

(*Note:* Sample summaries are provided for the first two chapters only. Follow these models in writing the summaries of the other eleven chapters.)

End-Chapter Exercises

I. A. *Author as person* (sample of how these questions might be answered)
       1. Don Akchin
       2. A student–high school, probably college
       3. U.S.
       4. Fitness, noncompetitive athletically
       5. Living
       6. _____
       7. Lively, probably slight (149 lb.), young
       8. Values fitness, but dislikes old fitness
       9. Yes—can laugh at himself
       10. Yes—writing to help other people
       11. Personal experiences
II. *Author's purpose*
    1. Inform
    2. Entertain, persuade
III. *Attitude toward audience*
    1. People like himself—nonathletes who would like to be fit
    2. Very well, except I'm not fit
    3. Try his prescription for fitness
IV. *Author's occasion*
    1. Assignment to write about fitness in a magazine read by college students
V. *Subject and development*
    1. How to practice new fitness
    2. Experience
    3. Old fitness limited to natural athletes; new fitness can be achieved by anyone. How to achieve it?
    4. Yes—comparison–contrast and chronology
    5. Yes—examples, description, quotes, statistics; to entertain, prove, and make clear
    6. Yes—underlined headings to set off parts and numbered steps; easier to find main ideas
    7. Informal: "Now as I say," and "(snicker, snicker)"

VI. *Questions about the text*
   1. Easy nonfiction
   2. Yes—I have had similar experiences and have read about aerobic exercise
   3. Familiar
   4. Yes—to well-known athletes
   5. Easy
   6. Mostly familiar—new ideas at end on how to achieve training effect
   7. Yes—headings are used
   8. Easy
VII. *Yourself as reader*
   1. Assigned to improve my reading
   2. I liked it; it was funny and informative
   3. To complete the assignment; to find out how to become fit
   4. Some background in the subject; similar experiences
   5. Entertained, informed, and persuaded to try new fitness
   6. Will start exercising three times a week and check pulse rate

Chapter 3   In-Chapter Exercises

1. *Passage 1*
   Purpose sentences: The three at the end that begin, "The purpose of this chapter is. . . ," and end "why they occur."
   Subject: listening
   Focus: how to improve listening
   Passage 2
   Purpose sentence: "The contribution of Rome to the development of Western civilization is tremendous."
   Subject: Rome
   Focus: its importance and contributions
2. *The Outline*
   Main Idea 1. Good readers follow conscious reading strategies
         A. They ask questions as they read
            1. For example, they might use . . .
            2. Professor Robinson says . . .
3. *Main idea:* first sentence, "The physical world . . ."
   Transitions: Also; Consider, for example
   Outline:
      I. Distractions make it hard to pay attention
         A. Sounds interfere
         B. Fatigue and discomfort interfered
            1. Hard to listen in hot, stuffy, noisy room
         C. Best intentions won't help
4. *Main idea:* "Everywhere penalties for sexual improprieties were severe; . . ."
   Transitions: About the same time, Sometime later, All three cases
   Outline:
      1. Massachusetts ex.
      2. Stanford ex.
      3. Barnard ex.
      A. All three from liberal institutions

       I. Penalties were severe
         B.   Army of housemothers
         C.   Elaborate security measures
         D.   Male and female dormitories

5. 1. Specific
   2. General
   3. General
   4. Specific
   5. Specific
   6. General
   7. General
   8. Specific
   9. Specific
  10. General

6. *Subject:* American violence
Focus: worse than before
   1. s.m. example
   2. s.m. example
   3. s.m. example
   4. s.m. example
   5. s.i.
   6. s.m. description
   7. m.i.
   8. s.m. quote
   9. s.m. quote
  10. s.m. example
  11. s.i.
  12. s.m. example
  13. s.m. statistics
  14. s.m. statistics and comparison
  15. s.m. comparison
  16. s.i.
  17. s.m. quote
  18. s.m. quote and description
  19. s.m. quote
  20. s.m. quote and statistics

Summary
   What is subject? Violence in America
   What did author say about it? Media suggest violence never stops.
   May be getting worse. Don't have good statistics to prove if better or worse.
   Heavy TV viewers expect more violence than they will meet. So can't say if
   worse—but not so bad as some expect.

End-Chapter Exercises

   I. A. 1. *It is simply reading, as men and women have always read, for the delight of*
          it, and for the consequent enrichment and enhancing of one's life.
       2. Three main ideas: Reading for delight, for education, and for philosophical
          enrichment
          Chunk 1, Paragraphs 1 through 6

Chunk 2, Paragraphs 7 through 10
Chunk 3, Paragraphs 11 through 12
3. a. Subideas: Delight of childhood reading
Lack of time
Magnetic centres
Buy own books
Keep open to new ideas
Read to develop human qualities
Read the best
   b. Supporting material: Quotation
Comparisons
Descriptions
Parable (anecdote)
Examples
   c. Transitions: And first, then, reading for the sheer delight of it; But with
delight there may be coupled something else. For one also reads to learn.
And about that and one thing more, I shall be very brief; One reads for
the sheer enjoyment of it; one reads to learn; and there is a yet more
excellent way.
6. *What is the subject?* Reading. *What did the author say about it?* One should
read for fun, for education, and for spiritual enrichment. Buy own books.
Look for new ideas. Be aware of associations. Read the best.
7. Questions at end
   1. Nonfiction essay
   2. John Livingston Lowes
      a. A book lover—wants to teach others to love reading
   3. Persuade people to read more
   4. Audience well-enough educated to read the books he refers to
   5. Purposes for reading

Chapter 4   In-Chapter Exercises

2. I. 1. Title
   2. Table of Contents
   3. Preface
   4. To the Student
   5. Text-marking symbols
II. 1. Vocabulary Builder (Appendix)
   2. Glossary
   3. Answer Keys
   4. Index
III. 1. Title and author
   2. Explanation of contents
   3. A system for close, critical reading
   4. A system for leisure reading
IV. 1. Chapter objectives
   2. In-chapter Exercises
   3. Key terms marked
   4. Headings
   5. Illustrations and examples

6. Final summary
7. Key strategies
8. End-chapter Exercises (practice, application, discussion, vocabulary)

3. 1. Preliminaries to active reading
    Ask questions
    Know what to expect
   2. The rapid-reading process
    How to skim, scan, survey, and so on
    How to read rapidly
   3. The close reading process
    How to analyze organization
    How to remember
   4. The critical, evaluative process
    How to judge value of texts
    How to detect bias and analyze persuasion

4. 1. How book is organized and why
   2. How chapters are set up
   3. How to do vocabulary improvement
   4. How to use key reading strategies
   5. How to use text-marking symbols

5. 1. How to become an active reader
   2. Ways to become an active reader
   3. Analyzing persuasive texts
   4. Ways authors try to persuade readers
   5. Introduce some good reading habits first; end with a complicated but important reading skill

End-Chapter Exercises

I. B. *Motivation:* dissatisfied with existing texts; wanted to teach scientific method and research
   How different: more on ecology and evolution
   Short chapters: easier for students; professor can rearrange
   How read and study: skim objectives, read chapter, study figures, read summary, review and answer objectives, do self-quiz
   Discussion questions: discuss in or out of class; may not yet have answers
   Types of references: all types, both difficult and easy
   Aids for reading: running glossary, cross-references, numbered sections, asterisks to identify vocabulary, index

Chapter 5 End-Chapter Exercises

I. A. 1. *Subject and focus:* splitting up the listening process. . . for clearer view. . . of the way. . . we listen
   2. *Main ideas:* 3 planes: sensuous, expressive, sheerly musical, and comparison with theater
   3. *Words to circle:*
       Plane 1: brainless, mere sound appeal, that plane, escape sensuous plane

Plane 2: expressive, meaning to music, meaning, definite meaning,
expresses, search for specific words
Plane 3: notes themselves, sheerly musical plane
Comparison with theater: sounds and movements, sensuous plane,
expressive plane, feeling, plot and development, sheerly musical
Conclusion: active, listen for something

4. *Transitions*
Paragraph 1–the numbered planes
Paragraph 2–Sentence 1
Paragraph 5–Sentence 1
Paragraphs 11, 12, and 16–entire paragraphs
Paragraph 17–Sentence 1
Paragraph 20–last 3 sentences

5. *Major chunks*
Paragraph 1. introduction
Paragraphs 2–4. first plane
Paragraphs 5–11. second plane
Paragraphs 12–15. third plane
Paragraphs 16–21. comparison with theater
Paragraph 22. conclusion

Chapter 7   In-Chapter Exercises

1. I. Introductory paragraph 1
   Statement of subject and focus
   Preoutline of ideas
   Will be organized according to topics
   II. Body paragraphs 2–21
   Main ideas:
   Sensuous plane
   Expressive plane
   Sheerly musical plane
   Analogy to the theater
   III. Conclusion, Paragraph 22
   Idea: Need to be an active listener

2. Branches of anthropology
   1. Physical
   2. Cultural
      a. archeology
      b. linguistics
      c. ethnology

3. General statement: first sentence
   General point: The individual has hundreds of reasonable moments in life.
   Details: Inspiration from many sources
   Inspiration from books most reliable
   Share wisdom with authors

4.

Outline of Differences

Republicans	**Democrats**
1. 400 attending	1. 200 attending
2. Took 3½ hours	2. Took 8 hours
3. Ran smoothly	3. Chaos
4. Passed resolutions in good time	4. Took 3 hours to get started
5. Bright auditorium	5. Dim, old hall
6. Speakers using microphones	6. Everyone shouting
7. Settled things ahead of time	7. Tried to work out everything there

5. Chunk 1. Attention—engages imagination and visualization
Chunk 2. Need—you want to know more; you are adventurous
Chunk 3. Satisfaction—you can join our organization to satisfy your needs
Chunk 4. Visualization—our special generation and how we can make it better
Chunk 5. Action—fill out form and send in

End-Chapter Exercises

I. A.
1. Inductive, or specific to general—a list of specific instances and examples leads up to main idea
2. Topical—introduces topic in introduction with "first"; indicates will be others
3. Topical—preoutline in introduction names the topics
4. Problem–solution—problem stated in first paragraphs and solutions offered in rest of essay
5. Process—steps listed in the order they should be followed

I. B.
1. Classification (or topical)
   How family influences consumer
   Behavior is subdivided into two ways
2. Problem–solution
   Record-keeping a problem; microfilm one solution
   (or deductive: general statement and example)
3. Process
   Step-by-step enumeration
4. Classification (or topical)
   Five benefits of active listening
   Listening
5. Chronological
   Describes what happened over a period of time

IV. D.

1–4	6–14 (or 12)	11–2
2–7	7–12 (or 14)	12–3
3–10	8–11 (or 9)	13–5
4–13	9–9 (or 11)	14–6
5–8	10–1	15–15

Chapter 8   In-Chapter Exercises

1. 1. Interesting quote
   2. How advertisers study the effects of their efforts
   3. Advertising—methods of measuring its effectiveness
2. 1. m.i.—Caravaggio's work is tender
   2. s.m.—example of *Madonna of Loreto*—description of painting
   3. s.i.—why contemporaries found disrespectful
3. 1. m.i.—computer had major impact
   2. s.m.—cheaper—$2000 or less
      comparison with progress in transportation (there is additional s.m. in this paragraph)
   3. Summary idea: Every college student needs to know about computers
4. 1. Readers are all different, which causes them to read differently
5. 1. How divorce arrangements are made in different societies
6. 1. How divorce arrangements are made in various societies
7. 1. Rococo to neoclassicism
8. 1. Chromosomes come in pairs
   2. What happens to chromosomes during fertilization
9. 1. We must use reason to combat injustice

End-Chapter Exercises

I. A. Paragraph 2
   1. First sentence
   2. Study midterm to help with future tests
   3. Learn kinds of questions
      Doublecheck study skills
   4. Main idea
   Paragraph 3
   1. You can then plan your day
   2. Find your best times to study
   3. Keep a chart
      Study when alert
   4. Main idea
   Paragraph 4
   1. First sentence
   2. Aztec social order—divisions and descriptions
   3. Nobles
      Commoners
   4. Main idea
   Paragraph 5
   1. First sentence
   2. Possible to "bug" private conversations
   3. Police find useful
      Citizens object
   4. Main idea

Paragraph 6
1. None
2. Subject changes from intuitive to formal paragraph markers
3. None
4. Transitional

Paragraph 7
1. First sentence
2. Subject of book: management process
3. Additional main topics in book
   Questions to be answered
4. Introductory

Paragraph 8
1. First sentence
2. Main topic of chapter: organization
3. Parts of a speech
   Purposes of introduction
4. Summary

Paragraph 9
1. First sentence
2. Genetic engineering as an *example* of technology
3. Using bacteria to change sunlight into energy
   Using life-forms to replace nuclear power plants
4. Subidea of main topic: technologies that affect business

I. B.   a.   Divorce rates and customs in various societies
   b.   Divorce is a source of concern in all societies
   c.   Types of divorce in different societies
        Divorce in other societies seems sensible compared to ours
        Causes of divorce in our society
   d.   Gusii of Kenya divorce for sterility
        Zuni put belongings outside
        And many others
   e.   A wonder that divorce in our society is not more common

Chapter 9   In-Chapter Exercises

1. 1. Run-off election—second election between two top candidates
   2. Demographic analysis
      Analyzing such factors as age, sexual balance, ethnicity, and other characteristics of a group
   3. Trephining
      Cutting a hole in skull to let evil spirits escape
   4. Cloture
      A vote of 60 senators to end debate and prevent filibuster
   5. Theorems
      Proven statements about mathematics
   6. Cohesion
      Holding like substances together
      Adhesion
      Holding unlike substances together

2. 3. Subject:　　reason
　　　Verb:　　　must be
　　　Object:　　definition, axiom, theorem
　4. Subject:　　evidence
　　　Verb:　　　shows
　　　Object:　　that reverse reaction occurs
　5. Subject:　　political scientists
　　　Verb:　　　speak of
　　　Object:　　party systems

3. Example: The ancient, lonely book ^s sat ^v on the library shelf, where no one read it for years.

　Example: When the rock star in his tight jeans and open shirt, with his guitar hung around his neck, began to sing, the crowd ^s cheered ^v.

4. Example of 3: I ran over the pedestrian because he was wandering aimlessly and seemed not to know where to go.

　Example of 4: The pedestrian I hit, who seemed to bounce off the hood of my car, can best be described as a sad-faced, slow-moving old gentleman.

5. Change in student population made professors feel they no longer had a profession

End-Chapter Exercises

I. A. a. Seller's market　　　　Not enough things to buy
　　　　 Buyer's market　　　　Lots of things to buy
　　 b. Hardware　　　　　　Physical computer
　　　　 Software　　　　　　Programs in computer
　 A2.　　Meanings for words agreed upon by the majority of people
　　　　　Dictionary: the study of word meanings
　 A3. 2. Good and evil
　　　 4. Psyche—had to sort seeds—like sorting good and evil
　　　　　Adam and Eve and apple—knew good by knowing evil
　　　 5. Can be a better person if know both good and evil and still choose good

I. B. 1. *Sixteenth century.* Sentence 1, base clause: they have hospitals
　　　　　　　　　　　　　Sentence 2, base clause: hospitals well appointed
　　　　　　　　　　　　　Paraphrase: the hospitals are so excellent that people would rather go there when they are sick than stay at home. (Your paraphrase will not be identical. Check to see that it is close in meaning.)
　　　 2. *Seventeenth century.* Eating—we do not eat everything the same way and we should not read everything the same way either.
　　　　　　　　　　　　　Think about what you read and read some books more carefully than others.
　　　 3. *Eighteenth century.* The first time Boswell met Johnson was in someone else's house. He was impressed and thought of the painting he had seen of him.
　　　　　　　　　　　　　The ghost was awe-inspiring and so was Johnson.
　　　 4. *Nineteenth century.* Unfair to silence anyone who believes something different from the majority. The extremists who give impromptu speeches in the streets should still have the freedom to speak.

5. *Twentieth century.* Teenagers often want to change the establishment and try to improve the world.

6. Yes
Cause: Metallic atom tranfers electrons to nonmetallic atom
Effect: strongly attracting ions
No
Cause: universal joint broke
Effect: automobile accident
My universal joint broke and caused me to have an accident while I was driving to the doctor's office.

I. C. 1.

	Vampire Toad	Giant Tree Toad
Subject:	vampire toad	giant tree toad
Audience:	popular, general	scientific
Purpose:	inform and entertain	inform
Occasion:	inform public in popular magazine article	inform students and scientists in scientific book
Word choice:	startling, emotional, informal	specialized, scientific, colorful, concrete, formal
Supporting material:	vivid, emotional description	unembellished description
Sentence structure:	simple, compound, and complex; long sentences	short, direct, precise sentences
Punctuation:	dashes, commas, periods	semicolons; standard
Standard effect:	startling; negative emotional response	informative

I. C. 2.
Word choice: old, archaic
Supporting material: analogy
Sentence construction: long, complex
Punctuation: commas and semicolons to clarify long sentences
Effect on reader: somber, inspiring, thoughtful

Chapter 10   In-Chapter Exercises

2. 1. Anti-Vietnam War demonstrations
2. Numbers of demonstrations
3. Times of demonstrations
4. Increased from 1965–1968
5. Hundreds of thousands
6. 100,000
7. 300,000
8. More people participated as the U.S. became more involved in war.
9. There was increasing dissatisfaction with the Vietnam War during the 1960s, and hundreds of thousands were willing to express it.

3.

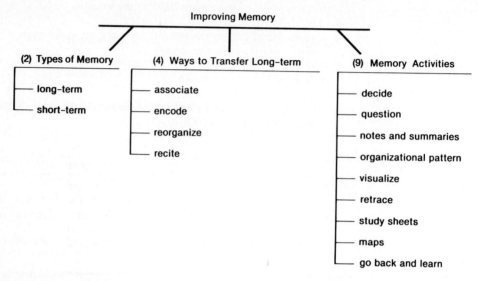

End-Chapter Exercises

I. C.   1. Five
   2. One; one whole wall, grey glass
   3. High in a castle tower
   4. A vine that covers the wall and part of the window
   5. Gloomy, high, curved
   6. An incense burner—fires—red, blue, yellow. Yes—of incense.
   7. Ottomans, candelabra, bed with canopy, ancient tombs (sarcophagi)
   8. Hung on all the walls, floor, ottomans, bed, and canopy—gold cloth
      spotted with black figures
   9. Black and gold
   10. Artificial wind behind drapes keeps them in constant motion

   D.   1.   1. Who watched different types of television programs
      2. Different audiences and numbers
      3. Types of programs
      4. Millions of people watch a great deal of television
      5. Minimum—children 2 to 5 go to bed early or are not interested in adult
         programs
         Maximum—women 55+ at home without many other responsibilities
      6. Situation comedies are most popular with people of all ages, followed by
         drama and movies. Women watch more than men and like drama best.
         Teenagers like situation comedies best. Men prefer adventure and
         movies.

   D.   2.   1. Decline of farm population 1930–1980
      2. Population by thousands; years in ten-year increments
      3. Diminishing population
      4. In 50 years, farm population has decreased by 25,000 people.
      5. 1930 maximum—country rural. 1980 minimum—technology and
         industry drew people away from farms.
      6. In fifty years the farm population has decreased steadily from 32,000 to
         less than 10,000 people.

E. *Ways the family influences consumer decisions:*

Individual traits

Family responsible for early traits
Causes people to buy as they do

Assigned roles

Children—cereal
Husband—cars and insurance
Wife—food, clothes, appliances
husband and wife share some

F. *Advantages of active listening:*

To understand others (2)

Receive messages
Pay attention

To help others (4)

No burden
 listen, not advise
Speaker understands self
Lowers threats and barriers
Catharsis for problems

Chapter 11   In-Chapter Exercises

1. 1. Executive Director of Yale–China Association
   2. Lecturer at Yale
   3. Director of East Asian Projects at UN and coauthor of book on Mao
2. 1. An understanding lawyer
   2. Has authored a book on the subject

Chapter 12   End-Chapter Exercises

I. A. 1. Author agree
       2. Author agree
       3. Kennedy agree
          Hatch disagree
          Author no opinion stated
I. B. 1. *Facts:* McNaughtan shot Drummond in January 1843
               Drummond worked for Sir R. Peel
               He died five days later
               Cockburn argued from state of mind, not act of shooting
               McNaughtan was charged with murder
               Solicitor General did not combat testimony by nine medical witnesses
               McNaughtan tried in Central Court, Old Bailey
          Opinions:
               McNaughtan victim of delusion
               McNaughtan imagined Tories to be enemies
               Tindal directed jury to acquit
               Criminal's responsibility rests on right and wrong
               No difference with McNaughtan
          Hidden Persuasion:
               "Practically directed" and selection of details suggests author
                   disagrees with findings of the court

2. *Facts:* Book is about Africans brought to America
                Blacks came from Africa
                Sartre and Wright did state quoted material
  Opinions:
                America a country of contradictions between ideals and practice
                Blacks are the quintessential Americans
                History of Blacks is history of all Americans
  Deliberate persuasion:
                Choice of words, quotes, examples show authors are obviously sympathetic to Blacks and are trying to persuade

Chapter 13   In-Chapter Exercises

1. 1. Persuade. Was trying to get sympathy for migrant farm workers.
   2. Poor, scruffy agricultural town. . . not far from luxury; she was a child of farm worker parents who had committed herself (and other examples).
   3. Appointed by Federal court; traveling with government officials; his insight and sympathy; his unwillingness to let first impressions rule (and other examples).
   4. He saw special qualities in her even though his first impression was negative. This speaks well for his judgment.
   5. He probably favors government aid because of his sympathetic portrayal of the woman and his empathy with the farm workers' poverty.
2. (1) Just and limited war that can be controlled is conceivable.
   (2) No. Social environment has a strong effect on assassins.
3. Democratic Party
5. 1. Sentence 1
   2. Sentence 2
6. 1. Everyone should have one
   2. No one should have one
   3. See the danger of making handguns accessible to everyone
7. 1. All guns should be registered
   2. Persuade readers to want to control the use of hand guns
8. 1. Use of Anectine to control prisoners
   2. There are several kinds of prison violence
   3. Describes in loaded language the effects of the drug
   4. Against the use of such drugs—calls it violence
   5. For it. Believes it helps control prisoners

End-Chapter Exercises

I. A. 1. Grossly demented, cowering bureaucrat
     a. They are insane and weak
     b. No. Engages emotions—but it doesn't prove
  2. a. Federal Government and southwestern states
     b. Exaggerates the fight and shows how difficult it will be to resolve it
  B. 1. All of them. Loaded language in titles suggest controversy, forming opinions, taking sides. Choices f. and l. are hardest to guess unless you already know these subjects are controversial.

C. 1. a. Working class wanted and needed more independence in 1940s
    b. Stacked to suggest chaos among workers at that time
    c. Yes and no. Newspapers are supposed to be objective, but we know they publish slanted and exaggerated accounts. Citing these sources proves the incidents happened and were reported, but stacked and emotional examples cause the reader to question the truth of main idea.

D. 1. a. Stopping narcotics sales and emptying the ocean with a teacup
    b. Impossible to stop narcotics traffic
    c. No. Two totally unlike things are being compared. Engages emotions, but does not logically prove

E. 1. a. No. Irrelevant material does not prove

F. 1. a. Should Federal funds be spent to rehabilitate heroin addicts
    b. They are ineffective
    c. Yes and no. They suggest gigantic increases in funds with no results. No statistics on results, however.
  2. a. Child care
    b. There is and will be a tremendous need for child care.
    c. Yes and no. Broad statistics. One might question their validity.

G. 1. a. Pity for a helpless prisoner
    b. He was a murderer without a conscience
    c. Irony

H. 1. a. Day care, television, new drugs
    b. Historical analogy
    c. No. Because two things being compared may not be alike in all respects. End result of one may not be the end result of the other.
    d. It is of tremendous importance.

I. 1. a. Against
    c. Using one's own judgment to decide when to kill. Yes.
    d. Emotional. Hamburger in the stomach, experiments. . . on live fetuses, and so on.
    e. Quotes, vivid description, loaded comparisons. Slanted and emotional.
    f. Softens and avoids the issue
    g. Yes. Last paragraph
    h. All human life should be protected, including the unborn
    i. Dr. Kass (anti). Planned Parenthood (pro). Dr. Kass. Planned Parenthood avoids issue by using neutral, inaccurate language. Dr. Kass argues vividly and cites the thalidomide issue.
    j. Ironic and sarcastic. He is against abortion and those who advocate it.

IV. C. 1.— 8
    2.—14
    3.— 3
    4.—11
    5.— 4
    6.— 7
    7.—13
    8.— 9
    9.— 2
    10.— 1
    11.— 6
    12.—12
    13.—10
    14.— 5

IV. D. *Author and source:* author's affiliations, source of the text, author's
         assumptions, organizational pattern
         Emotional appeals: emotionally loaded language, vivid, emotional description,
         figurative analogies, emotionally loaded examples, tone, irony
         Incomplete or faulty reasoning: selected and stacked supporting material,
         historical analogies, literal analogies, irrelevant data

Appendix

Vocabulary Test
1. a
2. b
3. a
4. b
5. c
6. c
7. d
8. d
9. b
10. a

Matching

1. 10		11.	9
2. 15		12.	18
3. 8		13.	12
4. 13		14.	16
5. 5		15.	20
6. 3		16.	6
7. 17		17.	19
8. 11		18.	4
9. 7		19.	2
10. 14		20.	1

INDEX